MODERN LIBRARY

Currently A

KAREN ARMSTRONG on Islam
DAVID BERLINSKI on mathematics
RICHARD BESSEL on Nazi Germany
IAN BURUMA on modern Japan
PATRICK COLLINSON on the Reformation
FELIPE FERNÁNDEZ-ARMESTO on the Americas
LAWRENCE M. FRIEDMAN on law in America
PAUL FUSSELL on World War II in Europe
ALISTAIR HORNE on the age of Napoleon
PAUL JOHNSON on the Renaissance
FRANK KERMODE on the age of Shakespeare
JOEL KOTKIN on the city
H
MARK KURLANSKY on
EDWARD J. LARSON on the theory of evolution
MARK MAZOWER on the Balkans
JOHN MICKLETHWAIT AND ADRIAN WOOLDRIDGE on the company
ANTHONY PAGDEN on peoples and empires
RICHARD PIPES on Communism
MICHAEL STÜRMER on the German Empire
GEORGE VECSEY on baseball
MILTON VIORST on the Middle East
A. N. WILSON on London
ROBERT S. WISTRICH on the Holocaust
GORDON S. WOOD on the American Revolution

Forthcoming

ALAN BRINKLEY on the Great Depression
JAMES DAVIDSON on the Golden Age of Athens
SEAMUS DEANE on the Irish
JEFFREY E. GARTEN on Globalization
MARTIN GILBERT on the Long War, 1914–1945
FRANK GONZÁLEZ-CRUSSI on the history of medicine
JASON GOODWIN on the Ottoman Empire
PETER GREEN on the Hellenistic Age
JAN T. GROSS on the fall of Communism
RIK KIRKLAND on capitalism
BERNARD LEWIS on the Holy Land
FREDERICK LOGEVALL on the Vietnam War
MARTIN MARTY on the history of Christianity
PANKAJ MISHRA on the rise of modern India
COLIN RENFREW on prehistory
JOHN RUSSELL on the museum
ORVILLE SCHELL on modern China
CHRISTINE STANSELL on feminism
ALEXANDER STILLE on fascist Italy
CATHARINE R. STIMPSON on the university

Also by Kevin Starr

Coast of Dreams:
California on the Edge, 1990–2003

Americans and the California Dream series

Americans and the California Dream, 1850–1915

Inventing the Dream:
California Through the Progressive Era

Material Dreams:
Southern California Through the 1920s

Endangered Dreams:
The Great Depression in California

The Dream Endures:
California Enters the 1940s

Embattled Dreams:
California in War and Peace, 1940–1950

Land's End: A Novel

Over California
(photography by Reg Morrison)

O California!
Nineteenth and Early Twentieth Century California
Landscapes and Observations
(with Stephen Vincent and Paul Mills)

CALIFORNIA

A History

KEVIN STARR

A MODERN LIBRARY CHRONICLES BOOK

THE MODERN LIBRARY

NEW YORK

2007 Modern Library Paperback Edition

Published in the United States by Modern Library, an imprint of
The Random House Publishing Group, a division of Random House, Inc., New York.

Originally published in hardcover in the United States by Modern Library,
an imprint of The Random House Publishing Group,
a division of Random House, Inc., in 2005.

ISBN 978-0-8129-7753-0

LIBRARY OF CONGRESS CATALOGING-IN-PUBLICATION DATA
Starr, Kevin.
California : a history / Kevin Starr.
p. cm.—(A Modern Library chronicles book ; 23)
Includes bibliographical references and index.
ISBN 978-0-8129-7753-0
1. California—History. I. Title. II. Modern Library chronicles ; 23.
F861.S83 2005
979.4—dc22 2005043857

Printed in the United States of America

www.modernlibrary.com

6 8 9 7 5

Book design by Mary A. Wirth

for

Kathryn and Steven Sample

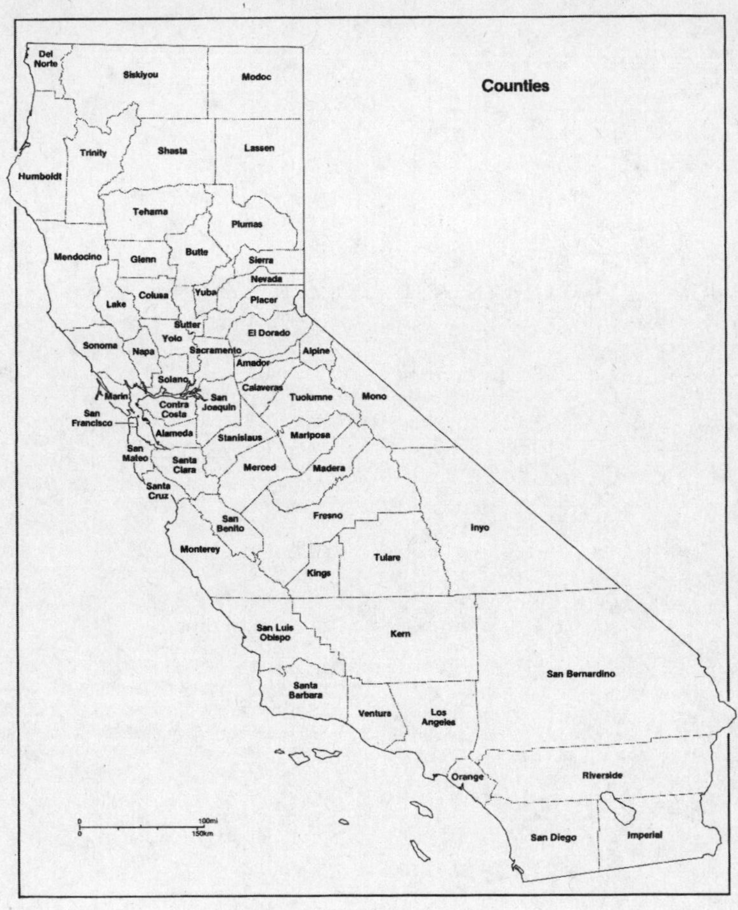

The Counties of California

CALIFORNIA STATE LIBRARY

Contents

Cypress Point, Monterey County, the 1860s

CALIFORNIA STATE LIBRARY

Preface

A Nation-State

Where did it come from—this nation-state, this world commonwealth, this California? How did an American state, one in fifty, rise to such global stature, with its $1.5 trillion economy making it, as of 2005, the fifth-ranked economy on the planet? Never before in human history, it could be argued, had such a diverse population assembled itself so rapidly under one political system. By 2004, the Los Angeles Unified School District alone was reporting some ninety-two languages in use in its student population. The city itself, meanwhile, had become the second largest Mexican city on the planet and a ranking Korean, Iranian, Armenian, and Ethiopian metropolis. With a population of thirty-six million in 2004, California contained 12.5 percent of the population of the United States as of Census 2000. Metropolitan Los Angeles was the second largest urban region in the nation, the San Francisco Bay Area the fourth. If the five-county Los Angeles metropolitan region alone were a separate state, its 20.6 million people would make it the fourth largest state in the country.

Where had these people come from? And why were they here? What forces of war and peace, of economics, what shifts of demography and social aspiration had caused the population of California to shoot up from seven million in 1940, to seventeen million in 1962 (when California surpassed New York as the most populous state in the nation), to nineteen million by the mid-1960s when immigration laws were reformed, allowing for new migration from Asia, Africa, Latin America, and the Middle East? Sponsored by Spain and Mexico in its colonial and early frontier eras, California—with 32.4 percent of its population Latino as of 2000—was in the process of becoming the most important center of Mexican culture and society outside Mexico itself. Facing the Asia-Pacific Basin, California was likewise becoming an epicenter of Asian American civilization, with nearly 11 percent of its population of Asian origin and San Francisco on the verge of becoming the first prominent American city with an Asian American majority.

Here was an American state that by the twenty-first century had become a world force in terms of people, trade and commerce, tourism, and technology, and, more subtly, a state possessed of a certain glamor, a magic even, rich with the possibilities of a better life. Here was a crossroads commonwealth. By the millennium, California was exporting some $1.7 billion in goods worldwide—mostly to Mexico, Japan, Canada, Taiwan, South Korea, the United Kingdom, the Netherlands, and mainland China, its leading trading partners (in that order), but also to twenty-six other ranking trading partners as well. The Port of Los Angeles–Long Beach on San Pedro Bay was the busiest port in the nation and one of the ranking ports of the world. Five million overseas visitors were pouring into California each year by the late 1990s, and the travel and tourism economy of the state was generating more than $75 billion annually from domestic and international travelers and employing more than a million Californians before the terrorist attacks of 9/11. What did the nonbusiness travelers come to see? Disneyland in Anaheim, first of all, and Universal Studios in Hollywood, followed by an array of amusement parks and outdoor attractions including the Golden Gate National Recreation Area and Yosemite National Park.

These dual attractions—the entertainment industry and natural beauty—virtually define the state. In the early twentieth century, California had won the contest over the best site for the emergent motion picture industry. And this in turn established a matrix for the development of other new entertainment media—radio, records, television, video, CDs, DVDs—that were to follow. The main reason California was attracting so many visitors, foreign and domestic, was that California had long since been presenting itself to them via the various entertainment media as a land of enchantment and dreams. Much of the world tended to perceive the United States itself as, somehow, California, thanks to television programs such as *Baywatch,* which broadcast to millions a Day-Glo version of life on the sunny beaches of the Golden State.

At times, California seemed imprisoned in a myth of itself as an enchanted and transformed place: a myth that, in one way or another, had its origins in the Spanish colonial era. The very acceleration of California into an American commonwealth had been the result of a gold rush, with all that such beginnings implied for the perception of California as a place where human beings might break through the constraints of day-to-day life and come into possession of something immeasurably better. Such a utopian expectation also brought with it, when things did not go well—when California was wracked by earthquake, fire, and flood; when its prisons filled to overflowing; when its economy went into sudden collapse; when its politics grew dysfunctional; or merely when Californians experienced the inevitable human tragedies, shocks, and setbacks they had come to California to escape—the common complaint that California had been hyped beyond recognition: that for all its media-driven pretenses to glitz and glamor, California was, all things considered, just another American place, and sometimes even worse than that.

Still, it had to be admitted—even in bad times—that California *noir,* as disappointing as it might be, could not negate the cumulative achievement of California as a fused instance of American and global cultures. Here, among other things, nature had been supplemented and heroically rearranged so as to make possible a population of thirty-six million—an estimated fifty-five million by 2040—which natural conditions alone could never have supported. Not since ancient Rome or the creation of Holland had any society comparably subdued, appropriated, and rearranged its water resources. Or used this water-related infrastructure, including hydroelectricity, to establish—again, so swiftly—the foundations for a mass society at once agricultural and industrialized. Or created such extensive cities and suburbs in such short order. Or linked these built environments in an equally rapid time with highways, freeways, and bridges of comparable magnitude.

California emerged as a society with a special capacity for technology. In the nineteenth century, the locally invented Pelton turbine increased water-driven power sixfold. Pioneered in California by the heavier-than-air glider flights of John Montgomery in 1883, aviation was localized in California a few short years after Kitty Hawk, and the great names of California aviation—Lockheed, Curtis, Douglas, Northrop—became synonymous with the very planes they designed and built. In the 1930s and early 1940s, California played more than its part in the release of atomic energy. In what later would be designated the Silicon Valley, the semiconductor was invented, and from this came the digital revolution, including the Internet, also perfected in California. The millennium found California on the cutting edge of yet another revolution: biotechnology.

The great universities and research institutes of California were the cause and the result of this aptitude for science and technology. It began in the American frontier era with the technology of mining, which led to the establishment of an academy of science and a state geological survey. And then, when barely out of its frontier phase, California turned to the purest science of them all—astronomy—with the construction of the first of three world-leading astronomical observatories. From this arose a scientific community that demanded—and achieved—some of the best universities and research institutes in the nation.

The very same society that was ordering and rearranging its environment through technology was also learning to revere nature as its primary symbol of social identity. From the beginning, American California was at once what human beings had made of it and what they had found there in the first place: a region of magnitude and beauty, encompassing all the topography, climate, and life zones of the planet (with the exception of the tropical), from the seashore to the desert, from the Great Central Valley at its center to the snowcapped Sierra peaks guarding its eastern flank. From the beginning, American California was caught in a paradox of reverent awe and exploitative use. As early as 1860, the state had urged the setting aside of the Yosemite Valley not just because it was so grand and so beautiful, but because its very grandeur and beauty established the expectation of what California should become in its social and moral existence. A streak of nature worship—sometimes mawkish and sentimental, sometimes neopagan in its intensity, and, toward the millennium, frequently Zen-like in its clarity and repose—runs through the imaginative, intellectual, and moral history of California as a fixed reference point of social identity. A society that had consumed nature so wantonly, so ferociously, was, paradoxically, nature's most ardent advocate.

California is an American story that from the beginning has been a global story as well. Despite its quasi-autonomous existence—the power of its economy on the world stage, the overseas offices maintained by the state government to promote international trade, the continuous diplomacy demanded by its worldwide investments—California remains an American place, perhaps the most American of American places, prophesying the growing diversity of the United States. In the mid-nineteenth century, the American people, operating through their federal government, brought American California into being. By the millennium, the national importance of California had become far more than the fifty-three Californians who sat in the House of Representatives or the two women who sat in the United States Senate. California had long since become one of the prisms through which the American people, for better and for worse, could glimpse their future. It had also become not the exclusive, but a compelling way for this future to be brought into existence. California, noted Wallace Stegner, is like the rest of the United States—only more so. How California came to be such a representative American place, what has been gained and what has been lost, is the theme of this brief chronicle.

KEVIN STARR

SAN FRANCISCO AND LOS ANGELES

June 2005

Chronology

1510 Garci Ordóñez de Montalvo describes California as an island near the Terrestrial Paradise.

1513 Vasco Núñez de Balboa discovers the Pacific Ocean.

1519 Ferdinand Magellan commences first circumnavigation of the globe.

1519 Spaniards under command of Hernán Cortés commence the conquest of Mexico.

1532 Fortún Jiménez is perhaps the first to use the name "California" to describe the isthmus west of Mexico.

1535 Hernán Cortés founds a settlement on Santa Cruz Bay.

1539 Francisco de Ulloa explores the mouth of the Colorado River and discovers that Baja California is a peninsula, not an island.

1540 Hernando de Alarcón ascends the Colorado River. He or Melchor Díaz becomes the first European to cross into Alta California.

1542 Navigator Juan Rodríguez Cabrillo, sailing for Spain, commences reconnaissance of Alta California coast.

1564 Miguel López de Legazpi establishes Spanish presence in the Philippines.

1565 First Manila galleon crosses the Pacific from Philippines to Mexico.

1577 English flotilla under the command of Francis Drake commences second circumnavigation of the globe.

1579 *Golden Hinde* enters Drake's Bay on the Point Reyes peninsula.

1595 Spanish galleon *San Agustín* is driven aground at Point Reyes.

1602 Sebastián Vizcaíno explores California coast to Cape Mendocino, after which the Spanish government abandons exploration of the region for 167 years.

1697 Jesuits establish first of eighteen missions in Baja California.

1768 Jesuits are expelled from the Spanish empire and replaced in Baja California with Franciscans.

1769 In January, the Sacred Expedition sails and marches north to Alta California. That July, Father Junípero Serra dedicates Mission San Diego de Alcalá.

1774 In January, Captain Juan Bautista de Anza leaves Tubac, Arizona, to reconnoiter a land route from Mexico to Alta California.

1775 Spaniards discover the Golden Gate and sail into San Francisco Bay.

1776 In June, the second Anza expedition reaches the shores of San Francisco Bay. In October, Father Francisco Palóu dedicates Mission San Francisco de Asís.

1777 In November, Pueblo de San José de Guadalupe is founded as the first civil settlement in Alta California.

1781 In July, the Yuma attack and slaughter a party of Spaniards en route to California, sealing off the recently opened Anza trail. In September, the Pueblo de Nuestra Señora la Reina de Los Angeles is founded as the second civil settlement in Alta California.

1784 In August, Father Serra dies at Mission San Carlos Borromeo.

1786 In September, two frigates of the Royal French Navy under the command of Captain Jean François Galaup Comte de La Pérouse spend ten days in Monterey Bay, the first non-Spanish expedition to reach Alta California.

1791 In September, a Spanish scientific expedition under the command of the Italian-born navigator Alejandro Malaspina sails into Monterey Bay.

1792 In November, an English naval expedition under the command of Captain George Vancouver anchors in San Francisco Bay.

1796 In October, the American ship *Otter* drops anchor in Monterey Bay.

1806 In April, the Russian ship *Juno,* under the command of Count Nikolai Petrovich Rezanov, arrives in San Francisco Bay.

1812 The Russian American Fur Company establishes Fort Ross on the coast one hundred miles north of San Francisco Bay.

1816 In October, the Russian naval ship *Rurik,* under the command of German-born Otto von Kotzebue, arrives in San Francisco Bay.

1818 In November, the French-born privateer Hipólito de Bouchard, flying the flag of the revolutionary Republic of Buenos Aires, raids Monterey and the south coast.

1824 California (Alta and Baja) is designated a territory of the newly established Federal Republic of Mexico. The Miwok Indians of the San Joaquin Valley rise in rebellion.

1826 Trappers from the Hudson's Bay Company, under the command of Peter Skene Ogden, explore the interior of Northern California. In August, American trappers led by Jedediah Smith make the first overland penetration of California from the east.

1827 In May, Jedediah Smith and two companions become the first white men to cross the Sierra Nevada.

1833 California governor José Figueroa appoints Mariano Guadalupe Vallejo commander of the northern district.

1834 The Híjar-Padrés colony arrives in Alta California. In August, Governor Figueroa calls for the secularization of the missions.

1834 In April, Rachel Larkin gives birth to the first California child born to American parents.

1836 In November, Californios revolt against Mexico and declare California a republic. Mexico co-opts the movement by upgrading California from a territory to a department and making the leader of the revolt, Juan Bautista Alvarado, the new governor.

1839 Governor Alvarado makes a 48,000-acre land grant to Swiss émigré John Sutter as a buffer against incursions from the northeast. British consul general Alexander Forbes proposes that Mexico eliminate its debt to Great Britain by ceding Alta California to the British-owned California Company, modeled on the Hudson's Bay Company.

1840 In *Two Years Before the Mast,* Richard Henry Dana, Jr., calls for the Americanization of California.

1841 Comte Eugène Duflot du Mofras scouts Alta California as a possible colony for France.

1841 Sir George Simpson, governor-general of the Hudson's Bay Territories, negotiates trading agreements with Mexican California.

1842 In October, American commodore Thomas ap Catesby Jones apologizes for raising the Stars and Stripes over Monterey.

1845 Irish priest Eugene McNamara negotiates to send ten thousand Irish colonists to Alta California.

1846 In January, Army captain John Charles Frémont raises the American flag atop Gavilán Peak outside Monterey. In May, Frémont meets with Marine lieutenant Archibald Gillespie on the shores of Klamath Lake, Oregon. Five days later, American settlers in Sonoma declare the California Republic. In July, U.S. sailors and marines raise the Stars and Stripes over Monterey and

Yerba Buena on San Francisco Bay. At the end of the month, the *Brooklyn* arrives from New York with Mormon immigrants. In August, American forces occupy Los Angeles. In November, the Donner party is trapped by early snows near Truckee Lake (now Donner Lake) in the Sierra Nevada. In December, Californio horsemen under the command of Andrés Pico defeat American dragoons at the Battle of San Pasqual.

1847 In January, the Battle of La Mesa finalizes the conquest of California. Three days later, the Californios sign the Capitulation of Cahuenga. Later in the year, Jasper O'Farrell surveys a street plan for the newly established city of San Francisco.

1848 In January, carpenter James Marshall discovers gold on the South Fork of the American River. In February, the Treaty of Guadalupe Hidalgo cedes all Mexican lands north of the Río Grande to the United States. In December, President Polk confirms to Congress that gold has been discovered in California.

1849 In June, the governor of the military territory of California, Brigadier General Bennett Riley, calls upon the American citizens of California to form a government. In September, elected delegates convene at Colton Hall in Monterey to draft a constitution. In October, the convention calls for the creation of California as the thirty-first state. In November, voters ratify a constitution for the newly created state and elect officials. In December, the legislature convenes in San José.

1850 In January, Congress begins a nine-month debate regarding the admission of California to the Union. In April, the state legislature approves the indenturing of Native Americans to whites. In May, Army troops massacre Pomo Indians in Lake County. By June, 635 vessels float abandoned in San Francisco Bay. In August, squatter riots break out in Sacramento. In September, President Millard Fillmore signs the bill admitting California to the Union as the thirty-first state.

1851 In March, Congress passes the Land Act, requiring the validation of all Spanish and Mexican land grants. In June, the first Vigilance Committee seizes control of San Francisco. In July, miners hang Josefa in Downieville. In September, Louise Amelia Knapp Smith Clapp writes the first of twenty-three letters to her sister in Massachusetts. Santa Clara and California Wesleyan colleges and a female seminary at Benicia are founded.

1852 In April, the high-pressure hydraulic hose is introduced to mining. Construction begins on a state prison at Point San Quentin.

1853 The California Academy of Sciences is founded in San Francisco. Andrew Jackson Grayson begins work on *Birds of the Pacific Slope.*

1855 In January, a railroad is completed across the Isthmus of Panama. The

College of California in Oakland and St. Ignatius College in San Francisco are established. Carleton Watkins opens his Yosemite Art Gallery in San Francisco. The *Annals of San Francisco* is published. Josiah Royce is born in Grass Valley.

1856 In May, the second Vigilance Committee seizes control of San Francisco. James Mason Hutchings establishes *Hutchings' Illustrated California Magazine.*

1858 The California Supreme Court rules against the freedom of alleged slave Archy Lee.

1859 In September, California chief justice David S. Terry mortally wounds U.S. senator David Broderick in a duel on the shores of Lake Merced in San Mateo County. That same month, a state-sponsored convention meeting in San Francisco calls for the construction of a transcontinental railroad.

1860 Engineer Theodore Judah lobbies Congress to subsidize a transcontinental railroad. Geologist Josiah Whitney establishes the California Geological Survey. Anton Roman opens a publishing house in San Francisco. German immigrants establish the Olympic Club. Construction begins on the state capitol building.

1861 Republicans and pro-Union Democrats form the fusion Unionist Party and capture the legislature and governorship. The Central Pacific Railroad is incorporated in Sacramento. Napa winemaker Agoston Haraszthy acquires 200,000 grapevine cuttings in Europe for shipment to California.

1862 The Pacific Railway Act authorizes and finances the construction of a transcontinental railroad. Drought devastates the cattle economy of Southern California. A normal school for the training of teachers opens in San Francisco.

1863 Governor Leland Stanford breaks ground on construction of the transcontinental railroad.

1864 The second Pacific Railway Act increases land-grant and financial incentives. President Lincoln signs a bill protecting Yosemite and the Mariposa Big Trees. William Chapman Ralston and Darius Ogden Mills found the Bank of California. Samuel Clemens moves to San Francisco.

1865 St. Vincent's College opens in Los Angeles.

1868 Legislature establishes the University of California. John Muir arrives in San Francisco and immediately departs for Yosemite.

1869 Union Pacific and Central Pacific meet at Promontory Summit, Utah. Pico House opens in Los Angeles.

1870 A second state normal school opens in San José.

1871 Eighteen Chinese men, including a boy of fourteen, are lynched in Los Angeles.

1872 Charles Nordhoff publishes *California for Health, Wealth, and Residence.* Photographer Eadweard Muybridge photographs the trotting horse of Leland Stanford. Mark Twain publishes *Roughing It.* Clarence King publishes *Mountaineering in the Sierra Nevada.*

1873 In January, the Modocs of Northern California rise up in organized rebellion. Andrew Hallidie of San Francisco invents and introduces the cable car.

1874 The California School of Design opens in San Francisco.

1875 The failure of Bank of California precipitates a financial panic.

1876 St. Vibiana's Cathedral is dedicated in Los Angeles. Market Street, San Francisco, is illuminated with electrical arc lights and reflectors for the Centennial celebration.

1877 Unemployed workingmen hold nighttime rallies in San Francisco sandlots. Denis Kearney preaches violence and revolution. Young hoodlums sack Chinatown. Alarmed businessmen of San Francisco form the Committee of Public Safety. Disaffected labor leaders organize the Workingmen's Party.

1878 Legislature passes the Drainage Act, calling for comprehensive study of water resources. Delegates meet in Sacramento to rewrite the state constitution.

1879 Voters pass the rewritten state constitution by a slender majority. Agriculture replaces mining as chief element in the California economy. Henry George publishes *Progress and Poverty.* George Davidson establishes the first astronomical observatory on the West Coast.

1880 Lester Pelton patents the water turbine. The University of Southern California opens in Los Angeles.

1883 John Montgomery makes the first heavier-than-air glider flight.

1884 U.S. judge Lorenzo Sawyer orders an end to hydraulic mining. Helen Hunt Jackson publishes *Ramona.*

1885 Atchison, Topeka & Santa Fe Railroad reaches San Bernardino. The Federated Trades and Labor Council and the Coast Seamen's Union are formed in San Francisco.

1887 Lick Observatory opens atop Mount Hamilton. Wright Act authorizes irrigation districts. Brewers and Maltsters launch a successful strike in San Francisco. Pomona College opens in Southern California.

1890 Pasadena inaugurates an annual New Year's Day floral parade.

1891 The Sailors Union of the Pacific is formed in San Francisco. The Fourth Cavalry assumes responsibility for Yosemite. Charles Dudley Warner publishes *Our Italy.* Newly constructed Leland Stanford Junior University admits its first students. Boss Chris Buckley flees San Francisco. Whittier College opens in Southern California.

1892 Peter Remondino, M.D., publishes *The Mediterranean Shores of America.* John Muir is elected the first president of the Sierra Club. Gentleman Jim Corbett defeats John L. Sullivan for the heavyweight boxing championship of the United States.

1895 The Southern California Fruit Growers Association is established. Charles Fletcher Lummis launches the magazine *Land of Sunshine.*

1896 Phoebe Apperson Hearst sponsors a master plan for the University of California.

1897 Katherine Tingley arrives in San Diego to found Point Loma Theosophical Institute.

1898 In November, Stanford president David Starr Jordan calls for the reform of California culture and politics.

1899 In January, the *San Francisco Examiner* publishes Edwin Markham's poem "The Man with the Hoe."

1901 The Teamsters Union leads a citywide general strike in San Francisco. Water from the Colorado River reaches Imperial Valley via aqueduct.

1903 The Pacific Coast baseball league is organized.

1904 Fresno wagoneer Benjamin Holt invents the tractor.

1905 Water from the Colorado River floods Imperial Valley. California Fruit Growers Exchange markets oranges under Sunkist label. Japan Society of Northern California is founded in San Francisco.

1906 In April, an earthquake measuring 8.3 on the Richter scale shakes the Bay Area for forty-five seconds, followed by seventeen serious aftershocks. In October, San Francisco outrages President Theodore Roosevelt by sending Japanese children to segregated public schools. Later that year, graft trials begin in San Francisco.

1907 Southern Pacific contains Colorado River water flooding into the newly created Salton Sink. The movie industry arrives in Los Angeles. George Freeth introduces surfing to Southern California.

1908 The Great White Fleet visits California. The Carnegie Institution opens an astronomical observatory atop Mount Wilson.

1909 Homer Lea predicts a Japanese military invasion of California.

1910 The Los Angeles Chamber of Commerce organizes an air show at Dominguez Hills. Bombing of *Los Angeles Times* offices kills twenty. Progressive reformer Hiram Johnson is elected governor. IWW forces free-speech confrontations in Fresno. D. W. Griffith begins filming in Southern California.

1911 The Lockheed brothers design, produce, and fly a passenger-carrying seaplane.

1912 Bitter dock strike rages in San Diego. Lee de Forest carries out vacuum tube experiments in Palo Alto. Mack Sennett films the first Keystone comedy.

1913 Legislature passes the Alien Land Law. Water from the Owens River arrives via the Los Angeles Aqueduct. Sheriff's deputies and strikers clash in Wheatland. Cecile B. DeMille films *The Squaw Man.*

1914 The U.S. Navy establishes the Pacific Fleet.

1915 Panama Pacific International Exposition in San Francisco and Panama California International Exposition in San Diego run concurrently.

1916 Bomb kills ten and injures forty during Preparedness Day parade in San Francisco.

1917 The 100-inch Hooker Telescope in Mount Wilson Observatory increases the observable universe by 300 percent.

1919 Governor William Stephens signs the Criminal Syndicalism Act. United Artists is organized.

1920 Legislature expands the scope of anti-Japanese legislation. The California Institute of Technology is named. Donald Douglas opens an aviation company in Santa Monica.

1923 Evangelist Aimee Semple McPherson dedicates Angelus Temple in Los Angeles. Fire sweeps the Berkeley hills.

1924 Immigration Act prohibits Japanese from emigrating to the United States. Los Angeles Basin is producing 230 million barrels of crude oil and 300 million cubic feet of natural gas.

1927 T. Claude Ryan builds *Spirit of St. Louis* in San Diego. Mexican field workers organize the Mutual Aid Society and submit demands to growers. *The Jazz Singer* introduces sound in film.

1928 St. Francis Dam collapses, creating a flood that kills four hundred. Philo T. Farnsworth makes the first television transmission from San Francisco laboratory.

1929 In February, oil heir Edward Doheny, Jr., is murdered in Beverly Hills. Western Airlines announces service to New York via Kansas City. *Graf Zeppelin* arrives in Los Angeles.

1930 Eight thousand field workers strike in Imperial Valley. Edward Doheny, Sr., is acquitted of bribery.

1931 Two thousand cannery workers go on strike in Santa Clara Valley. UC Berkeley physics professor Ernest Lawrence develops the cyclotron. Naval air service establishes Moffett Field. Albert Einstein begins the first of three visits to Southern California. Millard Sheets paints *Angel's Flight.*

1933 Ten thousand cotton pickers go on strike in San Joaquin Valley.

1934 Longshoremen launch a coastwide maritime strike. Seventeen agricultural strike leaders are tried on charges of criminal conspiracy. Upton Sinclair runs for governor as a Democrat. William Saroyan makes his literary debut.

1935 Boulder (later Hoover) Dam on the Colorado River is put into operation. Douglas Aircraft announces the DC-3.

1936 Associated Farmers, Inc., provokes Salinas lettuce strike. San Francisco–Oakland Bay Bridge is dedicated. Dorothea Lange photographs *Migrant Mother.*

1937 Golden Gate Bridge is dedicated. Russell and Sigurd Varian devise the klystron tube at Stanford laboratories.

1938 "Ham 'n' Eggs" pension plan goes before the voters.

1939 Newly inaugurated governor Culbert Olson pardons Tom Mooney. Golden Gate International Exposition opens on Treasure Island. Publication of *The Grapes of Wrath* by John Steinbeck, *Factories in the Field* by Carey McWilliams, *The Big Sleep* by Raymond Chandler, *Ask the Dust* by John Fante, *The Day of the Locust* by Nathanael West, and *After Many a Summer Dies the Swan* by Aldous Huxley.

1940 California's first freeway, the Arroyo Seco Parkway, is dedicated. Walt Disney Productions uses audio oscillator from newly formed Hewlett-Packard Company to enhance music for *Fantasia.*

1941 America First rallies are held in Los Angeles and San Francisco. Japanese attack Pearl Harbor.

1942 In February, FDR signs Executive Order 9066; Japanese submarine fires on an oil storage facility in Santa Barbara Channel; bogus reports provoke an air-raid scare over Los Angeles. In March, Lt. General John DeWitt orders the removal of all Japanese, including American citizens, from the West Coast; FDR issues Executive Order 9102 creating the Civilian War Relocation Authority. In April, Lt. Col. Jimmy Doolittle leads his California-based B-25 bombers on an air raid over Tokyo; Major General George Patton prepares for the invasion of North Africa at the Desert Training Center; War Department purchases Rancho Santa Margarita y Las Flores for Marine Corps advanced training center to be called Camp Pendleton. In August, Sleepy Lagoon defendants are sentenced. In October, the Hollywood

Canteen opens, and the first of one million soldiers are processed through Camp Stoneman north of San Francisco for service in the Pacific.

1943 The Zoot Suit Riots break out in Los Angeles.

1944 Ammunition ships explode at Port Chicago. Henry Miller moves to Big Sur.

1945 Bank of America employs ENIAC computer.

1946 Incumbent governor Earl Warren wins Democratic and Republican nominations for a second term.

1947 House Un-American Activities Committee holds hearings on the film industry. Chuck Yeager breaks the sound barrier.

1948 Bob Mathias wins the decathlon at the London Olympics.

1949 Radio station KPFA-FM begins broadcasting in Berkeley.

1953 Varian and Associates becomes the first company to move into the Stanford Industrial Park.

1954 L. Ron Hubbard founds Church of Scientology in Los Angeles.

1955 In July, Disneyland opens in Anaheim.

1956 The poem *Howl* by Allen Ginsberg consolidates sentiment of the Beat movement.

1958 NASA establishes the Jet Propulsion Laboratory in Pasadena. *The Dharma Bums* by Jack Kerouac helps launch the Zen movement. Giants and Dodgers move to San Francisco and Los Angeles. In November, Warren Harding climbs the sheer face of El Capitan in Yosemite.

1959 Fairchild Semiconductor announces integrated circuit chip.

1960 Master Plan for Higher Education envisions California as higher education utopia. Demonstrators riot against HUAC hearings in San Francisco. Caryl Chessman is executed.

1963 Jonas Salk establishes the Institute for Biological Studies in La Jolla.

1964 In September, the Free Speech Movement erupts at UC Berkeley.

1965 Rioting breaks out in Watts district of Los Angeles.

1966 Under leadership of César Chávez, United Farm Workers launches strike and nationwide boycott. Ronald Reagan is elected governor.

1967 In January, Human Be-In is held in San Francisco.

1969 Oil spill off Santa Barbara pollutes some thirty-five miles of coast. In August, Charles Manson and followers go on a killing spree.

1971 Intel Corporation brings microprocessor to market.

1972 Wallace Stegner wins the Pulitzer Prize for *Angle of Repose.*

1974 Gary Snyder wins the Pulitzer Prize for *Turtle Island*.

1976 Apple I computer goes on sale.

1978 Voters pass Proposition 13 reducing property taxes. In November, mass suicide at Jonestown in Guyana. In November, Mayor George Moscone and Supervisor Harvey Milk are assassinated in San Francisco.

1982 Voters reject the Peripheral Canal.

1986 Voters pass Proposition 63 declaring English the official language of California.

1989 Loma Prieta earthquake results in sixty-six deaths and $7 billion in damage.

1991 Firestorm in Oakland hills kills twenty-five, injures 150, and destroys 2,700 homes.

1992 Acquittal of police defendants in the beating of motorist Rodney King provokes five days of rioting in Los Angeles.

1993 Fires break out from Malibu to San Diego.

1994 Northridge earthquake kills fifty-seven and causes $20 billion in property loss. Voters pass Proposition 187 denying benefits to illegal aliens. Three-strikes-and-you're-out law mandates lengthy sentences for third-time offenders.

1995 UC Regents vote to end affirmative action. Jury acquits O. J. Simpson of murder.

1996 Voters pass Proposition 209 outlawing affirmative action in all state and local public programs.

1997 Earth First! activist Julia Butterfly Hill begins a two-year vigil atop a thousand-year-old redwood tree. In late March, thirty-nine members of the Heaven's Gate cult commit suicide in San Diego County.

1998 El Niño rainstorms cause dozens of deaths and $500 million in property losses. Voters pass Proposition 227 banning bilingual education.

2001 California experiences blackouts as the deregulated energy system goes into meltdown. Pacific Gas & Electric files for bankruptcy.

2003 Voters recall incumbent governor Gray Davis and elect film actor Arnold Schwarzenegger to complete Davis's term.

2004 Voters approve $3 billion bond issue for stem cell research.

2004 In April, Governor Schwarzenegger chooses the image of John Muir in Yosemite for the California quarter to be issued by the U.S. Mint.

2005 In May, city councilman Antonio Villaraigosa is elected the first Hispanic mayor of Los Angeles since Cristóbal Aguilar left office in 1872.

CALIFORNIA

1

QUEEN CALAFIA'S ISLAND

Place and First People

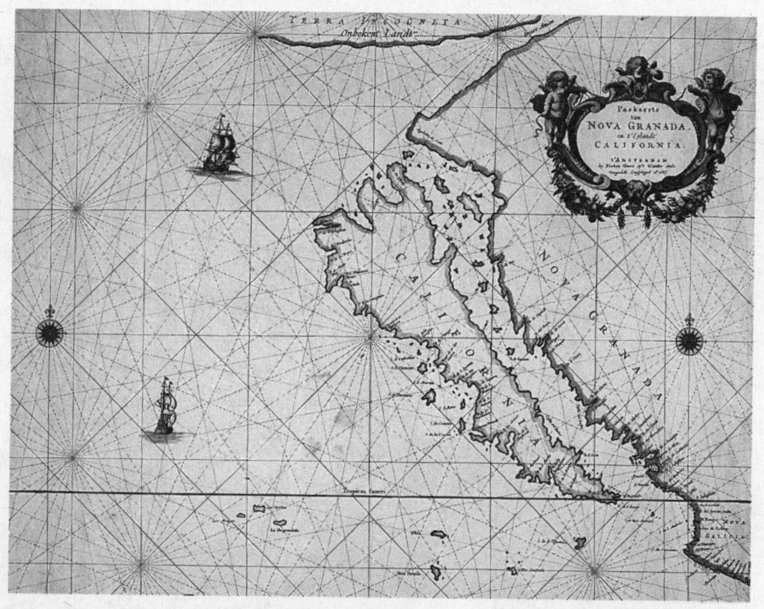

Wenceslaus Hollar, "A New and Exact Map" (London, 1666)

CALIFORNIA STATE LIBRARY

First described in a bestseller, California entered history as a myth. In 1510 the Spanish writer Garci Ordóñez de Montalvo issued a sequel to his 1508 prose romance *Amadis de Gaula,* which Montalvo had in turn based upon a late thirteenth- to early fourteenth-century Portuguese narrative derived from French sources. Published in Seville, Montalvo's *Las Sergas de Esplandián* (*The Deeds of Esplandián*) chronicled the exploits of Esplandián, son of the hero Amadis of Gaul, at the siege of Constantinople. Among Esplandián's allies at the siege were the Californians, a race of black Amazons under the command of Queen Calafia. California itself, according to Montalvo, was "an island on the right hand of the Indies . . . very close to the side of the Terrestrial Paradise," abounding in gold and precious stones. The Californians rode griffins into battle and fought with golden weapons. Queen Calafia herself was "very large in person, the most beautiful of all of them, of blooming years, and in her thoughts desirous of achieving great things, strong of limb and of great courage."

Equipping a fleet, Calafia had sailed to Constantinople to join the other great captains of the world in the siege against the Turks. By the end of the story, Queen Calafia and the Californians have become Christians (which involved, one surmises, giving up their promiscuous ways and the feeding of their male offspring to their griffins), and Calafia herself marries one of Esplandián's trusted lieutenants, with whom she goes on to further adventures.

In 1863 the Boston antiquarian Edward Everett Hale, author of the well-known short story "The Man Without a Country," sent a paper to the American Antiquarian Society in which he provided translations of key passages of *Las Sergas de Esplandián* and cited the prose romance as the source of the name "California." Hale's report was in turn reported on by *The Atlantic Monthly* in March 1864. Montalvo's two tales, Hale noted, were instant bestsellers and remained so for the rest of the sixteenth century. Not until the publication of *Don Quixote de la Mancha* by Miguel de Cervantes Saavedra in two parts in 1605 and 1615 were Montalvo's romances superseded in popularity. Don Quixote, furthermore, was not the only one to take these stories as literal fact. The Spanish in general had a tendency to conflate fact with fiction when it came to these prose romances.

In 1533 a party of Spanish explorers, sailing west from Mexico across an unnamed sea at the command of Hernán Cortés, conqueror of Mexico, landed on what they believed to be an island in the recently discovered Pacific. After 1539 they began to call the place after the mythic island of California, half believing and more than fully hoping they would find there as well the gold and precious stones described in Montalvo's romance, and perhaps even an Amazon or two. Not until 1539–40 did the Spanish discover their geographical mistake. California was a peninsula, not an island, and north of this peninsula—eventually called Antigua or Old California—was a vast northern region that the Spaniards, for one reason or another, would be unable to settle for another 230 years.

The American state of California faces the Pacific Ocean between latitude 42 degrees north (at the border of the American state of Oregon) and latitude 32 degrees north (at the border of the Mexican state of Baja California Norte). On a clear day, photographed from a satellite, California appears as a serene palette of blue, green, brown, white, and red. This apparent serenity, however, masks a titanic drama occurring beneath the surface, in the clash of the two tectonic plates upon which California rests. California itself resulted from a collision of the North American and Pacific plates. Across a hundred million years, the grinding and regrinding of these plates against each other, their sudden detachments, their thrusts above or below each other—together with the lava flow of volcanoes, the bulldozing action of glaciers, and, later, the flow of water and the depositing of alluvial soil—created a region almost abstract in its distinct arrangements of mountain, valley, canyon, coastline, plain, and desert. As the California-born philosopher and historian Josiah Royce observed, there is nothing subtle about the landforms and landscapes of California. Everything is scaled in bold and heroic arrangements that are easily understood.

Fronting more than half the shoreline of the western continental United States, California—all 158,693 square miles of it—offers clear-cut and confrontational topographies. First of all, there is the 1,264-mile Pacific shoreline itself. Thirty million years ago, tectonic action formed this shoreline by detaching a great land mass from the southern edge of the Baja California peninsula, moving it northward, and attaching it back onto the continent. At four strategic intervals—the bay of San Diego in the south, Monterey and San Francisco bays in the midregion, and Humboldt Bay in the north—this appended land mass opened itself to the sea and created four harbors. Formed as recently as thirty thousand years ago when mountains on the shoreline collapsed and the sea rushed in, San Francisco Bay is among the two or three finest natural harbors on the planet.

Rising from this coastline, from north to south, various mountain ranges run boldly into the Pacific. At latitude 35 degrees 30 minutes north, in the county of San Luis Obispo, these coastal mountains bifurcate into two ranges: the Transverse Ranges, veering in a southeasterly direction into southern Kern County in the interior, and the Peninsula Ranges, continuing southward down the coast. In the far north, the Klamath Mountains and the southern tip of the Cascades move in an easterly direction toward the Modoc Plateau on the northeastern corner. Running south from the Modoc Plateau is another, even more formidable mountain range, the Sierra Nevada—John Muir's "Range of Light," four hundred miles long, eighty miles wide—sealing off the eastern edge of California from the Great Basin until these mighty mountains yield to the Mojave Desert in the southeastern corner. Forty-one California mountains rise to more than ten thousand feet. The highest—Mount Whitney—is, at 14,496 feet, the second highest mountain in the continental United States. Mount Shasta in the north—rising from its plain to a height of 14,162 feet, its crowning glaciers still grinding against each other—was once an active volcano. Nearby Mount Lassen, also a volcano, was active as recently as 1921.

Thus in eons past did mountains set the stage for the essential drama of the California landscape: an interplay of heights, flatland, and coast. Coastal plains adjoin the bays of San Francisco and Monterey, and a great basin, the Los Angeles Plain, flanks the coast south of the Transverse Ranges. Four hundred and thirty miles in length, the Central Valley runs through the center of the state in two sequences, the San Joaquin Valley to the south, the Sacramento Valley to the north. Open and sweeping as well are the moonlike Modoc Plateau in the northeastern corner of the state, the high desert Great Basin on the eastern edge of the Sierra Nevada, the Mojave Desert in the southeast, and the Salton Trough thrusting itself up from Baja.

Here it is, then: a landscape of stark contrasts, vibrant and volatile with the geological forces that shaped the western edge of the continent. Numerous fault lines—the San Andreas, the Hayward, the Garlock, the San Jacinto, the Nacimiento—crisscross the western edge from San Francisco Bay to the Mexican border, keeping the region alive with tectonic action. Within human memory—in 1857 at the Tejon Pass in Southern California, in 1872 in the Owens Valley, in San Francisco in 1906, in

Long Beach in 1933, in the San Fernando Valley in 1971, again in the San Francisco Bay Area in 1989, and again in the San Fernando Valley in 1994—great earthquakes shook the land, destroying lives and property. At magnitude 8.3 on the Richter scale, the San Francisco earthquake of April 18, 1906, like the Lisbon earthquake of 1755, precipitated the destruction of an entire city.

Just sixty miles from Mount Whitney, the highest point in the state, is Death Valley, the lowest point on the continent at 282 feet below sea level. Here temperatures can reach as high as 134 degrees Fahrenheit, as they did on July 10, 1913. In midsummer the Central Valley can be as hot as the Equator. Fortunately for California as a place for human settlement, however, two factors—the California Current coming down from the northwestern Pacific, and the Pacific High, a high-pressure zone a thousand miles off the coast—help moderate the heat of the interior. From the point of view of human preferences, coastal California—where settlement began and maintains its greatest density—sustains a mosaic of salubrious climates. Few climates in North America, if any, can equal that of coastal California from the point of view of human use. Like the Mediterranean, the southern littoral is warm and dry. This Mediterranean climate continues up the coast and veers inland until it meets the forested regions of the north. From Monterey Bay to the Marin headlands north of San Francisco, however, this Mediterranean climate is moistened and softened by morning sea fogs and the other mitigating influences of maritime weather. In general, coastal California rarely gets below 40 degrees in January or above 72 degrees in July, in dramatic contrast to the inland heat.

There are two seasons in California, wet and dry. Rain (and, in the mountains, snow) falls typically from October to March, mostly between December and February. The rest of the year is generally sunny. Two thirds of the total precipitation falls in the northern third of the state, where some locations average as much as eighty inches of rain (or its equivalent in snow) in a year. This rainfall and the melting snowpacks of the Sierra Nevada and other ranges water the state through a series of streams that feed into the Sacramento River running north to south and the San Joaquin River running south to north, the two converging in Suisun Bay in the Delta country on the northeastern edge of San Francisco Bay. The interior Central Valley was once an extensive inland sea, hence its rich fossil deposits. Other river systems drain the Coast, Transverse, and Peninsula ranges north and south. In comparison to the arid Far West, then, California has more than its share of water, although it is not always where it is most needed.

The barriers of mountain and desert, together with its patterns of water and climate, render California a distinct bioregion. Even before it was depicted as an island in early Spanish maps, California was a kind of island on the land, sealed off by the Pacific, the Sierra Nevada, the Klamath and Cascade ranges in the north, and the Mojave Desert in the southeast. Off Monterey looms an undersea chasm as wide and deep as the Grand Canyon, and the effects of such depths—aside from the sapphire blue of the Bay—can be seen in the forests of kelp hugging the shore and the biotic exuberance of innumerable tide pools. Offshore, gray whales make their annual migrations north and south to feeding and breeding grounds. Salmon, sardines, halibut, tuna, bonito, crab, and abalone abound. Dolphins, sea elephants, sea lions, seals, and sea otters find abundant feeding in the fish-rich coastal seas. Sharks, barracudas, and samurai swordfish prowl, hunt, and feed through these waters.

Then there is the seacoast—a world unto itself, more than twelve hundred miles in extent. In certain regions—the North Coast, for example, or Big Sur south of Monterey—the land plunges precipitously into the sea. At other points, such as the Delta region on the eastern edge of San Francisco Bay or the south central coastal regions, a rich complexity of estuaries, tidelands, and marshes intercedes between land and sea. This littoral is in many ways its own life zone, with grunion running ashore, sandpipers skirting the dunes in carpets of low-flying silver, pelicans and herons rooting for frogs and small fish in the wetlands, and everywhere, overhead, the white light and bright cries of seagulls, egrets, and other seabirds.

Just inland, extending from San Francisco Bay to the Oregon border, there once commenced a primeval forest of redwoods, which also stretched across the upper portions of Monterey Bay on the Santa Cruz peninsula. These trees (*Sequoia sempervirens*) and their first cousins (*Sequoiandendron giganteum*), flourishing in some thirty-five groves in the Sierra foothills, were the most ancient living entities on the planet, some of them four thousand years old. Equally distinct to California were great oak trees, millions of them. A vast woodland, a river of oak nearly four hundred miles in length, circled the interior of the region, with a stately procession of great trees moving up along the eastern flank of the Coast Range, then sweeping eastward across the top of the Central Valley before flowing southward through the foothills of the Sierra Nevada. Found here as well, in the coastal mountainous regions, was the madrone: a thick hard red tree, clinging close to the earth, that also bespoke California as a distinctive region, as did the Monterey pine and the Monterey cypress: trees evocative of the classical past, standing in Virgilian dignity along the shorelines of the Central Coast.

Above this coastal region and its adjacent interior—above, that is, the mountains of Big Sur, the oak-dotted rolling hills of the south Central Coast, the sagebrush and chaparral of the southern region—glided the mighty condor, ancient survivor of the Pleistocene, borne aloft on its nine-foot wingspan by updrafts from the Pacific. Eagles, ospreys, hawks, and the lowly buzzard, alert for carrion below, shared these skies as well. Looking down from great heights, these soaring birds caught sight of the multitudinous herds of tule elk which, by the hundreds of thousands, roamed the Coast Ranges and the marshes of the Central Valley: the western wetlands that were all that was left of the ancient sea that once filled the interior.

Because California was mountain country, it was bear country as well: the black bear, the brown bear, and the great grizzly that could rise to full height, master of all it surveyed. Shambling through the state, primeval demigods in an unwritten epic, grizzlies stood at the apex of the food chain, the omnivorous predator of elk and deer on the plain, salmon and trout in the northern rivers, the fat-tailed beaver plying their ancient craft in the rivers of the interior. Even mountain lions gave way when grizzlies drew near. Native Americans considered the grizzly another kind of human being, a creature from the mythic past, a survivor from the dawn of creation.

Because California was an island on the land, its bird life was distinct, especially in the mountain forests that dominated the region. Flourishing in the vast pine woods, the mountain birds of California were lighter, paler, grayer than their counterparts in the interior of the continent, although the blue-fronted California jay seemed robust enough and, like the mighty condor, a worthy symbol of the state to come. Abundant as well were the quail flourishing in the underbrush, the flights of ducks over the wetlands, and, in the interior, over the vast Central Valley, the temporary birds of the state—flocks of Canada geese especially—flying in migration, north and south, along the Pacific Flyway. To put the matter in a nutshell (or rather, in an acorn shell, since the oak acorn was a primary nutrient for bear and Native American alike), California sustained throughout its many life zones the same plants and animals as were flourishing in the rest of the continent, albeit they had been transformed over time by the island-on-the-land nature of their habitat.

Such a teeming plenitude of plant, animal, and bird life was quite conducive to human habitation, as the Native Americans of the region had been discovering to their satisfaction for the more than twenty-five generations since their ancestors had first settled down at various points and in various ways in this mountain- and desert-guarded enclave, a semicontinent unto itself. At the initial moment of European contact in 1492, something approaching one third of all Native Americans living within the present-day boundaries of the continental United States—which is to say, more than three hundred thousand people—are estimated to have been living within the present-day boundaries of California. This claim has been disputed by those who argue for a much larger Native American population for the continental United States, but no matter: the figures, however they compare to the rest of the continent, are still impressive. For centuries, hundreds of thousands of Native Americans had been making their homes, living their lives, in the place now called California. In time, anthropologists would describe this Native American culture according to ethnographic categories based on linguistic distinctions. The Native Americans of California, they tell us, belonged to twenty-two linguistic families. Within these categories were some 135 separate languages.

No two authoritative ethnographic maps of Native American California are ever exactly alike, but the general outline of settlement—as in the case of the landforms, flora, and fauna that helped determine patterns of Native American life—are generally agreed upon. In the mountainous, stream-rich northwest were the fishing peoples: the Yuki, the Tolowa, Karok, and Yurok, the Hoopa, Wiyot, Mattole, and Wailaki, each skilled at netting and spearing trout and salmon, each builders of impressive settlements and totems. To the west were the Wintun, the Shasta, and the Yana, the last native peoples to survive in aboriginal circumstances, their final survivor, Ishi, emerging from the forest in August 1911. Farther south, encountered from the coast into the interior, were the Pomo, the Maidu, the Lile'ek, and the Wappo. The Miwok people throve in three enclaves: the Lake Miwok around Clear Lake north of the Bay Area; the

Coast Miwok in what would eventually be known as Marin County; and the Miwok of the northern San Joaquin Valley. Southeast along the coast from San Francisco Bay flourished the Costanoan. Like the Coast Miwok, the Costanoan were a shellfish-gathering people, and over the centuries they left behind great mounds of shells from innumerable feasts. To the south of the Costanoan were the Esselen people of Big Sur, adept at mysticism and the healing arts, and south of them were the Salinan, followed by the Chumash, who lived in long lodges in complex social arrangements and took to the channel off the Santa Barbara coast in seagoing canoes resembling those of Polynesia. The Gabrielino were centered in what would later be known as Orange County. To the east, along the mountains and plains of San Bernardino, lived the Serrano, an inland people with connections to the coast. The Yokut inhabited the center of the Great Central Valley. The northern Paiute, Washo, Mono, and Panamint peoples lived along the eastern edge of the Sierra Nevada, seasonally dividing their time between the mountains and the plain. The Tubatulabal held to the mountains of the southern Sierra, spilling into the southwestern desert. Here could also be found the Ute-Chemehuevi, a desert society related to the other peoples of the southwest. The Luiseño-Cahuilla and the Yuman occupied the southern tier of the southeastern desert.

With so many languages, so many tribes and tribelets, so many autonomous communities, Native American California offered a paradigm of linguistic and cultural diversity anticipating the population patterns of a later era when the peoples of the world arrived in the region. Certain generalizations, however, can be made that are valid for all the Native American peoples of California. The early inhabitants of California found in their various regions more than enough flora and fauna to sustain their lives; they were, therefore, not warlike in their relationships with each other, although quasi-ritualistic conflicts over disputed territories were not unknown. Large-scale political organizations were equally unnecessary. With no need to make war, they did not develop elaborate hierarchies. With nature relatively abundant, simple and effective technologies for hunting and gathering sufficed—although in their woven storage baskets, the Native Californian women achieved an art form that was also eminently practical. Theirs was a world of river, creek, or desert oasis, and of settlements that could easily be moved. Their therapy—their sociology even, and certainly their communal life—was centered on sweat lodges, where they warmed themselves with steam from water poured on fire-heated stones before plunging into a nearby river or lake, emerging renewed. In matters of property, they tended to be communal. In matters sexual, they tended toward balance and restraint, with full regard for the rearing of children. Their ego, as far as we can tell, was not the self-conscious, self-regarding ego of post-Renaissance Europe, but rather an awareness of self through the rhythms of daily life, the pageant of nature, the companionable presence of spirits, and the creation myths that gave them a cosmology and a history and fixed for them a place in the world. With the exception of the acorn, a universal food, the sustenance of each region in this mosaic—distinct in its topography, its climate, its varieties of fish and game—determined the gross and subtle differences of life: the fishing people of the northeast, the shell gatherers of the Central Coast, the hunter-gatherers of the interior, the agriculturists of the southeast all had their cultures determined over the centuries by what was there in the first place, by California itself.

While external organization tended toward the simplistic, the internal cultures of the various groups offered a highly developed heritage of creation myths, totems, and taboos, together with rituals and protocols for stylized warfare and the more pervasive peace, for coming of age, sexuality, family life, birth, and death. For these people, the world was alive with spirit, and the web of life—the linkages, dependencies, and interactions among humans, animals, and plants—was a continuum. The world itself was anchored in a story that had first been told when Coyote created the world and the human beings in it, and it was a continuing story in which they also were participating, from birth to death, in a flow of time that was circular, pervasive, and nonlinear. In the early twentieth century, pioneering anthropologists such as Alfred and Theodora Kroeber, Thomas Waterman, and Saxton Pope would marvel at the intricate linguistic, material, mythological, and moral culture achieved by these First Californians, especially as so vividly incarnated in Ishi, the last of them to come of age in aboriginal circumstances. The late twentieth century would witness the reemergence of these First Californians as a financial and political force in a postmodernist state. For a long time to come, however, theirs would not be an easy life as first Europe and then the United States invaded their lands, wiped out their food supply, uprooted their culture, and decimated their numbers. After twenty-five generations, the First Californians would soon be encountering social forces, diseases, and genocidal violence that would bring them to the brink of extinction.

2

LAWS OF THE INDIES

The Spanish Colonial Era

Franciscan Friar Jeremiah O'Keefe, Mission San Juan Capistrano, 1900

SEAVER CENTER FOR WESTERN HISTORY RESEARCH

LOS ANGELES COUNTY MUSEUM OF NATURAL HISTORY

From Columbus onward, the exploration and conquest of the New World by Spain was motivated by dreams of places equally as far-fetched as the island ruled by Queen Calafia. First of all, the Spaniards, having arrived in the Caribbean, had to find out what was on the other side of the Isthmus of Panama flanking its western edge. In 1513 a young adventurer, Vasco Núñez de Balboa, fleeing his creditors, seized command of the settlement of Darién on the eastern edge of Panama and organized an expedition into the interior. In September 1513, Balboa and his men made the breathtaking discovery of the Pacific Ocean. The extent of this vast sea remained unknown to the Spaniards for nearly a decade; yet even in the midst of such mystery, it was apparent that this newly discovered sea might very well be the pathway to the Indies that had eluded Columbus. Suddenly, the riches of Cathay and Chipango (China and Japan) seemed tantalizingly close.

Within the decade, however, the Spanish sailing expedition commanded by Portuguese navigator Ferdinand Magellan would dramatically qualify this hope for a quick connection to the wealth of the Indies. Having served the crown of Portugal in India and Morocco, Magellan knew these mysterious regions firsthand. He believed, moreover, that he could reach the Moluccas, a region fabled for its riches, by sailing directly west. King Manuel I of Portugal rejected the plan, but King Carlos I of Spain (later Holy Roman Emperor Charles V) backed Magellan's proposal. Setting sail from Spain on September 20, 1519, with five vessels and 265 men, Magellan reached the coast of South America by January. Sailing southward, he entered the strait below South America that would later bear his name, rounded the tip of the continent, and on November 28, 1520, reached the Pacific. Setting a northwest course, Magellan then sailed across the vast ocean discovered by Balboa seven years earlier. He reached the Marianas on March 6, 1521, and the Philippines ten days later. There, on April 27, 1521, he was killed while trying to arbitrate a dispute among the natives. One of his ships, the *Victoria,* sailed across the Indian Ocean, rounded the Cape of Good Hope, and reached Europe on September 6, 1522. In accomplishing this first circumnavigation of the globe, the Magellan expedition linked Spain, the Atlantic, the Caribbean, South and Central America, Mexico, the Pacific, and the Philippines into a continuum that would hold its unity until the collapse of the Spanish empire in the early 1800s. Set strategically in the center of this continuum was Mexico, and from Mexico would eventually be launched the exploration and settlement of California.

But first Mexico had to be made Spanish, which is to say, conquered. The very year, 1519, that Magellan began his epic voyage, another Iberian adventurer, Hernán Cortés, who had participated in 1511 in the conquest of Cuba, did exactly that. He sailed to Mexico in February 1519 and—in an epic campaign of daring, courage, cruelty, deceit, pathos, and splendor, which would fascinate historians from that time forward—reached the Aztec capital of Tenochtitlán in November 1519, seized the Aztec emperor Montezuma, retreated from the capital, made alliances with other Indian nations, campaigned once again across the Mexican peninsula, and on August 13, 1521, occupied Tenochtitlán once and for all, thereby laying the foundations of the viceroyalty of New Spain. Spain now held a strategic foothold on the Pacific, yet the question remained: was that opening to the Pacific direct and unimpeded, or were there other landforms—islands, most likely—to the west? For the time being, as the Spaniards consolidated their hold on Mexico proper, the question remained moot. Still, Cortés nurtured within himself the persistent Spanish dream of sailing directly to the Indies.

In 1532, Cortés, then nearing the final years of his New World career, commissioned an expedition under the command of Fortún Jiménez to sail west from Mexico and report on what he discovered. Crossing an inland sea that would later be called the Sea of Cortés or the Gulf of California, Jiménez encountered what he believed to be an island. Shortly thereafter, he was killed by natives. It was perhaps Jiménez or one of his associates who first called this supposed island "California."

When Cortés himself arrived in Baja California at La Paz in 1535, he named it "Santa Cruz." Spending two years trying to found a colony, Cortés seemed obsessed with this arid and rocky place. To understand why, one must understand the credence given by the Spanish to reports of fabled cities of gold that might very well be found across the next mountain. Rumors of such riches had brought Cortés into the heart of the Aztec empire, just as they had motivated the conquest of the Inca empire by Francisco Pizarro in 1532. Other reports believed to be true by the conquistadores—why else would such intrepid explorers as Hernando de Soto and Francisco Vásquez de Coronado plunge themselves into the very heart of the North American continent?—included the seven cities of Cíbola, the equally rich kingdom of the Gran Quivira, and the lands ruled by El Dorado, the Gilded Man, a king who had himself coated in gold dust each morning. Today it is easy to dismiss such stories as fairy tales, but in the early sixteenth century, among a people not yet fully emerged from a medieval mindset and gifted with vivid imaginations, such myths and legends possessed the power to motivate some of the most arduous and heroic overland and maritime expeditions in human history.

Passed over for the post of viceroy of the very same New

Spain he had founded with his conquest of Mexico, Cortés was dreaming of one last big score: the golden cities that might lie to the north, even the possibility of reaching the Strait of Anián believed to offer a direct maritime corridor from Atlantic Europe to the Spice Islands and the fabled kingdoms of the Far East. And so in 1538 Cortés sent yet another of his able lieutenants, Francisco de Ulloa, to explore the sea between Mexico and the alleged island of California and perhaps discover the seven cities of Cíbola. In 1539 Ulloa reached the head of this sea. It was a land mass continuous with Mexico, broken only by the mouth of a mighty river (the Colorado), which Ulloa also partially explored. The sea was a gulf, and Baja California was a peninsula, not an island.

The very next year, 1540—as Hernán Cortés returned to Spain to press his case for higher appointment—the very able administrator who was serving as the first viceroy of New Spain, Antonio de Mendoza, commissioned Hernando de Alarcón to explore the lands north of the Gulf of California that had been discovered the previous year by Ulloa. Heroically, Alarcón ascended the Colorado River for more than two hundred miles. Either he or another explorer, Melchor Díaz, crossing the Colorado River near the present-day city of Yuma, Arizona, became the first European to set foot in Alta, or Upper, California.

Thus, by the early 1540s, the Spaniards—thanks primarily to forces set in motion by Hernán Cortés—had moved the borders of New Spain northward as far as Alta California. In mid-1542, Viceroy de Mendoza commissioned the experienced navigator Juan Rodríguez Cabrillo, who had served with Cortés during the conquest of Mexico, to sail north along the western edge of Baja California, to explore the coastlands, and—Cabrillo's main mission—to reach the Strait of Anián purportedly linking the Atlantic and the Pacific. On June 27, 1542, the Cabrillo expedition—consisting of two small ships, the *San Salvador* and the *Victoria*—sailed from the port of La

Navidad on the Mexican coast north of Acapulco, rounded the tip of the Baja Peninsula, then moved slowly north, anchoring when possible for onshore explorations. On September 28, 1542, Cabrillo anchored in San Diego Bay, thus initiating European contact with the first of the three harbors of California (San Diego, Monterey, and San Francisco) that would prove of use to Spanish California.

Coming ashore at San Diego Bay, Cabrillo and his men became the first Europeans to reach California from the sea. On Christmas Eve 1542, on the island of San Miguel in the Santa Barbara Channel, Cabrillo fell and broke his arm near the shoulder. (Some sources say it was his leg.) The wound grew gangrenous as Cabrillo took his ships still farther north, to a promontory later called Point Reyes. Forced to turn back by heavy seas and bad weather, Cabrillo returned to San Miguel Island and there, on January 3, 1543, died from his infection. Cabrillo's dying wish—expressed to his chief pilot Bartolomé Ferrer, a native of the Levant in the service of Spain—was to continue the expedition northward as originally planned, once the seas and the weather got better. Burying Cabrillo beneath an incised rock on the nearby island of Santa Rosa, Ferrer took his ships north, and on March 1, 1543, he reached latitude 42 degrees north, later the boundary between California and Oregon, before turning south and returning to La Navidad.

For more than two decades, interest in the Californias went into remission—until the conquest of the Philippines. In 1564, Luis de Velasco, the able and honest viceroy of New Spain based in Mexico City, commissioned conquistador Miguel López de Legazpi to establish a Spanish presence in the Philippines. It was a breathtaking, near-impossible transpacific assignment; but Legazpi achieved it within seven years and thus linked New Spain and the Philippines across the Pacific. New Spain would continue to rule the Philippines from Mexico City until 1822. Once established in the Philippines, the Spaniards traded throughout the region—in Japan, China, the Moluccas, Siam—gathering into Manila the riches of Asia for shipment to Mexico by galleon, starting in June 1565. These great ships were at long last bringing the wealth of the Indies to Spain—not directly, but via the Pacific, Mexico, the Caribbean, and the Atlantic.

The Caribbean sea-lanes, known as "the Spanish Main," soon proved especially attractive to freebooters and pirates such as the English navigator Francis Drake. In late 1577, Drake organized a five-ship expedition that had multiple goals. First, he planned to reach the Pacific by rounding South America through the Strait of Magellan. Once there, he would plunder Spanish cities and ships on the Pacific coast. Having done that, he would proceed north in search of the Northwest Passage (as the English called the mythical Strait of Anián), claiming territory en route for England. He would then cross the Pacific, reach the Indies, and thereby achieve for England a connection to the fabled Spice Islands of the Far East.

It was a heroic program: the first circumnavigation of the globe since Magellan's. Preparing his ships in Plymouth Harbor, Drake was more than a pirate (although the Spaniards could legitimately consider him one!); he was the maritime embodiment of Elizabethan civilization itself, destined to create in North America a colonial society that would eventually become the United States. The conflict between Spain and England, in which Francis Drake so enthusiastically participated, was nothing less than a titanic conflict between English and Spanish civilizations, the Reformation and the Counter-Reformation, as both religious and political forces contended to answer the implied question: just exactly who would dominate the North American continent?

Setting sail from Plymouth on November 15, 1577, the Drake expedition crossed the Atlantic, navigated the Strait of Magellan (the first English ships to do so), and proceeded to sack Valparaíso and other smaller settlements on the Pacific coast of

South America. They seized Spanish ships, plundered them for treasure and charts, and moved northward in search of the Northwest Passage, getting as far, possibly, as the present state of Washington. By then, however, Drake's five-ship flotilla had been reduced by loss or separation to only the *Golden Hinde,* and this small ship—a mere one hundred tons burden, loaded with thirty tons of Spanish treasure—was literally coming apart at the seams. And so Drake returned the *Golden Hinde* southward to a bay he had noted on his northward voyage, on a peninsula guarded by steep white cliffs that had reminded him of the Channel Coast. Pulling into this bay on June 17, 1579 (today it is called Drake's Bay, on the Point Reyes peninsula), the English spent five weeks resting, making friendly contact with the Coast Miwok people of the region (who most likely thought that Drake and his men were their ancestors, returning from the dead), conducting the first Book of Common Prayer services in North America (led by chaplain Francis Fletcher, who later wrote an account of the expedition published in *Hakluyt's Voyages,* 1598–1600), and repairing their overburdened ship. At one point in his stay, Drake named the region Nova Albion (New England) and erected a plate of brass claiming it for the crown. Crossing the Pacific, the *Golden Hinde* visited the Moluccas, the Celebes, and Java before rounding the Cape of Good Hope and sailing back to Plymouth, which Drake reached on September 26, 1580.

The 1579 California sojourn of Sir Francis Drake, knighted by Queen Elizabeth upon his return, reinforced the strategic importance of California as a place midway between the Spanish interests in Southeast Asia and the Far East (centered in Manila), and the imperial construct of New Spain (centered in Mexico City) and the viceroyalty of Peru (centered in Lima). Drake's claim on Nova Albion can be seen as mere bravado; but it was nevertheless a symbol of great importance as far as California was concerned and has always been treated as such by historians, for it underscored from an English point of view the competition between two great civilizations for California and other regions on the North American continent.

So, too, were the Spaniards discovering—tentatively, even feebly, given the vast distances and their slender resources—the importance of a California connection. In 1584 a galleon commanded by Francisco de Gali discovered that the best way to get from the Philippines to New Spain was to follow the Japanese current westward, head directly toward the coast of Alta California off Cape Mendocino, then sail down the coast of California (Alta and Baja) and round Cape San Lucas to Acapulco on the western Mexican coast. This route was followed regularly by the Philippine galleons in the years to come. Unfortunately, the voyage across the Pacific could take as long as two hundred days, and few crews escaped a deadly toll of scurvy, dysentery, beriberi, vermin, the usual round of shipboard accidents, and even death from lightning. Logically, then, there emerged a plan in the mid-1580s in the mind of Pedro de Moya y Contreras, viceroy of New Spain and archbishop of Mexico: find and develop a port on the coast of Alta California where the Manila galleons could land before continuing south.

In 1595 the viceroy entrusted an exploratory expedition to the Portuguese merchant-adventurer Sebastián Rodríguez Cermeño. Take the galleon *San Agustín* across the Pacific from the Philippines, the viceroy instructed, and explore the coast of Alta California for possible ports. On November 6, 1595, after the usual horrible voyage, the *San Agustín* anchored in the same bay where the *Golden Hinde* had found safe harbor. Cermeño named the harbor the Bay of San Francisco and formally claimed the region for Spain. Unfortunately, on November 30, 1595, a sudden storm drove the *San Agustín* aground at Point Reyes, scattering its treasure on the shore. For generations to come, the Coast Miwok would fashion ornaments from shards of shipwrecked china; eventually, one intact teacup would be discovered by an amateur archaeologist. All that was left to Cermeño and his crew of seventy after the shipwreck was a makeshift launch they called the *San Buenaventura,* constructed from the wreckage. In this fragile bark, Cermeño and his men poked their way down the California coast to Acapulco, missing the Bay of San Francisco entirely and subsisting on fish and acorns provided by friendly Indians.

There had to be a better way to explore the California coast, and that was a formally commissioned and provisioned expedition from Mexico northward, as opposed to the use of galleon crews exhausted by more than two hundred days at sea. And so the Spaniards made one last reconnaissance before—as it turned out—abandoning Alta California entirely for the next 167 years. This last effort was impressive: three vessels with a crew of two hundred accompanied by three Carmelite chaplains, under the command of Sebastián Vizcaíno, a merchant-navigator with long experience in Mexico and the Philippines. Commissioned captain general of the expedition, Vizcaíno sailed from Acapulco on May 5, 1602. Reaching and naming the Bay of San Diego on November 10, he methodically explored his way up the coast, arriving on December 16 at a bay that he named in honor of the viceroy, the Conde de Monterey. Moving north, the Vizcaíno expedition—once again, one is tempted to say!—missed the entrance to San Francisco Bay, although the Spanish ships did pass close to the Farallon Islands off the entrance to that great harbor. Vizcaíno sailed as far north as Cape Mendocino before bad weather and scurvy forced his return to Acapulco.

Never one to hide his light under a bushel, Vizcaíno made much of the maps and descriptions of the California coastline his crew had assembled. He was especially boastful of the Bay of Monterey as being the perfect harbor for Manila galleons arriving from the Philippines. Yet while Vizcaíno, promoted to the rank of admiral, went on to a distinguished career exploring and mapping the coasts of Japan, New Spain did nothing about Alta California for the next 167 years.

How does one account for this delay? Why was this California connection, once made, so utterly abandoned? Some of the answers are obvious. New Spain had neither the financial nor the human resources to make a settlement so far to the north, whatever the importance of Alta California to the Manila galleons might be. Such a purely economic explanation, however, is not sufficient. Spain was obviously interested in California, as these expeditions suggest, but it was not yet interested in the establishment of a civil society there, even if it were capable of such a foundation.

The Spanish empire in the New World was governed by the Council of the Indies under a series of regulations drawn up in the early 1570s and organized into the Laws of the Indies in 1680. In minute detail, including the specifics of town planning, the Laws of the Indies called for the integration and interaction of ecclesiastical and secular societies. Church and state were to cooperate in a program of settlement and development that would promote both the worldly and otherworldly well-being of the colonists. While the Spaniards could bring the Laws of the Indies as far north as the city of Santa Fe, founded in 1609 at the foot of the Sangre de Cristo Mountains on the site of an ancient Indian ruin, they did not have the resources to bring the Laws and the society they enabled any farther north. And besides, even if they had possessed the wherewithal to settle Alta California, another version of Spanish civilization, another theory of the state—that of the Jesuits—soon claimed the right to evangelize Arizona and Baja California, together with a future claim on Alta California, and this in turn established a barrier to civilian settlement.

Under the Laws of the Indies and accepted church practice, mission theory had as its goal the evangelization of Native Americans and their education in religion and the manual arts during a period of residency and transition in a mission, leading eventually to their introduction into secular society as *gente de razón,* which is to say, full-fledged "people of reason," baptized Catholics and useful citizens. At this point (at least in theory), the missions were to put themselves out of business and be replaced by a diocesan parish structure staffed by secular clergy under the control of a local bishop. So much for theory. The reality, especially in missions entrusted to Jesuits—the Reductions (mission colonies) of Paraguay, most notably—was far more complex. Founded (three years before Cabrillo was exploring the California coast) by Ignacio de Loyola, a Basque soldier turned priest-reformer, the Company (or Society) of Jesus, more commonly known as the Jesuits, rapidly developed into a powerful order of scholars, educators, missionaries, and advisers to the great and powerful. The Jesuits were also an international organization of far-reaching influence. As missionaries they were unsurpassed, beginning with the efforts of one of their original co-founders, Francis Xavier, in the Far East. The Jesuits believed in enculturation, that is, the adaptation of Catholicism (as far as orthodoxy permitted) to the culture of those being evangelized. They also sought to protect such peoples and their cultures from catastrophic disruptions by soldiers and civilians. Established in the late sixteenth century in Paraguay, the Jesuit Reductions were fashioned as theocratic communities blending Spanish and Native American cultures, quasi-autonomous as far as secular authority was concerned, but thoroughly under the controlling guidance of Jesuit missionaries. Such was the Jesuit strategy—the protection of Indians in enclave utopias—but it was also the problem as far as secular authorities were concerned, especially after Enlightenment attitudes began, however tentatively, to enter Spanish thinking and a growing resentment began to coalesce against the power of the society.

Not surprisingly, the Jesuits—specifically Eusebio Francisco Kino and Juan María de Salvatierra, two Italian-born missionaries assigned to New Spain—dreamed of establishing their order in California. Already, from 1683 to 1685, Kino—like all Jesuit priests, a highly trained university graduate—had spent two years in Baja California (as chaplain and cartographer) as part of an effort to establish a colony on the peninsula. The effort collapsed, but Kino never let go of the dream of establishing a series of Jesuit missions in Baja, then moving north. Kino devoted the next phase of his life to founding a string of missions north through Sonora into present-day southern Arizona, then west to the confluence of the Gila and Colorado rivers on the present border of California. The missions established by Kino in the course of this California-oriented movement north were impressive in terms of the solidity of their churches and attendant buildings and the successful cattle ranches, staffed by Native American *vaqueros,* which constituted the core of the mission economy.

In 1691 Kino was joined in his California crusade by another formidable Jesuit, Juan María de Salvatierra, visitor general to the Jesuit missions in northern New Spain. Like Kino, Salvatierra was a highly educated priest of upper-class background, in his mid-forties, and convinced that the Californias, Baja and Alta, had the makings of a Jesuit utopia. Salvatierra and Kino were both highly suspicious of mixing missionary with secular ambitions. During his brief sojourn on the Baja Peninsula, Kino had been shocked by the violent response of the Spaniards when the Native Americans had proven reluctant to do their bidding. What Kino and Salvatierra envisioned, by contrast, were establishments more on the order of the Paraguay Reductions or what they themselves had established in Sonora and Sinaloa: Jesuit-controlled communities, oriented toward and staffed by Native Americans, with only a minimal presence of secular soldiers or colonists. After long negotiation with the Council of the Indies, the Jesuits received permission to enter Baja California, and in 1697 Salvatierra supervised the construction of the first Jesuit mission on the peninsula, named in honor of Our Lady of Loreto. Eventually there would be eighteen Jesuit missions in Baja California, running north in tandem with the missions established by Kino in Sonora and southern Arizona on the other side of the Gulf of Mexico.

So the notion that Spain abandoned California after the Vizcaíno expedition of 1602 is misleading. What Spain did, rather, was to assign to the Jesuits the responsibility for the missions on the northern Mexican frontier, which included Peninsular and Upper California. In doing this, Spain was making a virtue of necessity, for it did not have either the people or the money to settle this region. The Jesuits, in turn, were acting as a northern flank of New Spain. With stone from local quarries, they built mission churches of extraordinary elegance. In Sonora, Arizona, and Peninsular California, they ran flourishing ranches and allied industries. Trained scholars, they explored, mapped, and described in copious reports to their Jesuit superiors in Rome the landscape, flora, and fauna of their assigned territories. But they did not foster the development of a secular society, nor did they report to the viceroy of New Spain. Thanks to Salvatierra, who continued to rise in influence within the Jesuit order, the Jesuit missions of the northern frontier were granted exemptions from the control of either the viceroy or the Jesuit provincial (regional superior) of New Spain. Even the soldiers of the Peninsular California missions were appointed by, and reported to, their Jesuit superiors.

For seventy years this theocratic system remained in place, with Jesuit missionaries dreaming of expanding northward but never quite managing to do so. The good news was that the Jesuits were protecting the Native Americans from exploitation. The bad news—or so by the 1760s was it increasingly believed—was a growing conviction that the Jesuits were running things on their own terms and, moreover, that they had become too powerful an order—a church within the Church, a state within the State—for the good of the Spanish empire. Enlightenment values and a desire to reform and expand the empire had come dramatically to Spain with the ascension to the throne in 1759 of Carlos III, the greatest of the Spanish Bourbons. Among other things, this meant banishing the Jesuits from all Spanish dominions and seizing their assets. In 1765, the crown sent an inspector general to New Spain, José de Gálvez, commissioning him to suppress the Jesuits, reform colonial administration, and—at long last!—organize the settlement of Alta California. Unless Spain settled Alta California, the crown believed, some other nation—most likely Russia—would seize it.

In 1768 Gálvez embarked upon the first phase of his plan: the expulsion of the Jesuits from Baja California, which involved their arrest, temporary imprisonment, and exile to non-Spanish territories. Gálvez replaced the Jesuits with Franciscans from the College of San Fernando in Mexico City, with Father Junípero Serra serving as father-president. To serve as governor of the Californians, Gálvez appointed Gaspar de Portolá, a Catalonian of noble descent, with a distinguished military record as a captain of dragoons in Italy, Portugal, and New Spain. With kindness and diplomacy, Portolá organized the expulsion of the Jesuits, which, as it had in Mexico itself, led to protests from a loyal Indian population and the execution of hundreds of dissidents resisting the loss of their Jesuit protectors.

With the Jesuits gone, three Spaniards—Inspector General Gálvez, Father Serra, and Captain Portolá—began the planning in 1768 of an enterprise that had long eluded the colonial empire: the settlement of Upper California. In recognition of the momentous significance of what they were doing, the trio called their enterprise "the Sacred Expedition." If Gálvez was a talented (albeit unstable) administrator, and Portolá a sane and steady military man, who was Junípero Serra in this triumvirate? Unlike his colleagues, Serra was not a noble, but a farmer's son, born in 1713 in the village of Petra on the island of Majorca.

Baptized Miguel José, he had taken the name Junípero when he joined the Franciscan order at the age of sixteen. Relishing their roles as scholars and schoolmasters, the Jesuits—formed by the Renaissance as well as by the Counter-Reformation—felt little tension between intellectualism and Catholic spirituality. The Franciscan tradition, by contrast, had a more ambivalent response. Franciscans tended to adhere to a more medieval brand of piety, prizing simplicity. Saint Francis of Assisi was not himself a scholar—indeed, he had never even become a priest; yet subsequent Franciscans—the theologian Bonaventure, the philosopher Duns Scotus, and the scientist Roger Bacon come immediately to mind—distinguished themselves as academics while remaining loyal Franciscans. Such was the path that Junípero Serra had initially taken. Showing academic promise, he had gone on to higher studies within the Franciscan order and by the late 1730s was teaching philosophy and theology at the Lullian University in Palma. Then, in his mid-thirties, in an about-face that can be compared to a similar decision by Albert Schweitzer in the early twentieth century, Serra requested a transfer from his cushy academic post to the missionary College of San Fernando in Mexico City, which assigned him to some of its most difficult Indian missions in the inhospitable northern region of Sierra Gorda.

In other words, the predominant side of Franciscan piety—expressed by a rejection of an academic career, with its honors and physical security, in favor of evangelical asceticism—had transformed Serra from a pious priest-professor into an intensely fervent priest-missionary. Landing in Veracruz in the company of his former student and fellow Franciscan, Francisco Palóu, who would eventually write his biography, Serra insisted upon walking all the way to Mexico City. A snake or insect bite suffered en route resulted in an ulcerated leg that would bother him throughout his life. No matter: the diminutive friar (slightly over five feet in height) relished physical suffering and mortification as part of the ferocious asceticism that would characterize the rest of his life. Serra slept on a board bed, scourged himself, and lacerated his flesh with stones in the course of highly emotional sermons. As such, he represented a paradox: a priest formed by an almost medieval piety given a crucial assignment to an enterprise intended, in some measure, to establish civil society in California. The tension involved in such a paradox would soon surface.

Gálvez, Portolá, and Serra decided that four separate parties—two by land, two by sea—would constitute the expedition. Rendezvousing on the shores of San Diego Bay, the Spaniards would establish a base camp there, from which an overland expedition commanded by Captain Portolá would move north to the Bay of Monterey, where another base camp would be set up. Because of Vizcaíno's exaggerated report 167 years earlier regarding the spaciousness of the bay, the Spanish saw this harbor as crucial to a successful settlement. As yet, no one had any knowledge of the vast inland harbor, the Bay of San Francisco, to the north. On January 9, 1769, three newly constructed packets—the *San Carlos,* the *San Antonio,* and the *San José*—set sail for La Paz, and two land parties set forth on March 24 on an overland journey from Baja to Alta California that no one in two and a half centuries had yet successfully completed. After 236 years of thinking about it—from the first landing in Baja California in 1533 to 1769—this was all Spain could manage: three small ships and three hundred men, heading into a land long dreamed of but only sketchily reconnoitered.

The Sacred Expedition was a phantasmagoria of physical hardship, deprivation, suffering, and death. En route to San Diego, the *San José* was lost with all aboard. While the *San Antonio* reached San Diego in fifty-four days, the *San Carlos* took twice that time, and when it arrived, its crew were either dead or dying or devastated by scurvy. So also did the overland expeditions suffer as they negotiated the hostile terrain of the desert regions flanking Alta California to the south. As might be expected, Serra chose to walk, not sail, to his new assignment. His ulcerated leg proved especially painful, until he told a muleteer to treat it as he would a comparable leg wound on a mule. The muleteer's poultice worked wonders, and Serra was able to complete the trip on his own two feet.

By the time the land and sea parties were fully consolidated on July 1, 1769, only half of the Sacred Expedition was left alive, and many of those who survived continued to die off as the *San Antonio* sailed back to La Paz for supplies and reinforcements. At some time during this long wait, Pedro Prat, the French-born surgeon of the expedition, suffered a nervous breakdown. Despite such miserable conditions, Portolá headed north with a military detachment and Father Juan Crespí, another former student of Serra's from Majorca, who wrote a compelling account of this northern journey. On or about the first of October 1769, the Portolá party reached the Bay of Monterey, but no one could believe that this barely adequate harbor was the capacious port described by Vizcaíno. Nor was the *San José* waiting for them there, as they had hoped, and so Portolá took his men farther to the north. On November 1, 1769, an advance party of scouts commanded by Sergeant José Ortega came to the crest of a hill, and there in the distance the Spanish soldiers spied a bay (later named San Francisco) which Father Crespí later described as big enough to offer anchorage to all the navies of Spain. The Portolá party explored the southern shores of this bay, but did not discover its entrance. By January 24, 1770, having gone as far north into Alta California by land as any Spaniard had ever gone, the Portolá party arrived back at the squalid encampment in San Diego, where the sick, the near-dead, and the dying were desperately waiting for the return of the *San Antonio.* Showing his usual resilience, Portolá found forty quasi-fit men in the group and organized a relief mission back to Baja California. For a while it seemed as if the Sacred Expedition would have to be abandoned, but on March 19, 1770, the *San Antonio,* loaded with supplies and reinforcements, was sighted off the coast of San Diego.

Father Serra, meanwhile, on July 16, 1769, dedicated Mission San Diego de Alcalá, the first of the nine missions he would personally found. It was no more than a log shelter with a thatched roof, but it would give rise to a series of twenty-one missions, many of them far grander, that would eventually line the California coast, a day's journey apart, from San Diego to Sonoma north of San Francisco. Equally prophetic, the mission was burned down by local Indians the following year, rebuilt in 1780, and destroyed once again in 1803 by an earthquake. Not until 1813 would the present surviving structure be built. Even though Portolá remained unimpressed with the Bay of Monterey, he returned there, once the *San Carlos* had arrived with supplies and reinforcements, to establish a settlement on June 3, 1770. This time, Serra was with him, and on the same day, the father-president dedicated Mission San Carlos Borromeo, the second California mission, which in the following year Serra moved to the mouth of the Carmel River, taking up residence there as his headquarters.

With the exception of Serra himself and his two former students from Majorca, Juan Crespí and Francisco Palóu (each of them an excellent writer), the Franciscan missionaries from the College of San Fernando who arrived in California over the next half-century to staff the mission system were ordinary men as far as their talents and education were concerned; yet they were dedicated to an extraordinary purpose, at least in their own eyes: the evangelization of the Native Americans of California, whether the Native Americans wanted to be evangelized or not. While the Jesuit missionaries of Baja California were clerics touched by the Enlightenment (at least as far as a scientific interest in their environment was concerned), the Franciscans of Alta California—with the exception again of Crespí and Palóu and another Majorcan, Gerónimo Boscana—left little behind them in the way of writing or scientific observation. Theirs was, rather, a more narrowly focused life, anchored in and structured by Franciscan piety and the immediate challenges of missionary life. Some of these missionaries were, by the standards of any age, admirable men. Others were narrow-minded, even bigoted, regarding Native Americans as little more than children. All of them were leading lonely, isolated lives in a frequently forgotten place. Some of them—Father José María Zalvidea, for example, a missionary at Mission San Gabriel—suffered nervous breakdowns, if not outright insanity.

From the beginning, Spanish California demonstrated the same fundamental flaw that had characterized the Jesuit missions of Baja: the lack of a secular civil society as a matter of either theory or practice. Only San José de Guadalupe, founded November 29, 1777, near a small river on the southern edge of San Francisco Bay, and Los Angeles, founded September 4, 1781, at a similar river site in the center of a great plain in coastal Southern California, were chartered as *pueblos,* which is to say, as secular townships, as opposed to either a mission or a presidio garrison. A third settlement given pueblo (town) status—Villa de Branciforte, established in 1796 by the viceroy, the Marqués de Branciforte, as a retirement town for soldiers and their families near Mission Santa Cruz—never got off the ground. No retired soldiers, much less their wives and families, wanted to come that far north to live on the edge of nowhere. Branciforte eventually wound up as a kind of Botany Bay for men convicted of petty crimes. Even if Spanish California had had a more capacious theory of itself—which is to say, even if the viceroy had granted more pueblo charters to more settlements—for nearly half a century, no one really wanted to come to California. People came to or remained in California because they had to. Three soldiers, for example, convicted of the rape of a Native American woman in San Diego, were sentenced to serve in California for the remainder of their careers, and this was considered harsh punishment.

Serra's constant quarreling with the military governors of California reflects not only legitimate points of contention—the chronic sexual abuse of Indian women by soldiers, most notably—but also the fundamental tension between Spanish California as a missionary society reporting to the Franciscans and California as a secular society reporting to the military governor. So frustrated was Serra by his relations with Portolá's successor, Lieutenant Pedro Fages, that the father-president made the arduous journey back to Mexico City to demand from the viceroy, Antonio María Bucareli, that Fages be removed. Yet Serra also quarreled with Fages's successor, Captain Fernando Rivera y Moncada, and Rivera's successor, Captain Felipe de Neve, a man of equilibrium and first-rate ability. Historians of the missions, many themselves Catholic ecclesiastics, have by and large taken Serra's side in these quarrels; yet such continual contention must also be seen as underscoring the fundamental problem of a society founded as a missionary enterprise, with little provision, in either fact or theory, for a secular polity.

The viceroy to whom Serra appealed in 1771 was himself, like Serra, a professed religious under vows. The member of a distinguished Spanish-Italian family whose Florentine branch had produced three popes and six cardinals, Fray (or Brother) Antonio Bucareli had at the age of twenty-four taken vows of poverty, chastity, and obedience in the Order of St. John of Jerusalem, more commonly known as the Knights of Malta. Serving in the Spanish army, Bucareli had risen to the rank of lieutenant general before becoming governor and captain general of Cuba in 1766 and viceroy of New Spain in 1771. As a professed religious, Bucareli was in sympathy with Serra's missionary ambitions. As an experienced general, however, and the former governor of the richly populated Cuba, Bucareli knew that a more developed civil and military presence would be necessary for Alta California to thrive. Working ceaselessly on behalf of California until his death in office in 1779, five years before the death of Serra, Bucareli can be considered—along with Serra himself, Gálvez, Portolá, and Juan Bautista de Anza—one of the founders of Spanish California, hence of California itself. Gálvez might have organized the Sacred Expedition, but it was Bucareli who strengthened and consolidated the feeble northern settlement. He backed Serra, of course, his fellow religious; but he also sent the distinguished soldier Juan Bautista de Anza north on two crucial expeditions intended, first, to reconnoiter a land route from northern Mexico to California, and second, to establish a settlement on San Francisco Bay.

On January 8, 1774, Captain Anza—a longtime veteran of frontier service with an outstanding reputation—set forth from the presidio at Tubac, south of the present-day city of Tucson, with thirty-four soldiers and one Franciscan, Francisco Garcés, himself an experienced explorer. Anza and his party found their route and on March 22, 1774, reached Mission San Gabriel on the Los Angeles plain, then continued north to Monterey before returning to Tubac. In one heroic trek, Anza had linked California overland to northern New Spain. A grateful Viceroy Bucareli promoted Anza to lieutenant colonel, then gave him new orders: take to San Francisco Bay a party of 240 soldiers and soldier-colonists, together with four civilian families, including women and children, cattle and horses for breeding stock, and ample supplies, and bring them safely across the deserts of Arizona and California, then up the coast to San Francisco. Three babies were born on this arduous fifteen-hundred-mile journey, and one mother died. As the Anza party was being organized, a launch from the ship *San Carlos,* sent north from Monterey to search for an entrance to San Francisco Bay, at long last (thanks to the sailing skills of José Cañizares, sailing master of the *San Carlos*) found what he called La Boca (the mouth) and sailed through what later would more euphoniously be known as the

Golden Gate. The very next day, August 6, 1775, the *San Carlos,* under the command of Juan Manuel de Ayala, entered the great harbor.

Ten months later, an augmented Anza party arrived in San Francisco. Moving up the coast from Monterey, the soldiers and settlers were bringing with them the possibilities of a civil society, although pueblo or civic status had not yet been granted to their settlement. They would, rather, establish a mission and a presidio, together with the beginnings of family life, and that, for the time being, had to suffice. And so north they came: skirting Monterey Bay, moving through the redwood forests of Santa Cruz, then up the coast of the as-yet-unnamed San Francisco peninsula, camping on the site of what later would be the campus of Stanford University, and arriving finally at a lake that would later be known as Mountain Lake, in the heart of a city called San Francisco. The settlement party arrived on June 27, 1776. That September, on the seventeenth, a presidio was established under the command of Lieutenant José Joaquín Moraga on the shores of San Francisco Bay; and the following month, on October 9, 1776, Father Palóu dedicated Mission San Francisco de Asís. In the years to come, the mission system would be extended north of San Francisco Bay through the founding of San Rafael Arcángel in 1817 and San Francisco Solano in 1823, but the general nature and extent of Spanish California now stood established. It was a fragile coastal enclave. The most interior of the missions, Nuestra Señora de la Soledad, founded in 1791, was a mere thirty miles from the Pacific.

It was, moreover, a deeply flawed and deficient society. The entire relationship of the Spanish settlers—Franciscans and soldiers alike—to the Native Americans was, by contemporary standards, problematic, indeed catastrophic. The Franciscans saw themselves as coming to California to save souls, and they must be judged, in part, as the men they truly were—Spanish Catholic missionaries—and by the standards of their time. Yet even a sympathetic observer, acknowledging the benevolent intent of the mission system, must see it by the standards of the twenty-first century, as a violent intrusion into the culture and human rights of indigenous peoples. For more than twenty-five generations, Native Americans had lived harmoniously in their own cherished places under the terms of the cultures they had evolved. They had their own myths and rituals, their own way of life, their own fulfillments and dreams. And now they were being forced from their homelands, brought into the mission system—frequently against their will—and treated as children not yet possessed of full adulthood, not yet *gente de razón,* people of reason. As children, they could be beaten when they proved recalcitrant or ran away from the missions, as they frequently did, and were recaptured. True, some of them made the transition successfully and were hispanicized into productive farmers, artisans, vaqueros, and choral singers. Yet many more died of shock at their displacement, or of Spanish diseases. The sexual exploitation of Native American females by Spanish soldiers and other men in the colony was especially devastating as a matter of both personal violation and venereal disease. In contrast to Mexico, intermarriage was infrequent. The Native American population dropped precipitously—was most likely halved, in fact—by the end of the Spanish-Mexican era. It is difficult, in short, to see the mission system as resulting in anything other than wholesale anthropological devastation, whatever the sincerely felt evangelical intent of the missionaries and the civilizing goals of the Laws of the Indies.

Indian resistance was immediate. The very first mission Serra established was burned down within months. In 1775 there was an even more violent attack on the San Diego mission, and the resident Franciscan there was murdered. On July 17, 1781, the Yuma people living along the Colorado River attacked a party of soldiers en route to California with their families, slaughtered thirty soldiers and the four Franciscans accompanying them, and carried off the women and children. This Yuma massacre sealed off for the next forty years the trail Anza had so recently opened. Spanish California remained a coastal enclave, not only because the Yuma massacre dissuaded migration from the south, but also because fugitive Native Americans fleeing the missions created a hostile no-man's-land on the eastern edge of Spanish settlement. Spanish California, in short, was ringed by a borderland of hostile indigenous peoples, and this encirclement prevented any expansion into the interior or repopulation from the south. Throughout the Spanish colonial era, a state of war existed between the Spanish settlers and the majority of Native Americans in the region. This in turn helps explain why Spanish soldiers so assiduously hunted down fugitives from the missions, punished them, and took them back into captivity.

His life's work complete, the mission system established, all that was left for Father Junípero Serra to do was die, which he did with the piety and panache of a Spanish mystic, with Francisco Palóu, his interim successor as father-president, on hand to witness and record the event. Some six hundred Indian converts were said to have formed a guard of honor for Serra at the solemn funeral held at Mission San Carlos Borromeo on August 29, 1784. Two centuries later, in a far different California, Native American activists would bitterly oppose the proposed canonization of the diminutive friar who had played such a crucial role in bringing Spanish California into existence.

3

A TROUBLED TERRITORY

Mexican California

The Lugo Family, Bell, Los Angeles County, 1888

SEAVER CENTER FOR WESTERN HISTORY RESEARCH

LOS ANGELES COUNTY MUSEUM OF NATURAL HISTORY

In 1821, Mexico achieved its independence from Spain. It took nearly a year for the news to reach Alta California. After a brief flirtation with a royalist-manqué dictatorship under the emperor Agustín Iturbide, Mexico became a federal republic in 1824, with California, both Alta and Baja, classified as a territory. During the fifty-two years of Spanish rule, little seems to have occurred outside the steady expansion of the mission system and the arrival of a few foreign visitors. In the brief span of Mexican California, by contrast—from 1822 to its annexation by the United States in 1846—the canvas is crowded with important events. The central narrative of Mexican California revolves around the effort to create a civil society through secularization of the missions, foreign trade, and land grants. Even as Mexican California tried to do this, however, a fusion of forces—international commerce, a growing population of non-Mexican residents, the collapse of local politics, the threatening presence of foreign powers in the Pacific, and, more subtly, the emergence of Enlightenment ideas in a generation of California-born Mexican leaders—was coalescing to make the desired civil society less and less feasible in purely Mexican-Californian terms.

Through its federal constitution, adopted in 1824, the United Mexican States sought to recast themselves as a federated republic modeled on the United States. This meant a civil society based upon the validity of the secular order and the political equality of each citizen. These were lofty goals, and—as in the United States—they were frequently compromised. Yet whatever the faults or failures of the Mexican Republic, its framers envisioned a prosperous and fair civil order welcoming all citizens, whatever their bloodlines or descent. The old order did not die easily, however, for the very Mexico that was now calling itself a secular and civil republic was also a social, cultural, and psychological labyrinth of caste based on race, a feudal land system, a Catholicism that had subsumed the Indian religions of the region, and an individualism verging on anarchy that brought with it a proclivity to military dictatorship when things got out of hand, as frequently happened.

Even as a sideshow, Mexican California exhibited the same instabilities as its host republic. First of all, the Franciscans were by and large Spanish-born royalists, and they did what they could to ignore, if not openly resist, the newly established republic. This meant continued, indeed exacerbated, tensions between the padres and the military officers sent by Mexico to govern the territory. Most of these military governors were unpopular with resident Californios, who wanted self-government or merely to be left alone on their *ranchos.* In 1831, the *rancheros* of Southern California went so far as to take to the field in arms against the current governor, Lieutenant Colonel Manuel Victoria, and even to shed blood, which rarely happened when Californios squabbled over politics. While the Californios might claim the rights of self-government, the politics they practiced among themselves was less than encouraging, as across twenty years Norteños and Sureños connived against each other in Monterey and Los Angeles and, occasionally, on the field of battle. Eventually, on November 7, 1836, the Californios—led by Juan Bautista Alvarado, an educated Monterey-born Californio, assisted by a ragtag group of American mountain men led by Isaac Graham of Tennessee—went so far as to proclaim California a free and sovereign state. Under this scenario, California might have become another Texas, but neither the population nor the political momentum was sufficient to sustain independence. Besides, Mexico cannily responded to the rebellion by upgrading California from a territory to a department and naming Alvarado governor; and for the next ten years the Californios enjoyed a high degree of autonomy.

While Mexico might talk of a civil society, it remained unsuccessful in promoting civilian settlement in California. Few people wished to come, and so, in desperation, Mexico began to treat California as a kind of Botany Bay for wayward soldiers. The non-Indian population of Mexican California never exceeded seven thousand, and of these only one thousand were adult males. Had the mission system proved successful—and by the 1830s it had had more than sixty years to do so—a steady stream of Hispanicized Native Americans should long since have been transferring into the civil population of California. This never happened. Either the Indians died off, or they became permanently missionized (which is to say, wards of the Franciscans), or they fled into the interior. Mission culture remained volatile. In 1824, Native Americans rose up and seized control of three missions; and in 1829 a onetime mission Indian by the name of Estanislão organized a full-scale revolt among the Miwok of the San Joaquin Valley that was never fully suppressed, despite a punitive expedition led by Lieutenant Mariano Guadalupe Vallejo. Another possibility—one that had played a powerful role in the creation of Mexico—might have been intermarriage; yet this also was very rare, with only one notable example: the marriage of the Scottish-born trader and ranchero Hugo Reid to a Native American woman from Mission San Gabriel, a union surviving in collective memory and nurturing the Ramona myth.

Mexico, in any event, was growing weary of the mission system as a *retardaire* royalist remnant incompatible with a republican system of government. In 1833 the Mexican Congress demanded that all missions be secularized and their lands distributed to Hispanicized Indians and, perhaps, to new colonists. Hearing the news, two Mexican entrepreneurs—José María Híjar, a wealthy landowner from Jalisco, and José María Padrés, an army officer from Puebla who had spent a year in Alta California as inspector of troops and customs—used their connections with acting president Valentín Gómez Farías to promote a colonization scheme in which certain secularized mission lands of Alta California would be assigned to a colony organized by Padrés and Híjar. From one perspective—the populating of Alta California with industrious civilians—the Híjar-Padrés colony was good news. Here were people who actually wanted to go to California! Acting president Farías went so far as to appoint Híjar governor of California, and in 1834 some 250 colonists, together with their promoters, arrived there. The Híjar-Padrés colony contained a number of men—Ignacio Coronel, José Noé, and Agustín Olvera, among others—who would distinguish themselves in the years to come.

The governor of California at the time, however, Brevet Brigadier José Figueroa—a distinguished soldier and civil administrator, correctly considered by historians to have been the most competent governor during the Mexican era—opposed the colony. The mission lands, Figueroa argued, should be secularized in favor of the Indians living on them and not merely for the benefit of arriving colonists. These were Indian lands, after all, held in trust for them by the Franciscans; and it was the formal intent of the mission system to transform Native Americans into full-fledged citizens. In his opposition to the Híjar-Padrés scheme, Figueroa was influenced in part by the fact that he himself was of Native American descent. Fortunately for Figueroa, the new president of Mexico, Antonio López de Santa Anna, canceled Híjar's commission as governor as Híjar was en route; and so on August 4, 1834, issuing a 180-page proclamation, Figueroa took personal charge of the secularization process. Half of all mission properties, he decreed, would be assigned to mission Indians, and the missions themselves would be secularized at the rate of ten in 1834, six in 1835, and the remaining five in 1836.

Unfortunately, Figueroa died the following year, and the secularization process he had outlined in his manifesto, with its fair-mindedness and strict accountability, was ignored. Only a small percentage of mission Indians ever came into possession of the properties they and their forebears had been working for half a century. The twenty-one missions themselves—built of adobe by Indians under the supervision of Franciscans guiding themselves from architectural books brought north from Mexico—survived as physical structures. A number of them—San Diego de Alcalá, San Juan Capistrano, San Gabriel Arcángel, Santa Barbara, San Carlos Borromeo, San Francisco de Asís (more commonly known as Mission Dolores)—continue to thrive today as active parish churches. Mission Santa Clara de Asís on the southern edge of San Francisco Bay became the nucleus of a Jesuit college. Starting in the late nineteenth century, preservationists would organize a decades-long program of restoration, seeing in the twenty-one missions romanticized emblems of the Spanish colonial past.

By the time the missions were secularized and the remaining padres were repatriated to Mexico City or Spain, a new social institution, the land grant rancho, had become predominant. All told, more than six hundred land grants were made during the Mexican era; and these vast holdings, extending across the rolling hills of coastal California as far north as Petaluma above San Francisco Bay, dominated the economy and defined the society of Mexican California. Now ensued the age of the dons: men such as Don José Andrés Sepúlveda, the feudal lord of the eighty-square-mile Rancho San Joaquín in present-day Orange County, granted to Don José in 1837 by Governor Alvarado. There, in his capacious hacienda called "Refugio" (the Refuge), Don José and his extended family lived a life that would later be celebrated in California legend. For a later generation, rancho life represented Mexican California at its best.

It was a prodigal existence, generous and unheeding. Innumerable longhorn cattle roamed the hills. Families were large and extended. It was common for more than twenty relatives, near-relatives, and retainers to sit down to plentiful meals of beef, tortillas, chili peppers, rice, tomatoes, garbanzo and green beans, pumpkins, onions, oranges, apples, pears, and imported chocolate and spices, all of it prepared by Indian cooks under the supervision of the mistress of the house. Families met for three full meals a day, and there were midmorning and midafternoon snacks. In a society challenged by a paucity of civil institutions—two or three schools, one active printing press, the absence of urbanism—family was everything, the fundamental fact and premise of social life. Everyone was connected by blood or baptismal relationships, and no child went uncared for. If one needed a horse, one borrowed it from one rancho and left it at the next, and made one's own horses likewise available to others. At designated times of the year—religious feast days, the completion of branding or slaughter—the rancheros would gather their families and retainers at one or another hacienda for weeklong festivities that included late nights of dancing to the music of guitars, violins, flutes, and castanets, the hilarity of the evening intensified by imported wine, a domestic brandy called *aguardiente,* and spiked punches. On such festive occasions, the dons would dress in elaborate *charro* riding suits and ride on silver-studded saddles that represented a significant portion of their wealth.

Rancho society had its cruel, even barbaric side. The treatment of Native American labor was frequently harsh. Despite such disadvantages, Native Americans and men of mixed blood developed into vaqueros who must be considered among the most skilled horsemen of all time. Only a small percentage of the population was literate, yet Monterey-born Mariano Guadalupe

Vallejo, educated in one of the few schools of the territory, was a lifelong and voracious reader, a collector of books, and an antiquarian historian of acknowledged skill. Governor Alvarado had been educated in the same schoolhouse as Vallejo, taught by the English-born schoolmaster William Hartnell, later himself a successful ranchero. The St. Augustine, Florida–born soldier-administrator Agustín Zamorano, acting governor from 1832 to 1833, brought printing to the remote province, beginning with the *Reglamento Provincial* he issued in 1834 for Governor Figueroa. Despite the pastoral simplicity of the society and its frequent harshness, the leading families of Mexican California lived lives of comfort and increasing civility, especially after a developing trade with New England, Latin America, and the Far East began to bring to California a growing number of domestic luxuries.

This trade, in fact, embodied and energized the very dynamic—namely, contact with the outside world—that was in the process of transforming Mexican California internally, further destabilizing it politically, and edging it in the direction of American annexation. This process began in the Spanish era. In September 1786, two frigates of the Royal French Navy under the command of Captain Jean François Galaup Comte de La Pérouse spent ten days in Monterey Bay, taking on water and supplies for a voyage to the Philippines. La Pérouse's ships, the *Boussole* and the *Astrolabe,* were only the second non-Spanish ships to anchor in California since the visit of the *Golden Hinde* in 1579. While in port, scientists attached to the voyage made a rapid but effective reconnaissance of the coastal interior. Five years later, in September 1791, the Italian-born navigator Alejandro Malaspina, sailing for Spain, led a second scientific expedition into Monterey Bay, and his scientists and artists likewise reconnoitered and documented the countryside. Malaspina had under his command an American, John Green, the first American to visit California, who died there and was buried in Monterey. The English naval explorer Captain George Vancouver, also on a voyage of scientific exploration, anchored in San Francisco Bay in November 1792, and returned to California twice the following year. Pointedly, Vancouver insisted upon calling the region "New Albion," thereby recalling Drake's claiming of the region for England.

The visits of the scientific exploring expeditions of La Pérouse, Malaspina, and Vancouver represented a brief but telling connection between Spanish California and the scientific ambitions of the Enlightenment. Each visit resulted in impressive publications. American visitors, by contrast, were interested in trade, not science. China-bound, the *Columbia* and the *Lady Washington* skirted the California coast in the late 1780s but did not land. In October 1796, however, the *Otter* of Boston, under the command of Ebenezer Dorr, dropped anchor in Monterey Bay and took on food, water, and supplies before continuing to China. In the years to follow, the growing trade between New England and China, the increasing number of New England whalers operating in the South Pacific, and the developing trade in sea otter pelts off the California coast brought more American ships to the region.

What were English intentions in the Pacific? the Spanish pointedly asked. Or the intentions of the Americans, for that matter, or the Russians, who had materialized in San Francisco Bay in April 1806 in the *Juno,* formerly an American vessel, under the command of Count Nikolai Petrovich Rezanov of the Alaska-based Russian American Fur Company. Rezanov informed the Spanish that he was interested in establishing a connection with California as a source of resupply for his colony in New Archangel (Sitka). While negotiating with the commander of the presidio in San Francisco, Don José Argüello, Rezanov softened Argüello's resistance by becoming engaged to the commander's fifteen-year-old daughter, Concepción, but Rezanov, age forty-three, died crossing Siberia before permission for the marriage could be obtained. Concepción later became a nun (she was the first Californian to take the veil), and the story of her ill-fated engagement conferred a certain luster on an otherwise remote province not known for its romance. Concepción was on hand to witness yet another Russian visit to San Francisco, this in October 1816 by the *Rurik* of the Russian navy, under the command of the German-born Otto von Kotzebue. The *Rurik* was embarked upon yet another voyage of scientific exploration and crypto-expansionist reconnaissance, characterized by the same hefty publications upon return.

Each of these visits proved troublesome to the Spanish government, which had officially barred any foreign ships from landing or trading on the California coast. A scientific expedition, after all—even a trading or resupply mission, as in the case of the Russians and the Americans—could be interpreted as an act of military reconnaissance. But at least the French, English, Americans, and Russians had come in peace, which was more than one could say for the French-born privateer Hipólito de Bouchard, who, flying the flag of the revolutionary Republic of Buenos Aires, sailed two black-painted vessels into Monterey Bay on November 20, 1818, and spent the following week sacking the town before heading south to loot two ranchos and Mission San Juan Capistrano. One of Bouchard's crew, Joseph Chapman, an American, must have been a charmer—or at least had a good story to tell. Captured in Monterey, Chapman was soon welcomed into Spanish society and lived happily ever after, as did two other erstwhile American sailors, an African American known as Bob, and Thomas Doak of Boston. Jumping ship in March 1816, the pair made their way to Monterey, where, in rapid order, they were baptized as Roman Catholics (Doak became "Felipe Santiago" and Bob became "Juan Cristóbal"), pledged their loyalty to the crown, and married, in Bob's case, a prosperous widow, and in Doak's case, the daughter of Mariano Castro, a prominent local citizen.

Despite Spanish suspicion of outside arrangements, a number of these visits resulted, in one way or another, in commercial relationships. Doing business, however reluctantly, began in turn—at first subtly, then with growing force—to modify the ecclesiastical nature of Spanish California, a process that intensified in the Mexican era. Throughout the twenty-four years of Mexican rule, trade and commerce promoted secularization as Mexican Californians found their values, prosperity, and lifestyle modified by contact with the wider world. A growing number of non-Mexicans, meanwhile—émigré rancheros, commercial agents, at least one self-styled physician, and a carpenter turned builder-entrepreneur—took up residence, married into local families, and thereby enlarged the definition of what it meant to be a citizen of Mexican California.

The non-Spanish occupation of Alta California began with the Russians. In 1808, two years after Rezanov's visit, operatives of the Russian American Fur Company began to hunt otters and trade for sea otter pelts in Bodega Bay. In 1812 the company established Fort Ross on the coast some hundred miles north of San Francisco Bay as headquarters for its Russian and Aleut employees hunting seals and sea otters from kayaks up and down the California coast. Thoroughly Russian in appearance—with a dome atop its chapel and a great bell cast in St. Petersburg ringing out the hours—Fort Ross disturbed the Spanish, the Mexicans, and the United States, especially after 1823, when President James Monroe declared the Americas closed to any further colonization.

Anxieties regarding Indian attacks and the Russian incursion from the north—the latter eventually becoming legitimized through enforced trade agreements—led Governor Figueroa in April 1833 to establish a military district north of San Francisco Bay under the command of Mariano Guadalupe Vallejo, a Monterey-born cavalryman in the Mexican army then serving as commandant of the San Francisco presidio. Born in 1807 and living on well into the American era before his death in 1890, Vallejo must be considered the single most talented and influential member of his generation of native-born Californios. Whether judged as a soldier, a ranchero, a politician (including a term as a state senator in the American era), an entrepreneur, a man who valued education and learning (his son Platón would take a medical degree at Columbia and serve with his uncle Salvador in the Union army), or a pioneering historian, Vallejo embodies the best possibilities of Spanish and Mexican California in terms of its efforts to establish a civil society before the American conquest and later to make a successful transition into the new American order. Commissioned by the equally impressive Figueroa to establish a buffer zone north of San Francisco Bay, Vallejo ensconced himself in the Sonoma Valley—the Valley of the Moon, it would later be called, set between the Mayacamas and Sonoma mountain ranges—as a ranchero, as the administrator of the nearby Mission San Francisco Solano, as director of colonization, and, most important, as comandante-general of the district holding civil and military authority. Vallejo's mission was straightforward: to protect the northern frontier of Mexican California against hostile Indians, incursions by Russians from Fort Ross, and—a new development—incursions by trappers from the Hudson's Bay Company and freelance American mountain men.

Chartered in 1670 as a commercial company with quasi-governmental power and reorganized in 1821, the Hudson's Bay Company established its Pacific headquarters at Vancouver in the early 1820s, and from there in 1826 Peter Skene Ogden, a Canadian in the service of the company, first explored the interior of Northern California. Alexander McLeod of the company made two further incursions, getting as far south as the present city of Stockton. Ogden himself returned to California in 1829, making a bold and triumphant progress down the Central Valley. By the mid-1830s, the interior of Mexican California had become a happy hunting ground for Hudson's Bay trapper-traders in search of beaver pelts. So extensive was this trade that Sir George Simpson, governor-general of Her Majesty's Hudson's Bay Territories, visited California in 1841 to negotiate formal agreements with Governor Alvarado. In the course of his visit, Sir George visited Vallejo in Sonoma, marveling at the fact that Vallejo's parlor was furnished with cane chairs from the Hawaiian Islands.

To protect the northeastern flank of Mexican California, as Vallejo was protecting the northwestern coast, Governor Alvarado in 1839 made a similar agreement with a naturalized German-born Swiss émigré by the name of John Augustus Sutter. If Vallejo embodied the best possibilities of Mexican California, Sutter embodied the sheer adventurism, the hope of striking it rich in a new place, that by the late 1830s was bringing so many ambitious immigrants—Yankee, English, European, Latin American—into the remote Mexican department. An unscrupulous buccaneer, a figment of his own imagination (among other tall tales, Sutter claimed that he had served as a captain in the Royal Swiss Guard, a nonexistent regiment), Sutter dazzled Alvarado, who conferred upon him a 48,000-acre land grant at the junction of the Sacramento and American rivers. There, on a site that would eventually become the capital city of Sacramento, Sutter built a European-style fort—thick walls, gun towers, a great gate, the most ambitious fortification in California to that time—and from there, as with Vallejo to the west, he ruled a vast domain, which he called Nueva Helvetia—New Switzerland. In 1841 Sutter expanded his empire by buying out the Russian American Fur Company properties at Bodega Bay and Fort Ross.

On the coast, in the interior, in the south (once again served by the Old Spanish Trail), on the northern frontiers guarded by Sutter and Vallejo: Mexican California was by the mid-1830s everywhere in a state of ferment pointing to an inevitable transformation. The Americans were the most notable presence, beginning with the arrival in August 1826 of a party of seventeen trappers associated with the Rocky Mountain Fur Company. Led by Jedediah Smith, age twenty-seven, a charismatic, clean-shaven, Bible-reading explorer-entrepreneur, the Smith party constituted the first American penetration of California overland from the east. After a period of quasi–house arrest at Mission San Gabriel, the American mountain men moved up the San Joaquin Valley, trapping beaver as far north as the Stanislaus River. On May 20, 1827, Smith and two companions moved east across the Sierra Nevada, the first white men to cross that formidable range. Rendezvousing with his partners in July at Bear Lake, Utah, Smith returned to Southern California with a second party of eighteen trappers, supplied for two years. Crossing the Colorado River, he lost ten men in an ambush by Mojave Indians. The second Smith party spent another brief period under house arrest, this time at Mission San José, before it moved north to rendezvous with the first party Smith had left behind in central California. The reunited party then proceeded north to Oregon. On the morning of July 14, 1828, on the Umpqua River, Kelawatset Indians massacred the expedition. Smith and two other survivors managed to stumble their way west to Fort Vancouver on the Oregon coast.

Smith's heroic journey—the double encirclement of the Far West—was the physical, moral, and geopolitical equivalent of the great voyages of exploration off the California coast in the sixteenth and early seventeenth centuries. The Spaniards linked California to the sea; Smith linked California to the interior of the North American continent. In the wake of Smith came other trapping parties: the James Ohio Pattie party in 1827; the Ewing Young party of 1829; the William Wolfskill party of 1831; the Ewing Young–Isaac Williams party of 1832; the Joseph Walker party of 1833, which made the first east-to-west crossing of the Sierra Nevada; the Isaac Graham party of 1834.

Aside from their shared skills as trappers, traders, and overland travelers, these newly arriving Americans were men of differing capacities and inclinations. Smith, Pattie, Walker, Young, and others were merely passing through. Their orientation was to the more geographically encompassing world of the Rocky Mountain fur trade. William Wolfskill, by contrast, settled in Los Angeles and reinvented himself as a rancher, a vineyardist, a grower of English walnuts, and the owner of the largest orange groves in Southern California. Wolfskill, in short, became part of the local establishment—something that Isaac Graham, a different kind of man, a garrulous braggart, could never do. Settling in Monterey, the Kentucky-born Graham opened a distillery, the first on the Pacific Coast. He also provided Governor Alvarado with a praetorian guard of equally unruly, whiskey-drinking mountain men and earned exile to the Baja Peninsula when Alvarado tired of this unmanageable bodyguard.

In contrast to such rough-hewn mountain men were the Americans of the maritime trading elite: New Englanders, in the main, of recognized lineage, even a Harvard man: John Marsh, a graduate of Phillips Academy at Andover and Harvard College, who arrived in Los Angeles in 1836, converted to Roman Catholicism, was naturalized, became the first practicing physician on the Pacific Coast (despite his lack of a medical degree), and acquired a land grant rancho east of San Francisco Bay. The commercial agents active in the hide and tallow trade in the 1820s and 1830s—among them William Hartnell, Alfred Robinson, Henry Fitch, Abel Stearns, Faxon Dean Atherton, Thomas Oliver Larkin, and the Englishman William Gale—were almost universally gentlemen traders, whether self-made or to the manner born, connected to reputable English or New England companies such as Bryant, Sturgis & Company of Boston, active in the California trade since 1822. These skilled businessmen administered an intricate four-way exchange—manufactured goods to California, sea otter pelts to China, then back to California with Chinese goods to pick up cattle hides and tallow for shipment back to Boston—linking two seas and three continents. Many of these traders married into established local families. Henry Fitch eloped with Josefa Carrillo of San Diego; Abel Stearns married Arcadia Bandini of San Diego; Benjamin Davis Wilson, a member of the William Workman party of 1841, married Ramona Yorba of Rancho Santa Ana and purchased part of the Rancho La Jurupa in present-day Riverside. Widowed in 1853, Wilson remarried, this time an Anglo-American widow, Margaret Hereford, and the two of them eventually became the grandparents of George S. Patton, Jr., who went to West Point and became a general during the Second World War. Alfred Robinson married Anita de la Guerra, and their colorful wedding at the de la Guerra adobe in Santa Barbara was described in detail by Robinson's cousin, Richard Henry Dana, Jr. (a Harvard undergraduate on leave in order to recover his health as a sailor in the hide and tallow trade on the California coast), in an account later published as *Two Years Before the Mast* (1840). Thomas Oliver Larkin of Massachusetts, recently of Charleston, South Carolina, brought his own wife along: Rachel Holmes, a widow, whom Larkin met and married on board ship en route to California. Rachel Larkin thus became the first American woman to live in California, and her son, Thomas Oliver Larkin, Jr., entering the world on April 13, 1834, became the first California child born to American parents.

Not only did Larkin have an American wife and an American child, he remained a Protestant and an American citizen even after settling permanently in Monterey as a storekeeper and trader. A skilled carpenter, Larkin also built the first two-story house in California, combining adobe walls, a wood frame structure, a second-story veranda similar to those in Charleston, and a tile roof. The resulting design, subsequently known as Monterey Colonial, in and of itself expressed the fusion of

Mexican and Yankee peoples and traits that was occurring up and down the California coast. As if to finalize his status as the embodiment of the growing American presence on the California coast, Larkin was in 1844 appointed American consul and confidential agent. His mission, communicated to him in secret orders from Secretary of State James Buchanan, was to encourage the Californios, if ever again they should declare their independence from Mexico, to align themselves with the United States and to become, if they wished, an American state.

American in one way or another, California was destined to be, Richard Henry Dana, Jr., argued in *Two Years Before the Mast.* The devil was in the details. Embarrassingly, Commodore Thomas ap Catesby Jones, commander of the United States naval Pacific Squadron, had in early fall of 1842 received an erroneous report that Mexico and the United States were at war. Even more disturbing, the report said that Mexico was planning to cede California to England, lest it be seized by the United States. Feeling that he should act decisively, the commodore sailed his squadron north from Peru, entered Monterey Bay on October 19, 1842, and raised the Stars and Stripes the following day, demanding the surrender of the city. Learning of his error, the red-faced commodore ordered the Stars and Stripes lowered from the Monterey customhouse and sailed south to Los Angeles to offer his personal apologies to Governor Manuel Micheltorena.

The commodore's mistake prophesied things to come. It also reinforced the growing naval activity in the Pacific of foreign powers—England, France, and the United States especially—who had California very much on their minds. In contrast to the legitimate and highly subsidized scientific expeditions of the Spanish era, foreign visitors to California now seemed overtly political in their interests, although the visit of the French ship *Le Héros,* commanded by merchant marine captain Auguste Bernard Duhaut-Cilly, which visited the California coast in 1827–28, did represent a legitimate scientific expedition, with Duhaut-Cilly issuing a two-volume description of his voyage in 1834 and his naturalist, Paul Emile Botta, an Italian physician, publishing an equally seminal description of Native American life and of the flora and fauna of the California coast.

The next Frenchman to visit California, by contrast—Comte Eugène Duflot du Mofras, an expert in Spanish history serving as an attaché at the French embassy in Madrid—was expansionist, not scientific, in his interests. Duflot du Mofras's confidential mission, assigned to him by the French foreign office in 1839, was to scout Mexico and its northern possessions for opportunities for French settlement. Touring California for five months in mid-1841, Duflot du Mofras returned to Paris and published the best single account of California by a European to appear in the pre-American era, *Exploration du Territoire de l'Orégon, des Californies, et de la Mer Vermeille,* an account that fully expressed the count's wit, learning, eye for detail, love of anecdote and gossip, and maritime ambition. Standing on the shores of San Francisco Bay, Duflot du Mofras—with Gallic panache—flung his arms in the direction of the as-yet-unnamed Golden Gate and waxed lyrical regarding the future of this grand harbor. Back in France, he appended a secret memorandum to his report, suggesting that California was ripe for seizure. Let French Canadians in the employ of the Hudson's Bay Company, he argued, infiltrate California, then congregate around New Helvetia under the protection of Sutter. An uprising could then be staged on the pretext that the rights of French Canadians were being violated. French ships of the line could then sail into the bays of San Francisco, Monterey, and San Diego and seize the territory. California might thus become a new Louisiana on the Pacific, restoring French sovereignty in North America.

Alexander Forbes, a Scots merchant operating from Tepic, Mexico, had similar ambitions for Great Britain. Since Mexico owed British subjects more than $50 million, Forbes argued in his *History of Upper and Lower California* (1839)—the first English book to deal exclusively with California—let Mexico meet this debt by forming a California Company modeled on the East India Company or Hudson's Bay Company and issue shares to its debtors. The company would in turn administer California as the East India Company governed portions of India and the Hudson's Bay Company portions of Canada.

A young Irish priest by the name of Eugene McNamara had, not surprisingly, Irish ambitions. In 1845 McNamara petitioned the president of Mexico for land in California on which he promised to settle some two thousand Irish Catholic families, or roughly ten thousand colonists. McNamara's argument, endorsed by the archbishop of Mexico City, pointedly claimed that the "Methodist wolves" of the United States, as McNamara characterized them, would soon be seizing California unless such an Irish presence were established. McNamara's arguments harked back to the Reformation/Counter-Reformation antagonisms of the sixteenth century; but they also reflected a growing framing of the California question in terms of Protestant-Catholic, Anglo-Hispanic tensions. In his *Plea for the West* (1835), the famed Presbyterian preacher Lyman Beecher of Connecticut had urged the United States to acquire the West on behalf of American Protestant civilization. Otherwise, Beecher argued, the West would be dominated by the Roman Catholic peoples and cultures of the Spanish-speaking world, moving north from Mexico.

Whether or not they were Methodist wolves, Americans of a new sort were now arriving in California: families with children, crossing the continent by wagon train and taking up residence. The Bartleson-Bidwell party came first, arriving on John Marsh's ranch near Mount Diablo in Northern California in November 1841. That same month, the Workman-Rowland party—which, fearing snow, had bypassed the Sierra Nevada in favor of the southern route across the Old Spanish Trail—

arrived in Los Angeles. Two years later, Lansford Hastings, an Ohio-born lawyer turned settlement entrepreneur, brought forty Americans down via Oregon into the Sacramento Valley. That same year, 1843, the Chiles-Walker parties, which had split up to take different routes, entered the Sacramento Valley via the Malheur and Pitt rivers and approached the San Joaquin Valley via Walker's Pass. In 1844 the Stevens-Murphy party opened a new route across the Sierra via Donner Pass. Part of the party was forced to spend the winter on the shores of Donner Lake. They made it through. Not so the Donner party of 1846.

Making winter camp near Truckee Lake (now called Donner Lake) in the High Sierra on November 4, 1846, the Donner party endured before its rescue the following April a phantasmagoria of horrors, including murder and cannibalism, that remains to this day a fixed and recurring statement of California as betrayed hope and dystopian tragedy. Yet the survivors of the Donner party managed to fit in, even to thrive, in California after their ordeal was over.

The American wagon trains were bringing into California men and women in search of a better life, which many were finding. John Bidwell, for example, became a rancher in Butte County, a general in the state militia, a founder of the city of Chico, a congressman, a noted agriculturist and philanthropist. Martin Murphy settled on the southern shores of San Francisco Bay, where he prospered as one of the largest landowners in the state, sending his offspring east to Georgetown College to complete their educations.

Something was in the air—an attitude, an expectation, a gathering focus—on the part of Americans and their government regarding Mexican California. It would be no exaggeration, moreover, to see something of the same expectation on the part of the Californios. Despite the prohibitions coming from Mexico City, Mexican Californians were allowing the Americans arriving by wagon train to settle in the country and make new lives. The Californios were also discussing, confidentially, with Consul Thomas Oliver Larkin the possibility of joining the United States. In New York and Washington, meanwhile—in the All-Mexico agenda being advocated by the New York journalist John O'Sullivan, and the theory of Manifest Destiny being promulgated by Senator Thomas Hart Benton of Missouri—an ideology was being formulated and sentiment was building that would lead, inevitably, to an American presence on the Pacific Coast. Let the United States, O'Sullivan urged, encourage the states and territories of northern Mexico voluntarily to associate themselves with the American Union.

In contrast to this All-Mexico program, Manifest Destiny had a more assertive edge. It was the will of Almighty God himself, Senator Benton and others maintained, that the United States become a continental nation, from sea to shining sea. The realization of such a vision could entail the peaceful acquisition of non-American territories in the West, but it could also entail their violent seizure. For Josiah Royce, such an aggressive conquest constituted the central moral problem of California's foundation as an American commonwealth. Today, it might very well be seen as the central moral question and continuing issue between Mexico and the United States, especially as California comes into its Mexican American majority. Texas had rebelled and become an independent nation in 1836; California had tried such a rebellion that same year but had not possessed the resources to sustain independence. Yet Mexican California remained open-minded regarding the possibility of an American identity, provided that such an identity be freely chosen and that the language, customs, religion, and land titles of Mexican California be respected by the United States following affiliation or annexation. Yet as 1845 became 1846—the Year of Decision, as historian Bernard De Voto later dubbed it—the signs were pointing increasingly toward military action and the violent seizure of Mexican lands north of the Río Grande.

Historians have been wont to see the annexation of California by the United States as an act of conquest, a sideshow in the larger drama of Manifest Destiny and the Mexican War. Any close reading of Mexican California, however, suggests that even if the United States had never invaded Mexico or seized California by force of arms, California—as Richard Henry Dana, Jr., first put it—would in one way or another have become American. At the very time that war broke out, the Californios were negotiating with the United States regarding the possibilities of a peaceful annexation. From this perspective, Josiah Royce, writing in 1886, considered the forcible conquest of California as the original sin of American California history. What was taken by force, Royce argued, had been on the verge of being peaceably surrendered.

In its extravagant cast of characters, its mad dashes through the countryside by regular and irregular troops, its bloody clashes of cavalry, and its overall mood of secret diplomacy, high stakes, and dramatic action, the Conquest of California—as the seizure of California during the Mexican War is commonly called—survives in retrospect as an opera scenario worthy of Hector Berlioz. The scenario included the quasi-Napoleonic posturing of John Charles Frémont, one of the great adventurers of mid-nineteenth-century America; the rebellion of American locals, including the declaration of the California Republic; the presence of the American navy, including the maneuvers of marines and naval infantry; a massacre of Indians; two instances of cold-blooded execution; two notable military engagements; a treaty; a quarrel over the governorship; and a court-martial.

The story of the conquest of California begins with John Charles Frémont, a flamboyant, reckless army captain, the son-in-law of Senator Thomas Hart Benton, the high priest of Manifest

Destiny. Of French descent, handsome and dashing, Frémont had by 1845 led two exploring expeditions into the Far West. Upon his return, his wife, Jesse Benton Frémont, in many ways the driving force behind her husband's career—a woman of great beauty and trilingual education with the Mesdames of the Sacred Heart in St. Louis—had written from his notes *Report of the Exploring Expedition to Oregon and North California* (1845), a masterly narrative that had helped create the mood of continental expansion coming to a climax in 1846. No sooner had the report appeared than Frémont was moving westward at the head of a still larger army expedition—sixty men, with Kit Carson serving as chief of scouts—which Senator Benton had helped persuade the secretary of war to finance.

Frémont, however, had more than scientific exploration on his mind as he approached Monterey in January 1846. Already he had overcome the stigma of his illegitimacy to win an army commission, marry into the highest of political circles, and—through his wife's reworking of his notes and journals—position himself as the Pathfinder of Manifest Destiny. Now he would play the role of Bonaparte as well. Like everyone else, Frémont knew that California was ripe for seizure. Its conquest, in fact, held dazzling possibilities for the young captain of topographical engineers: the governorship of the newly acquired province, followed by a national career in politics, perhaps even the presidency. At the time of Frémont's approach to Monterey, the capital of California—as the result of the perennial north-south conflict in Mexican California—had been moved to Los Angeles, with Governor Pío Pico serving there and José Castro, based in Monterey, serving as comandante in the north. As might be expected, Castro was incensed that an armed force of American troops and mountain men should be so boldly sojourning at Sutter's Fort, then riding toward Monterey.

Camped outside Monterey, Frémont held conversations with consul and confidential agent Thomas Oliver Larkin, thereby adding to the melodrama of the occasion. Larkin had, after all, been in touch with most of the leading rancheros about the possibility of taking California out of Mexico and into the United States. Not only was Comandante Castro affronted by the presence of American troops in California, he also had to worry that something larger was afoot, which might very well involve yet another local insurrection, this time in favor of the United States. Quite naturally, Castro in no uncertain terms ordered Frémont out of California. Rather than leave, Frémont took his men to the top of the nearby Gavilán Peak, set up a hasty barricade, and raised the American flag. In one sense, it was pure theater; but then again, given the growing tensions between Mexico and the United States, it was theater with a purpose. Six months before the American navy arrived, Frémont was signaling American intentions.

Late on the night of March 9–10, 1846, Frémont struck camp and moved his men north to Oregon. There, on the shores of Klamath Lake, the plot thickened—indeed, it assumed an aura of permanent ambiguity; for there Frémont met on May 8, 1846, with Marine Lieutenant Archibald Gillespie, who had arrived in California in the guise of a traveling merchant bearing confidential dispatches from President James Polk and Secretary of State James Buchanan for Thomas Oliver Larkin. Gillespie had been ferried from Hawaii to California on the American navy ship *Cyane* and, once his meeting with Larkin was accomplished, had pursued Frémont north to Oregon. For the rest of his life—and in the legend that lasted well beyond his death in 1890—Frémont suggested that Gillespie had brought him confidential messages that, in effect, ordered him to seize California. Most scholars have disputed such a claim; yet Josiah Royce would see in Frémont's suggestion and subsequent actions the original sin of California history.

In one sense, the point was moot, for the United States had already declared war on Mexico, on May 13, 1846; but this would not be known in California for some months to come. In the meanwhile, Frémont returned from Oregon in late May, and his reappearance in California—riding at the head of a mounted column in Napoleonic splendor, protected by a colorful bodyguard of Delaware Indians—incited a group of American settlers in and around Sonoma to rise up, imprison General Vallejo (while liberating his wine cellar), and declare the California Republic, for which they fashioned a star-and-grizzly-bear-emblazoned flag that, with some modifications, became the official flag of the state in 1911. The United States Navy, meanwhile, under the command of an aged and ailing Commodore John Drake Sloat, had arrived off the coast in full force. Hearing of the Bear Flag revolt and of hostilities between Americans and Mexicans in Texas, Sloat decided to act, although he as yet had no official notice that a state of war existed between Mexico and the United States. In any event, Sloat sent his marines and sailors ashore and raised the American flag at Monterey on July 7, 1846, and at San Francisco five days later. Frémont, meanwhile, assumed personal control of the Bear Flaggers, who pledged their allegiance to the United States, then dashed with a small party to the shores of the Golden Gate (which he had named in his 1845 *Report*) to spike the ancient cannons guarding the harbor.

On July 23, 1846, Sloat relinquished command to Commodore Robert Field Stockton, a decisive figure and—handsome, independently wealthy, socially connected, ambitious for fame—equally as flamboyant as Frémont. Taking charge of the conquest, Stockton authorized Frémont to serve as brevet major of the newly established California Battalion of Mounted Riflemen, with Marine lieutenant Gillespie, promoted to brevet captain, serving as second in command and Kit Carson joining as chief of scouts. An amalgamation of Frémont's army troops, mountain men, the praetorian guard of Delaware Indians, and a contingent of Bear Flaggers, the battalion moved south to Monterey, as colorful as any column of condottieri from the Italian

Renaissance. Whatever violence it wrought—the slaughter of a Maidu Indian village, the cold-blooded shooting of the two sons of Francisco de Haro and their uncle José Berryessa—can be directly traced to Kit Carson, whose bloodthirstiness matched Frémont's bravura.

At Monterey, Frémont's battalion of regulars and volunteers was loaded aboard naval ships for transport to San Diego, where it was re-horsed and re-provisioned for the conquest of the south. By August 13, 1846, the pueblo of Los Angeles, the largest settlement in Upper California, was under American rule, with Captain Gillespie in charge of the city and Governor Pío Pico fleeing in the general direction of Mexico. At this point, the conquest of California seemed complete. Gillespie's harsh administration of Los Angeles, however, precipitated an insurrection that seemed for a time capable of reversing the tide, at least in the south. Gillespie was forced to flee the city, and a detachment of marines was turned back by the Californios when it tried to retake the pueblo. Even worse, a column of 121 dragoons, riding as the Army of the West under the command of Brigadier General Stephen Watts Kearny, entered California from the southeast along the Santa Fe and Old Spanish trails and was decisively defeated on December 6, 1846, in San Diego County in the Battle of San Pasqual. Charging a force of mounted Californios under the command of Andrés Pico, brother of the governor, the dragoons broke formation in pursuit of a group of Californios who had rushed them and then pretended to flee. The Californio ruse worked. When the American dragoons broke formation, the Californios wheeled around and penetrated the scattered American column. In the fierce hand-to-hand fighting that followed, twenty-three American dragoons lost their lives to deft thrusts from the twenty-foot willow lances the Californios wielded with deadly skill. It took, finally, a concerted invasion of the Los Angeles plain by a large and well-organized force of army dragoons, marines, and sailors acting as infantry, together with segments of Frémont's mounted battalion and a unit of horse-drawn artillery, to retake Los Angeles on January 10, 1847, at the Battle of La Mesa. Three days later, the Californios surrendered to Frémont, believing him to be the most sympathetic of the American commanders. They met Frémont under an oak tree in the hills outside the city in a surrender ceremony subsequently known as the Capitulation of Cahuenga.

By then a brevet lieutenant colonel, Frémont believed himself to be the legitimate governor of California, named as such by Commodore Stockton before Stockton's departure for the East. General Kearny, however, believed himself to be the legitimate governor by virtue of his superior rank and specific dispatches from Washington. Fearing the wrath of Frémont's battalion, Kearny bided his time until the arrival of a clearly appointed military governor, Army colonel Richard Mason, voided Frémont's claim. Frémont was ordered to return to Washington in the van of Kearny's column, under arrest on charges of mutiny. In Washington, a court-martial found Frémont guilty, but President Polk—grateful that all had ended well—granted Frémont a full pardon; yet the aggrieved Pathfinder resigned from the Army, wrote yet another memoir with the help of his wife, and mounted a private expedition into the West in search of a railroad route, before returning to California to go into the mining business and pick up the threads of a political career.

After more than three hundred years of exploration, shipwreck, expedition, settlement, evangelization, political strife, trade, and reconnaissance, the destiny of Alta California had become clear. It would be an American province. The United States now extended from sea to shining sea. Just exactly how California should be politically organized in its new identity, however, remained an open question.

4

STRIKING IT RICH

The Establishment of an American State

Colton Hall, Monterey, shortly after the First Constitutional Convention

CALIFORNIA STATE LIBRARY

On February 2, 1848, the United States and Mexico signed the Treaty of Guadalupe Hidalgo, ceding to the United States all Mexican territories north of the Río Grande in return for $15 million in cash and a $3.25 million payment of claims by Mexican citizens against the United States. From the conquest of 1846 to the signing of the treaty, the United States administered California under international law as occupied enemy territory in time of war. In the normal course of development, the next step would have been territorial status for the annexed Mexican department. As an American territory, California would have remained under the supervision of the federal government, with a measure of home rule granted prior to eventual statehood. Congress, however, balked at granting California territorial status. The Northern states wanted California free of slavery; the Southern states wanted at least part of California, or a territory carved from its southern sector, open to their peculiar institution. Unable to compromise, Congress made no territorial provisions for its newly acquired Pacific empire, and so California stumbled on as a legal hybrid, with the military providing civil administration and Mexican California providing a workable system of local law under its *alcalde* system of governance.

Once again, as in the Spanish and Mexican eras, California was experiencing difficulties in the establishment of a civil society. As the American population grew, a succession of military governors—seven in all—found themselves increasingly reluctant to administer civilians. Civilians, in turn, found themselves increasingly restive with the necessity of living under the *alcalde* law of Mexican California as interpreted by the American military government. Originating in Islamic and Christian Spain, *alcalde* law was not based upon a separation of powers. It was, rather, more military in nature, with the *alcalde* functioning as judge, jury, and chief executive in the local community. Thus the American military officers and civilians who were appointed *alcaldes* in the interregnum years of 1846–50 held consolidated and centralized authority that would prove unworkable once the Gold Rush had created a population boom.

Still, many *alcaldes* managed to do good work in this interim period. Appointed *alcalde* at Monterey, Navy lieutenant Walter Colton—a Vermont-born Congregationalist chaplain educated at Yale and Andover Theological Seminary—brought a measure of Yankee order to the capital city of the recently acquired department. With convict labor, Colton built a school and a Greek Revival town hall, using a local yellow stone: the latter was the most ambitious building thus far erected on the Pacific Coast, soon to play an important role in the political evolution of California. Naval lieutenant Washington Bartlett, a Maine man who spoke fluent Spanish, having been appointed *alcalde* of Yerba Buena on the northern edge of the San Francisco peninsula, saw grand urban possibilities in the settlement. To bring into being the newly renamed city of San Francisco, Bartlett commissioned Jasper O'Farrell—an Irish-born civil engineer from Chile, now serving as surveyor-general of Alta California—to survey the tip of the peninsula and lay out a town plan that would guide the growth of San Francisco for the next 150 years. Two years later, Army lieutenant Edward Ord established a similarly long-lasting town plan for Los Angeles.

After the Treaty of Guadalupe Hidalgo, an effort was made to integrate more civilians into the *alcalde* system. Stephen Field, for example—a Connecticut lawyer with a degree from Williams College, later to be appointed by President Lincoln to the U.S.

Supreme Court—served as *alcalde* of the newly established settlement of Marysville, at the confluence of the Feather and Yuba rivers.

From one perspective, the *alcalde* era represented a fusion of Mexico and the United States that possessed—like the Monterey Colonial style of architecture invented by Thomas Oliver Larkin—its own charm and the promise of a successfully fused Yankee-Latino culture, already under development in the Mexican era when so many Yankee émigrés had settled in California and married into local families.

Was this process to continue, one might ask, especially as intermarriage continued through the interregnum period? Was American California destined to evolve gradually as a Yankee-Latino enclave, with an increasing number of Americans marrying Californios or otherwise absorbing Hispanic culture? All five of the Carrillo daughters from Santa Barbara, for example, married Yankees. From this perspective, the 1846–50 interregnum would later cast a spell of enchantment—a daydream of California as an Arcadian Yankee Mexico—that would eventually provide the state with some of its most salient myths. Already, a mood of reverie and lost romance can be detected in the memoir *Life in California Before the Conquest* (1846) by Alfred Robinson, the longtime representative of Bryant, Sturgis & Company whose marriage to the Santa Barbara heiress Anita de la Guerra was so extensively described by Robinson's cousin Richard Henry Dana, Jr., in *Two Years Before the Mast* (1840). Even the flinty Vermont Congregationalist Walter Colton could come under the spell of California, which Colton later described as rivaling the sunny shores of southern France or Italy in his memoir *Three Years in California* (1850), dedicated to his good friend Mariano Guadalupe Vallejo.

Far from being nostalgic regarding the passing Mexican era, however, Vallejo himself was very much concerned with maximizing the possibilities of the new American polity. For all of its existence, California had remained only sketchily developed, and now there was a chance—for such pre-Conquest residents as Vallejo, Larkin, Sutter, Charles Weber, and William Leidesdorff, together with such newly arrived entrepreneurs as Mormon leader Sam Brannan—to develop California as a forward-looking, money-making American place. A son of both Spanish and Mexican California, Vallejo entered into a business partnership with Larkin because the former consul and confidential agent had justifiably earned a reputation as the "gettingest" man in the province, busy across half a dozen enterprises: thirty new buildings in Monterey alone, designed and built for sale; contracts to supply the Navy; land for sale or lease; wheat and livestock; and, in partnership with Vallejo and Bear Flagger Robert Semple, the creation from scratch of the city of Benicia on the north shore of the Carquinez Strait leading into San Francisco Bay.

Slightly inland, meanwhile, on Mexican land grant property he owned where the Calaveras River flowed into the tidal waters of the San Joaquin, German-born Charles Weber, who had arrived in California in 1841 with the Bartelson-Bidwell party, was busy by 1847 establishing his own new city, Tuleburg, which he renamed the following year in honor of Commodore Stockton, conqueror of California. William Leidesdorff—an African Dane from the Virgin Islands (with a Danish father and a mother of African descent) who had come to California in 1841 from New Orleans, where he had worked as a cotton broker—was equally bullish on the newly established city of San Francisco, where Leidesdorff, exempted from the color line (if, indeed, his ancestry was known), was busy building a warehouse and the City Hotel, the first such hostelry in San Francisco, while serving as the treasurer of the new city government and, as chairman of the school board, building the city's first public school.

Another San Francisco–based entrepreneur, Samuel Brannan, a Mormon elder, was not only developing the city—a flour mill, the *California Star* newspaper, a provisions and hardware business—but was also embodying the socioeconomic boost the newly acquired province had received from the arrival of the ship *Brooklyn* in San Francisco Bay on July 31, 1846, with its 224 Mormon immigrants—men, women, and children—under Brannan's leadership. Persecuted in the East and Midwest, the Mormons were coming to California as the comparably persecuted Pilgrims had come to Massachusetts on the *Mayflower* and suppressed Roman Catholics had arrived in Maryland on the *Ark* and the *Dove.* Almost simultaneously, members of a battalion of Mormon volunteers who had reached San Diego on January 29, 1847, as part of the invading Army of the West were mustered out into civilian life. The Mormons brought to California, at a critical point in its development, social solidarity and much-needed manual skills as sawyers, carpenters, millwrights, farmers, and irrigationists. So too would the veterans of the 1st Regiment of New York Volunteers be soon available, once they were discharged in the summer and fall of 1848. Organized by New York lawyer Jonathan Drake Stevenson, who served as colonel of the regiment, the volunteers had come to California as soldier-colonists, with some of the men bringing along their wives and children, thereby adding to the social complexity of the newly acquired province.

A number of discharged Mormons and New York Volunteers found work inland in the employ of Captain John Augustus Sutter at New Helvetia. No one seemed better positioned to capitalize on the new American order than Sutter, master of the strategically located northeastern flank of the settled portions of Northern California. Already, overland immigrants who arrived at Sutter's Fort, just inland from the Sacramento River, did their re-provisioning from Sutter's stores, bought or leased their land from Sutter, or contracted from him the labor (and sometimes, it has been alleged, the sexual services) of Native Americans indentured to Sutter or otherwise under his control, many of them little better off than slaves. Sutter had great plans for the city (not yet named Sacramento) that would one day rise on his property, and to that end he began to plan for the expansion of the local infrastructure, including an *embarcadero* (wharf) on the Sacramento River and the construction of housing near the fort. That meant lumber, and lumber meant a sawmill—which is exactly what Sutter commissioned carpenter James Wilson Marshall to build.

A New Jersey native, Marshall had arrived at Sutter's Fort in July 1845, joined the Bear Flag revolt, and served with Frémont before returning to partner with Sutter in building a water-driven sawmill. Marshall provided the construction know-how, Sutter the cash. To meet a growing market for construction, Sutter and Marshall realized, the existing way of creating lumber—sawing each board painstakingly with a two-man whipsaw—would have to be replaced by a more efficient water-driven process. Once a sawmill was built alongside a river, running water could turn the wheels that moved the saws that cut the logs into usable lumber, which could then be brought down to Sutter's Fort for local use or floated downriver to San Francisco via barge. Selecting a suitable site on the South Fork of the American River where the water ran swiftly, Marshall and a team of Mormon carpenters recently discharged from the Mormon Battalion, together with a handful of Indian laborers, got to work on the sawmill they hoped would make their fortune. Instead, this sawmill changed the course of California history, provoking a mass migration and propelling California headlong into an accelerated future.

Inspecting the mill site on the morning of January 24, 1848, Marshall noticed some sparkling pebbles in the gravel bed of the tailrace his men had dug alongside the river to move the water as swiftly as possible beneath the mill. Marshall took little notice, thinking the pebbles were merely shiny pieces of quartz. Farther down the tailrace, however, where the water became shallow, he picked up from the gravel bed four or five more of the shiny rocks. Having some knowledge of minerals, Marshall decided that the shiny nuggets were either sulphuret of iron or gold. When he pounded a nugget between two rocks, it changed its shape but did not break apart. The nugget was gold, Marshall thought, but he needed further proof. Bringing the nuggets back to the mill site, Marshall announced to his Mormon workers—or so he later remembered—"I have found it!" Gathering around Marshall, the men examined the nuggets. One of them, at Marshall's direction, pounded one of the specimens into a thin sheet, using a hammer. Another, Peter Wimmer, took the pounded flake back to a cabin where his wife was making soap by boiling lye. Elizabeth Wimmer dropped the flake into the boiling lye, and it brightened. The application of baking powder proved equally positive. James Wilson Marshall had truly found it—found gold!—and California would never be the same.

Informed of the discovery by Marshall, John Sutter pulled his copy of the *Encyclopædia Americana* from the shelf and read the article on gold. He also treated Marshall's specimens with nitric acid. Once again, the nuggets passed the test. Sutter spent a sleepless night. This discovery of gold would change everything he had worked for! Already the Mormon carpenters had negotiated permission to search for gold in their off-hours. Soon that would be their full-time occupation. Sam Brannan, by then working as a storekeeper at Sutter's Fort, brought the news to San Francisco a few months later. Running through the streets, Brannan shouted at the top of his lungs that *gold, gold, gold* had been discovered on the South Fork of the American River!

Soon, just as Sutter had feared, his employees, Mormons and non-Mormons alike, were abandoning their jobs, purchasing stores and equipment from Sam Brannan, and taking to the riverbeds. By late spring, the first wave of the Gold Rush was under way. Hearing of these developments, Army colonel Richard Mason, the military governor, toured the goldfields that July in the company of his aide, Lieutenant William Tecumseh Sherman. Returning to Monterey, Sherman wrote a report, which Mason signed for delivery to President Polk. Army lieutenant Lucien Loeser was dispatched to Washington via the Isthmus of Panama with Mason's report and 230 ounces of California gold packed into an oyster can. Loeser left Monterey at the end of August and arrived in Washington in late November. On December 5, 1848, in a message to Congress, President Polk made it official. Gold had been discovered in California. Overnight, the regional Gold Rush of 1848 exploded into the international Gold Rush of 1849.

Within the following two years, the Gold Rush fast-forwarded California into what historian Hubert Howe Bancroft would later describe as "a rapid, monstrous maturity." Within a year of President Polk's announcement, the non–Native American population of California was approaching one hundred thousand, up from the less than ten thousand of 1848. Even more astonishingly, California had organized itself as a state, bypassing territorial status, had held elections, and was petitioning Congress for admission into the Union. Within three years of President Polk's announcement, the non–Native American population had soared to 255,000, and a new metropolis, San Francisco, had sprung into existence like Atlantis rising from the sea. In just about every way possible—its internationalism, its psychology of expectation, its artistic and literary culture, its racism, its heedless damage to the environment, its rapid creation of a political, economic, and technological infrastructure—the Gold Rush established, for better or for worse, the founding patterns, the DNA code, of American California. Josiah Royce believed that the Gold Rush offered a case study in American character and hence was of importance to understanding the nation. Like the Revolutionary War, the Great Awakening, the Louisiana Purchase, or the Civil War, the Gold

Rush, according to many historians, constitutes a defining moment in the development of the United States.

First of all and most fundamentally, it was exactly what the name implies: a rush, a mass migration, of mainly younger men and some of middle age from all corners of the earth, including China and Australia, who ventured everything, their lives included (one in twelve would die in the process), on the gamble that they could strike it rich and thereby break through to a better life. Such a hope, such a psychology of expectation, fused the California experience irretrievably onto a dream of better days: of a sudden, almost magical, transformation of the ordinary. Ironically, such an expectation was also reprising the dreams of the Spanish conquistadores, explorers, and maritime adventurers of the sixteenth and seventeenth centuries. The Spanish quest for El Dorado was now being Americanized with its psychological and mythic hold as powerful as ever.

Like the Spaniards, moreover, the forty-niners first had to get there, which remained a formidable task. While not as difficult as the voyages of Cabrillo and Vizcaíno, or the overland treks of Portolá and Anza in times past, reaching California in 1849 was still a daunting challenge. It could involve, at its longest, a voyage of five to eight months around Cape Horn or an overland trek of equal duration. Crossing the isthmus of Panama or Nicaragua (or in some cases Mexico) could cut down on this time by as much as two thirds by 1850; but the trip across the isthmus—from Chagres, then up the Chagres River by boat, then down to the Pacific by mule or foot (such a trek as a plucky Jesse Benton Frémont was making in the spring of 1849, en route to California to join her husband)—involved high risks and probabilities of accident, fever, snakebite, alligator attack, drowning, or various forms of mayhem including robbery and murder. Some overland travelers preferred an approach to California along the Old Spanish Trail through the deserts of the

Southwest, even to the point of crossing Death Valley as the William Manly party, after much travail, succeeded in doing in 1849.

In rapid order, however, a maritime voyage to California became, for those who could afford it, relatively safe and comfortable, with such companies as the Vanderbilt Line and Pacific Mail Steamship providing steamer-sail service from New York to Chagres and from Panama City on the Panama–Pacific Coast to San Francisco. When a railroad was completed across the isthmus in late January 1855, California became even more accessible, and the percentage of women in the non-Indian population rose to 10 percent. Eighteen forty-nine was, however, primarily a year of arrival by sail. By October a forest of masts rose from 308 abandoned ships crowding San Francisco Bay. By June 1850 that figure had doubled to 635 vessels, and a number of ships had been dragged ashore to serve as warehouses, saloons, hotels, and in one case—the brig *Euphemia,* left floating but permanently anchored offshore—a city prison.

By then, the Mother Lode—which is to say, the 120 miles of Sierra Nevada foothills and mountains centered on the Mokelumne River—teemed with mining camps of every description. In his report to President Polk and his subsequent actions and judgments, Colonel Mason, governor of California, established a social and political doctrine of overwhelming importance. The goldfields, Mason decreed, were under the jurisdiction of the federal government. They were freely available for prospecting and mining as long as certain filings and protocols were observed. The gold of California was not under private ownership. It belonged to everyone, provided one could find it, lay legal claim to it, extract it, and get it safely to one or the other of the many assay centers that were now springing up where nuggets could be weighed, valued, and melted into ingots for shipment to San Francisco and New York. All told, some $594 million in ingots—the equivalent of $10 billion in 2001 dollars—would over the course of the next decade be leaving the goldfields of California for the eastern United States.

Over the past 150 years, historians have interpreted the Gold Rush successively as a mid-Victorian epic of Anglo-Saxon progress (Hubert Howe Bancroft), a case study in American self-government (Charles Shinn), a moral crisis (Josiah Royce), a challenge to community building (John Caughey), a technological triumph (Rodman Paul), an outpouring of entrepreneurial self-actualization (J. S. Holliday), a case study in the persistent and shaping influence of American institutions (Malcolm Rohrbough), a transformation of America itself (H. W. Brands), and—from the perspective of young Turk New Historians—a nightmare of violence, lynch law, racism, genocide, xenophobia, class and sexual conflict, and brutal degradation of the environment. Each of these interpretations is true in its own way, but not the full truth. A protean and transformative event, the Gold Rush remains multiple in its meaning, with each generation finding in it corroboration for contemporary concerns.

Gold Rush California was primarily a man's world, at least until the mid-1850s; and, yes, it could be wild, free, unconstrained, exuberant. Such a vision of the Gold Rush as festival shivaree, as high jinks in the Mother Lode, can be found as early as the first humorists to cover the event—Alonzo Delano and Prentice Mulford, followed by Bret Harte and Mark Twain—and in the Gold Rush paintings of Charles Nahl. Hubert Howe Bancroft celebrated this point of view in *California Inter Pocula* (1888), which is to say, California in its cups. This interpretation of the Gold Rush as a fun-filled and affirmative adventure survived through numerous celebrations, including the 1949 centennial. It lingered in the movies (Gabby Hayes playing the comic prospector) and continues to sustain the ongoing revelry of a flourishing antiquarian drinking fraternity, the Ancient

Order of E Clampus Vitus, founded in 1857 and revitalized in 1931 by historian Carl Wheat, which places plaques at historic Gold Rush sites before adjourning to a nearby saloon.

There is something to be said for this interpretation, even when it is qualified. The Gold Rush did constitute a collective psychic release—a sense of youth, heightened expectations, freedom from constraints of all kinds—in the Argonaut generation of young men, and the smaller number of women, who came to El Dorado in search of the Golden Fleece. Yet life in Gold Rush California could also be nasty, brutish, and short. One out of every twelve forty-niners would lose his (or her) life en route to, in, or returning from the mines. Accidents were frequent. Cholera and other fatal diseases posed a constant threat. (An outbreak of cholera decimated Sacramento in 1850.) There was the ever-present temptation to drink too much, or to gamble away one's hard-won earnings or, if given the opportunity, to squander them on prostitution. Disputes regarding claims or any form of theft (a particular threat in a society in which miners were forced to leave their gear unprotected for most of the day) frequently led to violence; and because each man went armed and was willing to use his knife or pistol, brawls, stabbings, mayhem, and murder were commonplace.

As historian John Boessenecker has demonstrated, the murder rate in the mines was horrendous—an annual rate of 506.6 homicides per 100,000 population in Sonora, for example, in 1850–51, which is fifty times the national homicide rate of 1999. Outside the Mother Lode it could be even more dangerous. As historian (and former San Francisco deputy police chief) Kevin Mullen has documented, San Francisco averaged a homicide rate of 49 per 100,000 between 1849 and 1856, six times the 1997 homicide rate of that city. Los Angeles County, meanwhile, saw forty-four murders between July 1850 and October 1851, which translates to an annual rate of 414 homicides per 100,000. Between September 1850 and September 1851, the homicide rate in the city of Los Angeles and its suburbs spiked off the graph at 1,240 per 100,000, which remains the all-time high homicide rate in the annals of American murder. If California ever had anything resembling the Wild West—meaning cowboys and shoot-outs—it was Los Angeles County in the early 1850s; until, that is, the formation in 1853 of the Los Angeles Rangers, a permanent posse that would in the course of one year capture and execute more than twenty alleged miscreants. Between 1849 and 1853, Boessenecker estimates, there were more than two hundred lynchings in the Mother Lode. As courts and a criminal justice system began to assert themselves, that number fell to one hundred throughout the state between 1853 and 1857. Still, lynching remained an option in California down through the nineteenth century. The last old-fashioned Gold Rush–style lynching—that of five men in Modoc County—occurred as late as May 1901.

With the conspicuous exception of Josiah Royce, most nineteenth-century historians considered lynch law a tragic necessity, given the feebleness of legal institutions in the first years of the Gold Rush. To bolster their assessment, they pointed to the fact that most lynchings involved hearings before an elected tribunal, which heard evidence and pronounced sentence and hence possessed an element of legitimacy, indeed represented a resurgence of Anglo-Saxon legal traditions. Contemporary historians, however, combing through surviving records, have noted the disproportionate number of Hispanics being lynched and tend to link lynch law with larger patterns of race-based antagonism.

The Gold Rush, it must be remembered, represented the second extensive exposure on a personal level between Anglo-Americans and Hispanic peoples and cultures. The first such encounter had been the recently concluded war with Mexico. Therein lay a problem. While Gold Rush voyage narratives and journals contain expressions of regard for Latin American culture as represented by the ports of call en route to the goldfields, the overall attitude toward Hispanic civilization revealed in these documents is one of suspicion and disapproval, even contempt. In the case of Mexico, such attitudes were compounded by the recent war, in which Mexican troops had made a spirited defense of their homeland. In the goldfields themselves, three groups of miners—Peruvians, Chileans, and Mexicans from Sonora—possessed a mining expertise far beyond that of their Anglo-American counterparts; indeed, they frequently acted as tutors to the Anglo-Americans. Such a transfer of expertise might have resulted in gratitude born of collaboration. Instead, it rendered American miners hostile to the more skilled Hispanics, whom they envied yet held in contempt. One of the very first laws enacted by the California legislature after California had become a state was a license tax of twenty dollars a month on all foreigners in the goldfields. This levy was especially directed at Mexican miners at a time when there were some fifteen thousand Mexican miners in the southern Mother Lode. Repealed in 1851, the tax is nevertheless estimated to have driven some ten thousand Mexicans from the mines.

The Peruvians, Chileans, Sonorans, and Californios remaining in the mines—like the Native Americans and Chinese there as well—had a horrible time of it over the next few years. In San Francisco, Americans invaded and trashed Chilean encampments. In the mines, Mexicans were rounded up, fined, beaten, and driven from the diggings. The writer known as "Dame Shirley" (see Chapter 6) witnessed the whipping of a young Hispanic miner on unsubstantiated charges. He could be considered one of the lucky ones, for in one camp on the Calaveras River, sixteen Chileans were executed en masse on charges of murder after summary proceedings. Also in the Calaveras district, Edward Buffum witnessed an angry crowd of two hundred Americans, many of them drunk, string up two Frenchmen and one Chilean charged with robbery and murder after the most minimal of hearings, with none of the three accused understanding a word of English. In San Francisco the Vigilance Committee seized control of the city during the summer of 1851 in an effort to protect the inhabitants against the so-called Sydney Ducks, a group of Australian hooligans terrorizing the city. Four Ducks were hanged, one was whipped, and twenty-eight were sentenced to deportation.

Defenders of lynch law—or at least those trying to understand it—claimed that it represented a desperate attempt by miners and city dwellers to deal with a crime wave beyond the capacities of a government that was only then establishing itself. There is some truth to this view. Yet the large number of Hispanic victims argues that something else was at work as well: something that must be considered along with the way miners cleared the goldfields of Native Americans through wholesale slaughter, or restricted the Chinese to abandoned diggings. An ugly mood—racist and electric with sexual tension turned murderously misogynistic—seized the crowd in Downieville, Placer County, on July 5, 1851. That day, some two thousand American miners hanged a beautiful, spirited pregnant Mexican woman by the name of Josefa. The previous evening, a drunken miner had tried to break into Josefa's cabin, where she was living with her common-law husband, also a Mexican. Upbraided by Josefa the next day for his conduct, the miner called her a whore. Enraged, she stabbed him to death.

Scholars have recently been exploring the sexual instability of a virtually all-male society in the goldfields and finding in this tension significant causes for the volatility of life in the mines. The entire Gold Rush, argues historian Susan Lee Johnson, offers a case study in tensions, repressions, sublimations, and power relationships involving race, gender, and thwarted eroticism. Aside from the expected symptoms of such a situation—alcoholism, prostitution, the sexual enslavement of Chinese women, and something akin to slavery in the case of other prostitutes of color, all of them the frequent victims of disease and violence—there was also homosexual activity and related forms of homoerotic and/or sublimated behavior (all-male dances, for example, in which some miners assumed the woman's role) which, taken cumulatively, belie the Victorian and early twentieth-century assertion that the Gold Rush was peopled exclusively by Tom Sawyers and whores with hearts of gold.

In the larger landscape of domestic life, moreover, the Gold Rush reveals the emotional texture of mid-nineteenth-century American life. Respectable women, wives and sweethearts, were left behind, and this itself opened a landscape of loneliness, longing, and regret comparable to the separations of wartime. The respectable women who did make it to California, on the other hand—and their numbers increased steadily year by year—could experience an expansion of roles and opportunities. Louise Clapp (pen name Dame Shirley) learned to write. Mary Jane Megquier began to sell her pies to miners and eventually made a tidy fortune in the boardinghouse and catering business. Eliza Farnham, the onetime matron of women at Sing Sing, brought a group of respectable women around the Horn to San Francisco in 1849 as wives-to-be for the new community. Farnham later farmed for a few hardscrabble seasons in Santa Cruz before launching herself in San Francisco as a writer and crusading feminist. The scarcity of women, meanwhile, made for such anomalies as the acceptability of a married woman's being accompanied to a ball by four or five gentlemen in addition to her husband. Related to all this, the divorce rate rose steadily during these early years.

With the arrival of women came as well churches, synagogues, and schools, so many of them dating from 1849. The Royce family, for example, arrived overland that year after a trek of six months by covered wagon across the continent. Welcomed by a group of church ladies in the Mother Lode, Sarah Royce knew that she was once again in civilization. Her son

Josiah, born in Grass Valley in 1855, would later argue emphatically and from firsthand experience that cultural values were not lost on the California frontier; indeed, they became more precious than ever. Later teaching at Berkeley and Harvard, Royce was among the first to evaluate the Gold Rush as a social and moral event. While acknowledging all forms of misbehavior during this period, Royce also emphasized the spontaneous social organization that was also taking place in these headlong, heedless, prodigal years.

Mining, Royce emphasized, was by nature a social activity. Most miners came to California, whether from the Atlantic states or from Europe (especially France), as members of organized mining companies. While most of these companies dissolved amid the pressures of the goldfields, they did bring to California some form of social organization. Moreover, gold mining itself, as it progressed through increasingly complex stages of technology, in turn demanded more complex forms of social organization. While it might take one man to mine for gold with a pan, it took at least two to handle a Rocking Tom, which washed gravel through a hand-rocked device. And as placer mining (the search for gold in riverbeds) grew ever more ambitious, it would take ever more men—hence intensified social organization—to dam or divert a river, build sluices, or construct aqueducts across canyons. Dry-mining—digging into the earth for quartz—was an even more complex mining, hence social, enterprise. Then came the use of high-pressure hoses to wash away hillsides, starting in April 1852 with the jury-rigged improvisings outside Nevada City of Antoine Chabot, a French Canadian sailmaker: a technique immeasurably improved the following year by Edward Matteson, a forty-niner from Connecticut. Hydraulic mining soon emerged as an intrinsically complex industry, involving as many as a hundred men organized in corporate structures.

Regrettably, hydraulic mining further accelerated the destruction of the environment. California, noted Bayard Taylor, resembled a princess captured by bandits who cut off her hands to obtain the rings on her fingers. By the mid-1850s, the hills of the Mother Lode stood scarred and devastated by six years of assault. With the introduction of hydraulic mining, whole mountains were washed away. The resulting debris and silt clogged the rivers and creeks of the Mother Lode, which fed into the rivers of the Central Valley. Back in Massachusetts, Henry David Thoreau was especially affronted by this environmental depredation. California, Thoreau entered into his journal—he did not wish to go there! It was only so many miles closer to hell!

More positively, urbanization was another direct result of the Gold Rush; and urbanization precipitated in turn, decades before it might have been expected, the near-spontaneous organization of California into a state. While myth and legend might savor the folkloric image of the solitary miner, most miners lived and worked in common. They also created throughout the Mother Lode a string of mining settlements—Nevada City, Grass Valley, Dutch Flat, Georgetown, Jackson, Murphy's Camp, Sutter's Creek, and Sonora among them—which even today sustain a persistent and serviceable urbanism. The more strategically placed towns—Stockton, Marysville, Sacramento, San Francisco—rapidly became full-fledged cities; San Francisco was by 1870 the tenth largest city in the United States. True, these settlements were hastily thrown together and careless in their governance and management. San Francisco burned down seven times before it got around to establishing a municipal fire force. Sacramento was repeatedly flooded before it constructed a system of levees. Yet urban society had staked its claim, and this fact, especially in San Francisco, helped precipitate statehood.

WHICH BRINGS US TO politics and governance. All things considered, the Army performed quite creditably as the de facto civil government of California from 1846 to 1848. Some of the leading commanders of the Civil War—Ulysses Grant, William Sherman, Henry Halleck, Albert Johnston—spent time in California during the 1850s. As secretary of state in the military government, Halleck, a skilled lawyer, would play an important role in the creation of the civilian state. On leave from the Army, Sherman would prosper as a banker during the Gold Rush. As capable as the military governors of California were, however, the last such governor—Brigadier General Bennett Riley, appointed on April 12, 1849—had an increasingly complex problem on his hands. A growing population of urbanized American civilians was demanding self-government and such traditional rights as trial by jury. Already, that January, acting on its own authority, the newly formed city of San Francisco had drawn up plans for a fifteen-member legislative assembly and a judiciary. On March 5, 1849, just before Riley took office, this legislative assembly—in its own way, a kind of rump parliament—held its first meeting, elected a speaker, and began drawing up a code of laws.

Bluff, hardy, and plainspoken, the sixty-one-year-old governor decided to act. Neither military law nor the *alcalde* system currently in use, Riley decided, could cope with the complexity of California. And so the general acted as Congress had failed to act in 1846. On June 3, 1849, Riley issued a lengthy document in which he discussed the legal impasse California found itself in, with the military governing civilians under a hodgepodge of laws. Let the people of California elect thirty-seven delegates to a constitutional convention to be held in Monterey in September, Riley directed, and form a government. It was a breathtaking proclamation, one that forever secured Riley's place as a founder of the state; for that is exactly what the forty-eight delegates assembling in Colton Hall, Monterey (expanded from the thirty-seven delegates summoned by Riley owing to population growth in San José, San Francisco, Sacramento, and the San Joaquin Valley), proceeded to do: design California as an American state, using copies of the constitutions of New York and Iowa as guidelines. Riley's proclamation was bold and surprising enough. But here was something even more astonishing (presumptuous, even, according to certain congressional critics): the instant creation of an American state, fully functioning, as the goddess Minerva on the newly designed state seal had sprung full-grown from the brain of Jupiter.

The forty-eight delegates convening in Monterey were young (thirty-two of them were under the age of forty), white (seven were native-born Californios), and almost equally balanced between proslavery and antislavery contingents. A quarter of them had been born outside the United States. The president of the assembly, the towering (six foot six) Kentucky-born Robert Semple, embodied the collective experience of the delegates, being a veteran of the Lansford Hastings party of 1845, a leader in the Bear Flag revolt of June–July 1846, a co-founder (with Walter Colton) later that year in Monterey of *The Californian,* the first newspaper in the region, and one of the developers (along with Larkin and Vallejo) of Benicia, soon to be the state capital. Proceedings were in Spanish and English, with the English-born William Hartnell, a resident of California since 1822, serving as official translator. The talented writer J. Ross Browne was selected as reporter to the convention and kept meticulous records of the proceedings, later published in both languages; Spanish remained one of the two official languages of California until 1879.

It was not a perfect constitution, nor was it socially equitable. Only white males were granted the franchise, a point of contention given the Native American and African bloodlines of so many Californios, although the color line was never formally drawn in their case. African Americans, Chinese, and Native Americans were denied the rights of citizenship and prohibited from testifying against whites in court. The framers came dangerously close to banishing all African Americans, slave or free, from the state entirely. On the other hand, after much debate, slavery was prohibited in California, despite the knowledge that the admission of California as a free state would destabilize even further a shaky and fragile Union. Under the influence of Mexican law and previous Californio practice, women, including married women, were granted the right to own property in their own name, independent of fathers and/or husbands; this was a legal rarity at the time. The insistence that California be a free state necessitated new borders, for the delegates knew that Congress would never approve the admission of a free state the size of Mexican California. Hence the lands that would later become the states of Arizona, Nevada, Utah, and southern Colorado were trimmed away, leaving the suggestion that slavery might be introduced into these territories at a later date. Even then, the proposed state was a behemoth. If it were on the East Coast, it would extend from Maine to Georgia.

By Friday, October 12, 1849, California stood redesigned as an American state. Army major Robert Garnett designed a seal with the goddess Minerva at its center flanked by a miner at work and a grizzly bear feeding on grapes, against a backdrop of a ship sailing into San Francisco Bay and the snow-clad peaks of the Sierra Nevada. Thirty-one stars surrounded the seal, which presumed California's admission as the thirty-first state, together with the motto *Eureka,* classical Greek for "I have found [it]," which James Marshall later claimed were the very words he had used upon discovering gold on the South Fork of the American River.

That night, Friday, October 12, 1849, a grand ball was held in Colton Hall, presided over by delegate Don Pablo de la Guerra, soon to be state senator from Santa Barbara. Reporter Bayard Taylor was at the gathering and saw in its festive mingling of Hispanics and Yankees an image of hope for the future. The next day, the constitution was signed by the delegates, while cannons boomed a thirty-one-gun salute from the presidio. An English bark, the *Volunteer,* hoisted the Stars and Stripes in recognition. When Captain John Augustus Sutter presented the signed constitution later that afternoon to General Riley at his official residence, the old soldier had tears in his eyes. Choking with emotion, the military man who had precipitated statehood accepted the constitution, praised the work of his secretary of state Captain Halleck, and was given twice three cheers by the delegates gathered before the gubernatorial adobe.

That same day, Riley, still the governor of California, issued a second defining proclamation, this one calling for a general election on November 13, 1849, to ratify the constitution and to elect state officials and U.S. representatives. Should the constitution be ratified and such officials elected, Riley directed, the legislature should subsequently assemble on December 15 to elect two U.S. senators and continue the organization of the state. On a wet and dreary election day, only half of the eligible electors showed up at the polls—there was, after all, a Gold Rush going on!—but the constitution was ratified, 12,061 in favor, 811 against. Peter Burnett, a forty-two-year-old Tennessee-born Democrat who had already served as a supreme court judge in the Oregon Territory, was elected governor. Another Democrat, Ohio-born John McDougal, thirty-one, who had served as a captain in the Mexican War, was elected lieutenant governor. Two San Franciscans, George Wright and Edward Gilbert, were elected to the U.S. House of Representatives.

On Saturday, December 15, 1849, the newly elected state legislature duly convened in San José. Called the "Legislature of a Thousand Drinks" because one of its members, state senator Thomas Jefferson Green, liked to call out upon adjournment, "Well, boys, let's go and take a thousand drinks," this first legislature nevertheless set promptly about the business of organizing the legal and administrative infrastructure of the new commonwealth. On the twentieth, General Riley formally resigned as governor in favor of Peter Burnett. Riley also issued orders disestablishing the military as the government of California and relieved Halleck of his post as secretary of state. All in all, it had been an extraordinary performance on the part of the aging brigadier, who had acted in a legal and political void and had given legitimacy to the newly established state.

The key business now facing the legislature was the election of two U.S. senators, who would be responsible for negotiating the acceptance of California into the Union. John Charles Frémont was unanimously elected on the first ballot. It took three ballots, however, to elect the recent Tennessee lawyer-physician William Gwin, a key delegate at the constitutional convention, who had left Washington less than a year before with the express intention, so he had told his friend Senator Stephen Douglas of Illinois, of returning as U.S. senator from California.

California had need of Gwin's considerable political skills and rapport with the South, which held the veto on California's admission, and so it was perhaps fortunate for the would-be state that Gwin drew the straw giving him a six-year term, with Frémont drawing the shorter straw for a two-year term. The South knew that the admission of California as a free state would destabilize the Missouri Compromise of 1820 that had admitted Missouri as a slave state and Maine as a free, thus keeping the balance of free and slave states twelve to twelve and forever forbidding slavery above latitude 36 degrees 30 minutes north. This compromise had kept the Union stabilized for thirty years. Now, because of California, it was in jeopardy. Gwin was a Southerner by birth and proslavery in his general sentiment; Frémont, by contrast, was an avid Free-Soiler and in 1856 would be the first Republican candidate for president. It was thus up to Gwin to persuade Southern senators that it would be worth their while to find some formula that would allow for the admission of California into the Union. That was no easy task, for the great John C. Calhoun, senator from South Carolina, a dying invalid but still formidable, was leading the opposition.

The congressional debates and maneuverings between January and September 1850 regarding the admission of California to the Union constitute a drama of titanic intensity. Nothing less than the survival of the Union, already so fragile, was at stake in the minds of the key Senate players: Henry Clay of Kentucky, Daniel Webster of Massachusetts, Thomas Hart Benton of Missouri, Stephen Douglas of Illinois, and John C. Calhoun. Indeed, it had been the very maneuverings and compromises spearheaded in the past by Clay, Webster, and Calhoun—giants in the annals of American politics—that had time and again kept the Union together. Now that Union once again stood in danger.

In his last Senate speech, which had to be read for him, Calhoun was especially vehement regarding the illegality of California's having formed a state government without congressional authorization. California, Calhoun argued, was being used as a club against the South.

On March 7, 1850, Daniel Webster rose to answer the senator from South Carolina, thinking that the dying Calhoun was absent from the chamber, which was not the case. ("He is here," called out one senator. "I am happy to hear that he is," Webster replied graciously. "May he long be in health and the enjoyment of it to serve his country.") Webster proceeded to give a speech that was so conciliatory to the South that his Northern supporters considered it a great betrayal. With the sonorous eloquence that only he could command, Webster evoked the grandeur of the newly acquired empire of California, especially its great harbor at San Francisco, which would open the United States to the Pacific. California and New Mexico, Webster argued, were by climate and terrain unfit for slavery. To introduce slavery into these lands would be to defy the law of nature, hence to defy the divine will that had fashioned nature. Four days later, Senator William Seward of New York tackled, and somewhat demolished, the argument that the people of California had acted illegally in emancipating themselves from military rule. No free American people, Seward thundered, are obliged to remain indefinitely under military occupation.

William Gwin, meanwhile, was engaged in a series of behind-the-scenes negotiations with President Zachary Taylor, a Virginian and a slaveholder, who wanted California admitted to the Union without reference to the slavery question, which Gwin correctly saw as not an option. Taylor's death from gastroenteritis on July 9, 1850, and the elevation to the presidency of New Yorker Millard Fillmore, who appointed Daniel Webster secretary of state, removed the formidable barrier of presidential opposition. (Calhoun had died in late March.) An omnibus bill drafted by Douglas had meanwhile been introduced in the Senate on May 8 containing the elements of a compromise. Once again, Henry Clay, senator from Kentucky, the Great Pacificator who had spearheaded the Missouri Compromise of 1820, entered the lists on behalf of a disintegrating republic. California was to be admitted to the Union as a free state, Clay brokered, but New Mexico and Utah would be granted territorial status with no reference to the slavery question. Slavery would be abolished in the District of Columbia, but there would also be enacted a more stringent fugitive slave law. Lest the omnibus bill founder as debate continued, Senator Douglas reactivated his bill calling for the direct, immediate, and unqualified admission of California to the Union as a free state. Douglas's bill (Senate bill 169) forced the crisis. It passed the Senate on August 13, 1850, by a vote of 34 to 18, passed the House after three readings, 150 to 56, on September 9, 1850 (thereafter celebrated as Admission Day), and was immediately signed by President Fillmore.

News of statehood reached California via the mail steamer *Oregon,* which sailed into San Francisco Harbor on October 18, 1850, flying two banners announcing that California was a state.

The city went into celebration, and on the twenty-ninth a grand parade was held—the army, the navy, a marching band, mounted Californios in their splendid riding costumes, a contingent of Chinese in their finest silks, a float with a girl dressed in classical robes as California—followed by orations in Portsmouth Plaza, the reading of a celebratory ode, and the formal raising of a thirty-one-star flag.

Just as the South feared, however, the admission of California as a state destabilized the Union, despite the Compromise of 1850. North-South rivalry, in fact, would structure the politics of California for the rest of the decade as pro-Southerners, Whigs and Democrats alike, calling themselves "the Chivalry" and led by Senator Gwin, who controlled federal patronage, sought to keep the thirty-first state under the control of Southerners. Gwin managed to do this through the 1850s, even after 1857 when the newly elected Senator David Broderick, an Irish-born veteran of Tammany Hall and an antislavery Democrat, tried to outmaneuver Gwin and gain control of federal patronage and hence the state. Two years later, Chivalry stalwart David Terry, formerly chief justice, killed Broderick in a duel on the shores of Lake Merced on the outskirts of San Francisco. At Broderick's funeral, Edward Baker, later to die on the field of battle in command of a Union regiment, eulogized Broderick as a martyr to the cause of antislavery. The Terry-Broderick duel, together with Broderick's subsequent canonization, offered proof positive that even in far-off California the forces that would soon be threatening to break apart the Union were gaining strength.

Although slavery had been outlawed in California, Southerners continued to bring African American slaves into the mines. One of them, Archy Lee, refused to return to Mississippi with his master on the argument that by coming to California he had become a free man. The free black community of California, now four thousand strong, financed Lee's defense. While the California Supreme Court ruled in favor of Lee's master in February 1858—on the justly ridiculed grounds that Lee's young master, Charles Stovall, had not understood the implications of bringing Lee to a free state, and besides, Stovall was not a well man and needed Lee's assistance—a federal commissioner, William Penn Johnston, a Southerner, refused to apply the Fugitive Slave Law because Lee had not fled across state lines to escape slavery but had been voluntarily brought to California by his master. Still, to be on the safe side, Lee, together with hundreds of other African Americans living in California, decamped in the spring of 1858 to British Columbia, where gold had been discovered on the Fraser River. Not until 1863 would African Americans be allowed to testify in court, and not until the passage of the Fifteenth Amendment in 1870 would they acquire—at least on paper—the right to vote.

In Southern California especially there arose a form of Indian peonage, reinforced by the criminal justice system, that was slavery in everything save name only, with Native Americans sentenced for this or that alleged offense to long periods of indentured servitude to local contractors. The indenturing of Indians to whites, sanctioned by the state government in April 1850, fostered the rise of a slave trade, with slave raiders being especially interested in kidnapping Indian children. In the mines and northern counties, genocidal warfare was waged against the Indians—by the miners themselves, by state-supported volunteer militias, by various vigilante groups. Some massacres, such as those of hundreds of Pomos in the Clear Lake area in May 1850 by army troops, were recorded. Numerous others were lost to history, or remain only as tribal memories. Such slaughter, reinforced by the devastating effects of disease, reduced an estimated population of 150,000 in 1845 to less than 30,000 in 1870, with 60 percent of the deaths attributable to disease, the rest to murder. Tragically, the Native American peoples of California had been reduced by 90 percent since the arrival of the Spanish in

1769, and by 1870 they stood on the brink of extinction. Such vulnerability throws into bold relief the audacious rising of the Modocs of northeastern California in January 1873 under Chief Kientepoos, also known as Captain Jack. For half a year, led by their skilled chief, some fifty-three warriors, armed with rifles, held out in the lava beds of Modoc County against an army force that eventually reached a thousand soldiers. Strategically retreating into Oregon, Captain Jack was betrayed and captured that June and tried and executed in October. The Modoc War, as it is called, cost the commanding army general his life and represented a unique instance of organized resistance by Native Americans in the early years of the state.

5

REGULATION, RAILROAD, AND REVOLUTION

Achievement and Turmoil in the New State

Chinese worker on the transcontinental railroad, mid-1860s

CALIFORNIA STATE LIBRARY

In its first three decades, the newly established state of California invented and reinvented itself through law, politics, urbanization, institution building, agriculture, and the construction of a trans-Sierra railroad. In the strife-ridden 1870s, California approached the abyss, flirted with self-destruction, then regrouped. It was a busy twenty-three years.

Who owned the state, anyway? In the last five years of Mexican governance, there had been a flurry of land grants, many of them vague and indeterminate. A number of grantees had the good sense to retain the services of the professionally trained official surveyor of Alta California, Jasper O'Farrell, to survey and record title to their properties. During the military interregnum, Governor Mason commissioned Secretary of State Halleck to assess the situation. On April 13, 1849, Halleck filed a report questioning the validity of many land grants. In Sacramento, meanwhile, settlers had already begun to build on properties claimed by Sutter. In mid-August 1850, riots broke out when the sheriff sought to evict squatters from these lots. When the two-day confrontation was over, the sheriff, the city assessor, and several sheriff's deputies and squatters lay dead, and the mayor was seriously wounded.

This was no way to run a state, and this was certainly no way to meet the needs of the land-hungry Americans pouring into California. More than thirteen million acres of prime coastal acreage allegedly belonged to a few hundred grantees, many of them short on cash and devoid of initiative. It took little entrepreneurial ability to run longhorn cattle across the immensities of a rancho; how were cities and farms to develop when the land was being claimed by those who, for the immediate present at least, had little inclination to sell or to develop? The situation was even further complicated by the fact that during treaty negotiations, the American government had promised to honor land-grant titles from the Spanish and Mexican eras. In early 1850, the secretary of the interior dispatched to California attorney William Carey Jones—the son-in-law of Senator Thomas Hart Benton, hence the brother-in-law of John Charles Frémont—to investigate the whole situation. Unlike the report of Captain Halleck, Jones's report, filed on March 9, 1850, was generally favorable to the validity of most Spanish and Mexican land-grant titles, including his brother-in-law Frémont's claim to the Rancho Las Mariposas, which Frémont had purchased for $3,000 in 1847. Splitting the difference between Halleck and Jones, Senator Gwin introduced a bill, passed by the U.S. Senate in February 1851 and the House in March, establishing a three-member Board of Land Commissioners to sit in San Francisco and assess, title by title, the validity of all Spanish and Mexican land-grant claims in California.

Now began a long and agonizing ordeal, lasting for two decades, as each landowner argued his claim before the commission or before the federal district court or Supreme Court of the United States on appeal. While the majority of cases—604 claims out of the 813 brought before the commission—were confirmed, it could take as long as seventeen years for a case to move through the hearing and appeals process. That meant that lawyers got rich. Many of them were paid in land or revenue from land sales by cash-starved grantees. When it was over, very few of the original grantees had come through the process with their holdings intact. A significant transfer of wealth had occurred, and grantees from the Spanish and Mexican era, so many of them Hispanics, considered this a betrayal of the Treaty of Guadalupe Hidalgo and a legalized form of theft. The question of land grants—their origins in the Hispanic era, their validity or invalidity, the lives that were made or ruined by titles confirmed or denied—emerged as one of the important themes of nineteenth-century California, a situation that would be compounded when the railroad became the largest landowner in the state. For the rest of the century, much of California would remain resistant to small farming. The vast domains of the rancho might pass from Mexican to Yankee ownership, but these extensive landholdings, together with the quasi-feudal economy they encouraged, continued to dictate the structure of California agriculture.

Not surprisingly, the landowners of Southern California began to doubt whether they could survive in the new state, and to wonder whether it would not be better for them to separate into a territory of their own. Even as the constitution was being drafted in Monterey in September 1849, a number of Southern delegates, led by José Antonio Carrillo, argued for a separate territory south of San Luis Obispo. While the admission of California to the Union was being debated in Washington, a petition was circulated in Southern California asking Congress to admit the southern counties as a separate territory. In Congress itself, Senator Henry Foote, a Mississippi Democrat, was arguing that the Missouri Compromise line of latitude 36 degrees 30 minutes north should be extended to the Pacific, with the territory of Colorado being formed below that boundary. Southerners in the Senate and the House argued long and hard for such a Southern California territory, and Southern Californians spent the 1850s trying to form such a territory. Bills to divide the state were introduced in the legislature in 1851, 1852, 1853, 1855, 1858, and 1859. In September 1859 a successful referendum was held in the southern six counties, calling once again for the creation of the territory of Colorado, and Governor Milton Latham, appointed to the U.S. Senate, left for Washington promising to fight for federal approval of the measure.

Historians have tended to see in these efforts an attempt to extend slavery to the Pacific Coast. Perhaps that was true of the congressional debates of 1850. Other historians have seen in these proposals an effort, on the part of Yankees or Chivalry or both, to create a separatist Pacific republic. But the real impetus behind dividing California came from the fact that the state was truly two, and perhaps even four, distinct places: the urbanizing Bay Area and the mining districts; the Far North (one breakaway effort had called for the creation of the state of Shasta in that region); the Central Valley; and a sparsely settled Southern California, significantly Mexican, where ranch life and agriculture predominated. The outbreak of the Civil War scuttled separatist efforts in Washington, but the question of dividing California, while it has grown increasingly impractical over the years, has never fully gone away. It became a way of thinking and rethinking the developing identity of a nation-state.

Equally challenging was the threat posed to the legitimacy of the state by the San Francisco Vigilance Committee of 1856. In this case, the forces arrayed against the state were urban, specifically the Protestant businessmen of San Francisco, linked by Masonic association, out to rid the city of miscreants, especially if they were Irish Catholics. To the twofold political division of San Francisco—the Yankees and the Chivalry—must be added a third contingent: Irish Catholic Democrats from New York City, whose leader was David Broderick. By 1852, San Francisco was home to more than four thousand Irish-born immigrants and fourteen hundred Irish children of American birth. (By the late 1870s, more than a third of the city would be Irish Catholic.) The Vigilance Committee of 1851 had gone after the Irish-born Sydney Ducks from Australia. Now, in early 1856, a revived committee would usurp the police and judicial powers of the state in what Josiah Royce later described as the Businessmen's Revolution.

And a revolution it was, with all the protocols and panoply of a coup d'état, including a barricaded Fort Gunnybags in the center of the city, a semisecret committee of public safety, and some 2,500 well-drilled men marching with rifles and fixed bayonets. The flashpoint for the seizure of power was the public assassination of crusading newspaper editor James King of William (which was how King signed his name, to differentiate himself from other James Kings in the city)—a Protestant Savonarola with a special contempt for Irish politicians—by James Casey, a member of the Board of Supervisors, whom King of William had revealed to be a graduate of Sing Sing. Already, the business establishment of San Francisco was reeling from the equally shocking and public murder of a U.S. marshal by another Irishman, gambler Charles Cora, whose mistress had been insulted by the marshal's wife. Almost overnight, the Vigilance Committee was formed, under the direction of William Coleman, and seized the city. Coleman informed Governor J. Neely Johnson to his face that the committee now governed San Francisco. Cora and Casey were hanged on the very day of King of William's funeral, Thursday, May 22, 1856. And in the months to follow, the committee ruled the city as Governor Johnson stood by powerless. Hanging two more unfortunates as a final gesture, the committee disbanded itself with a great parade on August 18. Nothing like it had ever happened before in an American city: the seizure of power and open defiance of legitimate government by right-wing businessmen "reformers" backed by a paramilitary force.

Still, despite this humiliation and the continuing efforts to dismantle it, California—volatile, uncertain, a continuing question—survived and continued the development of its institutional life. Between 1850 and 1854, the capital of the state was moved around San Francisco Bay from San José to Vallejo, back to San José, then to Sacramento, then back to Vallejo, then to Benicia, before being brought back permanently to Sacramento. A state library was founded in 1850 with gifts of cash and books from Colonel Jonathan Drake Stevenson and Senator John Charles Frémont. In 1855 the library, the first comprehensive library in the state, issued an impressive printed catalog of its collection. In 1860 construction began on an ornate neoclassical capitol building designed by architect F. M. Butler. Given the newness of the frontier state, with its population of less than four hundred thousand, the sheer ambition of this Corinthian pile, completed in the 1870s, bespoke California's developing sense of itself.

So, too, did the founding of a number of institutions of higher education. In 1851, Jesuit missionaries from northern Italy founded a college at Mission Santa Clara, and the Methodists opened California Wesleyan College (later College of the Pacific) in nearby San José. In 1852 a female seminary, later Mills College, opened in Benicia. In 1855 the Jesuits opened a second college in San Francisco, and the Congregationalists received a charter for the College of California in Oakland, under the presidency of Yankee minister Henry Durant. In 1862 a state normal school for the training of teachers was established in San Francisco. In 1868 the state acquired the College of California as the nucleus of a newly established University of California, and in 1870 the state founded a second normal school for teacher training in San José.

The establishment of these colleges by Catholics, Methodists, and Congregationalists, together with the founding of Hebrew benevolent societies in San Francisco and in the larger settlements of the Mother Lode, underscored the fact that religion was not absent from the Gold Rush. Far from it: religion provided an immediate and compelling way for newly arrived settlers to organize themselves in their new environment. By 1850, just one year into the Gold Rush, California was sprouting churches and synagogues and was nurturing a distinguished clergy, who were at once reveling in and fearful of the intensities of the overnight foundation of American society on the Pacific Coast. For the Reverend Timothy Dwight Hunt of the First Congregationalist Church of San Francisco, California offered nothing less than an opportunity to replay the drama of the Pilgrims and Plymouth Rock. "Here is our colony," Hunt exhorted the New England Society of San Francisco on December 22, 1852. "No higher ambition could urge us to noble deeds than, on the basis of the colony of Plymouth, to make California the Massachusetts of the Pacific."

Many citizens fell short of such lofty ideals, and a number of them found themselves in state custody. In 1852 the legislature commenced plans to build a state prison at Point San Quentin on San Francisco Bay in Marin County, where the prison ship *Waban,* housing 152 convicts, was already anchored. Architect Reuben Clark, a veteran of Charles Bulfinch's studio in Boston, was chosen to design the structure. By 1854, the first cell block—called "the Stones"—was ready for occupancy. It remained in use until 1959. The management of San Quentin was subcontracted to James Madison Estell, who hoped to make a profit from convict labor. Estell vacillated from extreme cruelty to extreme leniency in his management style. An unknown number of convicts were killed, allegedly in the course of escape attempts. At one point, Estell locked down the entire prison for a week with no food service whatsoever. Guards drank on duty, so a later state audit claimed, and some of them exacted sexual relations from female convicts, also housed in the facility. On the other hand, politically connected prisoners were treated with deference and privilege. Some of them were spotted on the streets of San Francisco while serving their sentences. In November 1855, Estell's contract was canceled, and a state-appointed warden assumed responsibility for the prison.

In these early institutional developments, Californians were at once conceptualizing and actualizing their society. It was all happening so quickly! Not for California would there be—nor would there ever be, as it turned out—a deliberate process of development. California would, rather, develop impetuously through booms of people and abrupt releases of energy. Still, certain continuities have been apparent from the beginning. Mining—first for gold and later, in nearby Nevada, for silver—stimulated and paced the foundation and first growth of American California. But agriculture, also established in these Gold Rush years, was destined to dominate the next sequence of development, employing more people than mining by 1869 (47,863 to 36,339) and surpassing mining in 1879 as the leading element of the California economy, remaining so well into the twentieth century. In September 1851, one year into statehood, an agricultural fair was held in San Francisco, delighting one and all with a prodigality of fruits and vegetables three to four times the weight of comparable products in the East. In 1854 Governor John Bigler signed a bill establishing the State Agricultural Society of California, and James LaFayette Warren, a merchant and nurseryman from Massachusetts, began issuing the *California Farmer and Journal of Useful Sciences,* the first agricultural journal on the Pacific Coast. Throughout the 1850s, the hinterlands of San Francisco, as far south as San José and as far north as Healdsburg, were developing in productive farms. West Marin County sustained a thriving dairy industry operated by Portuguese, Dutch, Danish, and Swiss immigrants. Viticulture flourished in Napa and Los Angeles counties. In 1859, Hungarian-born Agoston Haraszthy, owner of the Buena Vista winery in Napa, produced the pioneering *Report on Grapes and Wines in California* for the State Agricultural Society, extolling the future of viticulture and wine-making in California. Two years later, at the request of the state legislature, Haraszthy spent a year in the wine regions of Europe seeking rootstocks for California. Haraszthy shipped some two hundred thousand cuttings, representing more than fourteen hundred varieties of grapes, across the Atlantic and around the Horn to California, the most delicate of them placed in raw potatoes submerged in water. Published by the legislature in 1862, Haraszthy's report of 1859, followed in 1862 by *Grape Culture, Wines, and Wine-Making, with Notes upon Agriculture and Horticulture,* also published by the state legislature, correctly earned him the title Father of California Viticulture.

In Los Angeles County, viticulture, together with fruit and vegetable production, had strong origins in the pre-American period. The Gold Rush, however, gave a strong second wind to the cattle industry—created, in fact, a cattle boom as thousands of cattle were driven north by vaqueros for sale and slaughter in the mines. The Gold Rush can indeed be said to have revitalized the rancho economy of Southern California and hence helped preserve a way of life that might have passed more swiftly had there not been such a flourishing cattle market in the north. The Great Drought of 1862–64 dealt a devastating blow to this revived cattle economy, replacing it with sheep-raising (there were more than 7.7 million sheep in California by 1876), but for the time being, the era of "cattle on a thousand hills," as historian Robert Glass Cleland so poetically described it, together with the rancho lifestyle it sustained, managed to hold its own.

Southern California, then, remained significantly Hispanic and rancho-based in its economy through the 1870s. On the one hand, a number of Hispanic males, displaced by the new order, took to the hills as bandits (no—they were freedom fighters, a later generation would claim), men such as the legendary Joaquín Murieta, who terrorized the Mother Lode in the early 1850s before being run to ground in 1853 near Panoche Pass and decapitated by Captain Harry Love of the California Rangers. The following year, San Francisco writer John Rollin Ridge in his narrative *Life and Adventures of Joaquin Murieta* (1854) recast the young bandit as a Robin Hood–like figure carrying on a guerrilla resistance to the new Yankee order. Whether as outlaws or freedom fighters, a significant number of Californios did take to the wrong side of the law in the 1850s, men such as Juan Flores, who terrorized Southern California until being apprehended and hanged in Los Angeles in 1857.

It would be a mistake, however, to characterize this era of Hispanic life in Southern California as one of banditry. On the contrary, most Californios adjusted successfully to the new American order, although they would experience a general pattern of decline over the next forty years. Most of the leading families of the Mexican era—bearing such names as Lugo, Pico, Domínguez, Yorba, Vejar, Sepúlveda, de la Guerra, Castro, Carrillo, del Valle, Estudillo, Pacheco, and Vallejo (in Northern California)—managed to hold on to their properties, although the process of selling land to pay lawyers or to meet other debts would eventually leave many of them impoverished. Figures such as Pío Pico, the last Mexican governor; his brother Andrés, who commanded the lances at the Battle of San Pasqual; ranchero Antonio Coronel; Peruvian-born Don Juan Bandini; his hispanicized son-in-law Abel Stearns; Pablo de la Guerra (who had played such an important role in the constitutional convention); and others continued to maintain their influence. Coronel served as mayor of Los Angeles in 1853. Andrés Pico, Pablo de la Guerra, and Mariano Guadalupe Vallejo served terms as state senators in Sacramento. Romualdo Pacheco of Santa Barbara was elected lieutenant governor in 1874 and served as governor for most of 1875—the only Hispanic (so far!) to have held this post in the American era—when the incumbent governor Newton Booth was elected to the U.S. Senate. Former governor Pacheco went on to serve seven years in Congress and three years as an envoy extraordinary to Central America. And yet even as prominent Californios maintained their positions—racing their horses, riding in splendor on festive occasions, marrying their daughters off to upwardly mobile

Yankees, seeking and holding political office—theirs was, ultimately, a time of gradual decline: a twilight of splendor that, even as it waned, would in the 1880s and 1890s be reappropriated by a generation of Anglo Southern Californians anxious to graft themselves onto the rootstock of a romantic past.

As the Civil War approached, then broke out, Hispanic sentiment was overwhelmingly Unionist, which testifies, one suspects, to the successful assimilation of Californios into American California. In Southern California, Pablo de la Guerra of Santa Barbara spearheaded a campaign against Chivalry sentiment as epitomized by district judge Benjamin Hayes, a pro-Southern Marylander, whom the de la Guerra faction unseated in a bitter election. When war broke out, Californios organized Company C of the 1st Battalion of Native Cavalry, which saw patrol duty in Arizona and New Mexico. Other Hispanic Californians joined the five hundred or so young men mustered in as the California Battalion of the 2nd Massachusetts Cavalry and saw action in Virginia. Platón Vallejo, holding an M.D. degree from Columbia University, served as a Union army physician. When his father, Mariano, visited various Union army headquarters during the war, he was received with honors as a fellow general by such high-ranking officers as Sherman, Halleck, Hooker, Sheridan, and Grant, whom he had known as captains and lieutenants years earlier in far-off California.

Legend has exaggerated the danger of California's declaring for the Confederacy or independence during the conflict. True, Albert Sidney Johnston, army commander on the Pacific Coast, did resign his commission in early 1861 to join the Confederate army, riding east from Los Angeles with a contingent of volunteers; and there were, initially at least, some pro-Confederate conspiratorial groups—the Committee of Thirty, the Knights of the Columbian Star, the Knights of the Golden Circle—that made a stab at plotting on behalf of the South. In general, however, political sentiment was overwhelmingly pro-Union. In

1861, Republicans and pro-Union Democrats, running as the fusion Unionist Party, captured the legislature and governorship, with Sacramento businessman Leland Stanford at the head of the ticket.

In military terms, California remained less than a sideshow. The draft was not enforced, and a significant number of young men moved west to escape the conflict. Yet the war did play a subliminal role in coalescing political identity. The agency for doing this—consolidating, that is, sentiment and identity in California on behalf of the Union, and thus grafting California even further onto the national experience—was the privately organized Sanitary Commission, responsible for raising money for the medical treatment of wounded soldiers; and the single individual who most dramatically led this effort was the San Francisco–based Unitarian minister Thomas Starr King, whose fiery speeches on behalf of the Sanitary Commission up and down the state (before his premature death from diphtheria at the age of thirty-nine in 1864) helped raise a quarter of all the support received by the commission from the entire nation while at the same time announcing to Californians that their state was now, irretrievably, an American place.

Proof positive of this fully consolidated identity was the construction during the mid-1860s of a transcontinental railroad. Throughout this epic of public-private finance and construction, Californians—sometimes ambiguously, even crookedly, according to many interpretations—more than played their part.

The 1850s witnessed the rapid expansion of railroad service throughout the United States. By 1860 more than thirty thousand miles of track linked the cities and hinterlands of the East and Midwest. It was also national policy to extend the railroad across the continent. In March 1853, Congress directed Secretary of War Jefferson Davis of Mississippi to commission the Topographical Corps of the United States Army to prepare a report recommending the five best routes for a transcontinental railroad line. Assembling a number of survey parties backed by a team of engineers and scientists, the Army prepared a three-volume survey titled *Pacific Railroad Reports* (1855), which represented a high point of federally sponsored research in the nineteenth century. Out in California, meanwhile, Oliver Wozencraft, M.D., a member of the constitutional convention of 1849, was extolling the necessity of linking California to the rest of the nation via rail. Engineer Theodore Judah, a graduate of Rensselaer Polytechnic Institute, took up the cause as a personal crusade. Judah had come to California in 1854 to build a railroad between Sacramento and Folsom, the first such connection in the state. As he supervised construction of the line, Judah became obsessed with the notion of continuing up the foothills, crossing the Sierra Nevada, and pushing eastward across the western half of the continent. In 1857, after surveying a number of possible routes, Judah published a pamphlet entitled *Practical Plan for Building the Pacific Railroad,* in which he laid out the specifics of his plan.

From the start, Judah knew that such a venture would have to be publicly subsidized. Largely as a result of his urging, the state legislature in April 1859 called for a railroad convention to meet in San Francisco in September to lay further plans. The convention called for the state of California to create a $15 million fund, augmented by $5 million from the state of Oregon, for construction of a line to the Nevada border, and commissioned Judah to go to Washington and enlist federal support. Sailing to the East Coast on the SS *Sonora* in October 1859, Judah spent the next two years tirelessly lobbying Congress for federal support of a transcontinental railroad. A master of lobbying tactics, Judah went so far as to establish a Central Pacific Railroad Museum in one of the rooms of the Capitol, filling it with sketches, surveys, and maps of the Dutch Flat–Donner Pass route Judah favored. After months of getting nowhere, Judah acquired his best and winning argument, namely, the outbreak of war in April 1861.

What if the English should come in on the side of the Confederacy, Judah asked, and land a fleet in California? How would the Union be able to counter such an invasion so far away? What if California and Nevada should drift into secessionist sentiment? And even if these states remained loyal, how were their gold, silver, and grain to be made available to the Union? Psychologically, how were California, Oregon, Nevada, and the other territories of the Far West to be stabilized in their relationship to the Union if they remained disconnected from the East for decades to come? Would not a transcontinental railroad, like the great Mississippi itself, unify the nation beyond disassembly? What more powerful agent and symbol of national unity could there be than bands of steel moving people, freight, agricultural products, newspapers, books, back and forth across a unified nation?

By 1861, both U.S. senators from California, James McDougall and Milton Latham, were solidly on board the project, as were the state's three congressmen, Timothy Phelps, Frederick Low, and Aaron Sargent. Through their influence, Judah was appointed secretary to the Senate Committee on Pacific Railroads, clerk to its counterpart in the House, and clerk of the House Main Committee on Railroads. The visionary turned lobbyist was now at the epicenter of congressional authority as the Pacific Railway Act of 1862 wended its way through each house en route to the desk of Abraham Lincoln. Passed by Congress and signed by the President, the act granted rights of way to the Union Pacific to build westward from Omaha and the Central Pacific to build eastward from Sacramento. In return, these two companies would be subsidized by an extensive federal package of loans, bonds, cash payments, and land grants. In 1864, in a second act, this incentive package was increased by an even more generous allocation of land grants on alternate sections, forty miles in length, of the entire line which would eventually make the Central Pacific and the Union Pacific, thanks to the federal government, two of the largest landowners in the Far West.

Incorporated in June 1861, the Central Pacific Railroad of California was the result of conversations that had begun a year and a half earlier between Judah and four Sacramento businessmen: Collis P. Huntington and his partner Mark Hopkins (hardware), Leland Stanford (groceries), and Charles Crocker (dry goods). Much was about to be accomplished by this group of seemingly ordinary men of ordinary backgrounds, with only Stanford, a lawyer, in the professional ranks. Raising a mere $15,800 in cash, the Big Four, as history would know them, formed an enterprise that over the next decades would earn them $200 million in profits. When Stanford took office as governor in January 1862, the pathway became even more clear as Stanford—untroubled in that age by modern notions of conflict of interest—promoted further state subsidies for the railroad project and named Crocker's brother, then serving as chief counsel to the railroad, to the state supreme court.

On January 8, 1863, Stanford—serving simultaneously as governor of California and president of the Central Pacific—broke ground in Sacramento on what turned out to be a six-year epic of construction. Already the respective roles of the Big Four had asserted themselves. Huntington would take care of lobbying in Washington, Stanford would see to the state government, Crocker would supervise construction, and Mark Hopkins would keep the books. Increasingly, Theodore Judah, the chief engineer of the Central Pacific, was finding himself odd man out as his four associates squeezed and resqueezed the project for every penny it was worth. When the Big Four awarded the construction contract to a dummy corporation which they owned, Judah bowed out with a $100,000 payment and an option to buy the company back for $400,000, if he could raise the money in the East. Sailing in October 1863 for New York, where he hoped to raise money from Cornelius Vanderbilt, Judah contracted typhoid fever crossing the Isthmus of Panama and died in New York, four months short of age thirty-eight, and a mere four days after the first rails had been laid in Sacramento.

Throughout its history, American California has always imported its labor when necessary. The construction of the Central Pacific offered the first case in point. It was one thing to build a rail line from Sacramento across the valley floor, even to nudge it into the foothills; but when it came to crossing the Sierra Nevada, construction chief Charles Crocker knew that he had a problem. There were not enough men in California willing to do this sort of backbreaking work at the price Crocker was willing to pay. Surveying the labor pool of California, Crocker could see that there were thousands of Chinese in the state, most of whom had, for reasons of racial exclusion, been marginalized out of mainstream employment. And yet Crocker knew that these Chinese men, as miners and agricultural laborers, had long since proven themselves strong and sinewy, disciplined and dedicated, persistent and inventive; and so in 1865 Crocker hired fifty of them as an experiment. He would eventually have some ten thousand in his employ, and cumulatively, over the next four years, these Chinese workers would achieve an epic of construction second only to the Great Wall of China itself: the crossing of the Sierra Nevada with bands of steel, including the penetration of a near-solid rock barrier with the Summit Tunnel, hewn by hand from solid rock. Moving ties and rails, pounding spikes with a force that seemed to explode from their muscular bodies, lowering themselves in baskets down sheer cliffs to dig holes for dynamite out of solid rock, taking direction meticulously despite barriers of language, dying in unknown (because unrecorded) numbers from accidents, day in, day out across six years, in one case laying ten miles of track in a day, "Crocker's pets," as the Chinese were derisively called, more than proved their mettle against the competing Irish workers of the Union Pacific. They established for all time (although it would take more than half a century for this to become clear in the minds of white California) the right of the Chinese to live and work in the Golden State: even more, to insert "Sino-Californian" into the essential formula of American California itself. On May 10, 1869, at Promontory Summit, Utah, ceremonies were held joining the Union Pacific and Central Pacific tracks. Embarrassingly, Stanford missed when he swung a silver sledgehammer to drive in the last spike; but no matter, the telegraph operator on-site did not miss his key as Stanford swung, and the announcement went out across the nation: the United States of America now stood unified by an iron roadway.

What kind of world would this postrailroad era be for California, now that it was less than a week's journey from the East Coast? Already, a year before the completion of the line, San Francisco newspaperman Henry George had been asking the same question in the pages of *The Overland Monthly* in an essay entitled "What the Railroad Will Bring Us." California was losing its splendid isolation, George lamented. The mining frontier of the 1850s and the self-governing province of the 1860s were passing. California was now joining the national economy, including the industrial culture that had been expanded and intensified by the Civil War. Hundreds of thousands of new immigrants could be expected to pour in. What would they find? A better life? Or the same dreary, grinding poverty that had motivated their immigration in the first place?

As it turned out, the negative aspects of George's scenario prevailed. The decade of the 1870s was in general not a good time for the nation, or for Europe for that matter, and many of California's problems were linked to the national and the international experience. In September 1873, Wall Street was gripped by a panic when the banking house of Jay Cooke went under. The New York Stock Exchange closed for ten days. The worst depression thus far in American history ensued, lasting the rest of the decade, with thousands of businesses, including most major railroads, falling into bankruptcy. In 1877 President Hayes sent federal troops into a number of cities to contain a series of strikes against railroad companies that set new standards for both organized and spontaneous strike action in the United States. In St. Louis, a committee of strikers seized city government for two weeks before federal troops regained control. Marxism, meanwhile, was making the transition from theory to practice beginning with the foundation in London in 1864 of the International Workingmen's Association, more commonly known as the First International, under the leadership of Karl Marx. A revolutionary commune seized control of Paris in March 1871 following the defeat of France in the Franco-Prussian War and the dissolution of the Second Empire. Numerous hostages, including the archbishop of Paris, were executed, and a number of public buildings burned. When the army regained control of the city, some seventeen thousand radicals and suspected sympathizers were executed.

From this perspective, California got off easy, although what did occur in the state in the 1870s must be linked to the destabilized national and European environments. The decade opened on a prophetically horrible note: the mass lynching in Los Angeles in October 1871 of eighteen Chinese men, including a boy of fourteen, followed by the looting of the Chinese quarter by a predominantly Anglo-American mob of five hundred. What could account for such murderous fury? Certainly, it was more than the riffraff of the city who were involved, as the official report of the incident tried to paint it. The violence of the frontier era had not been banished by the railroad. Far from it: violence seethed beneath the surface and was now resurfacing in a shocking manner. The Los Angeles massacre of Chinese must be seen as the social and psychological paradigm of what was happening in California as anti-Chinese agitation moved north to San Francisco and the Chinese became increasingly the scapegoats for collapsed expectations.

By 1870, San Francisco, with a population of 149,473, was the tenth largest city in the United States, a remarkable development for a city that did not formally exist in 1846. To understand this growth, one must look at San Francisco from two perspectives. It was the dominant urban concentration on the Pacific Coast, drawing upon and being energized by the extensive and varied economy of its hinterlands, which comprised most of the central and northern portions of the state. At the same time, San Francisco was also a maritime colony of the eastern United States and Europe. As such, it more or less instantly replicated the economic, social, and cultural institutions of advanced urbanism. Contemporaneous photographs of the city, such as those published by the English-born photographer Eadweard Muybridge in July 1877, reveal an amalgam of homes, churches, synagogues, warehouses, hotels, theaters, and public squares, fully comparable to the cities of the Midwest and the East. New wealth was pouring into the city from Nevada, where silver had been discovered in 1859 in the Comstock Lode in Virginia City, which would eventually yield some $400 million through the 1870s.

Joining the railroad Big Four in their ornate mansions atop Nob Hill (served since 1873 by cable cars) were the Silver Kings—James Fair, James Flood, John Mackay, and William O'Brien—a second wave of staggering wealth, Irish Catholic in contrast to the Anglo-Protestant Big Four. From their perspective, the 1870s constituted the apogee of capitalism; the sentiment was shared by such mega-entrepreneurs as Lloyd Tevis, James Ben Ali Haggin (a Kentuckian of Turkish descent), Milton Latham, William Sharon, George Hearst, Darius Ogden

Mills, François Pioche, Isaac Friedlander, and the other investors in the city busy amassing fortunes in complex developments of mining, banking, agriculture, and land and stock speculation; building mansions in Rincon Hill, South Park, and Nob Hill, with villas farther south on the Peninsula, and filling them with furniture and art; and marrying off their children to each other or to cash-challenged aristocratic Europeans whom they met on grand tours. The parodic antitype of this class was one Joshua Norton, a failed speculator who had most likely lost his mind after losing everything else in an effort to corner the rice market in the summer of 1857 and had thereafter styled himself as Norton I, Emperor of the United States and Protector of Mexico. Habitually attired in military garb, Norton survived on the largesse of the city, dining at public expense: a warning subconsciously understood, no doubt, regarding the dangers of the financial speculation that had become a way of life in the city.

Most representative of this ultracapitalist class was William Chapman Ralston, Ohio-born, who in 1864 founded the Bank of California in partnership with Darius Ogden Mills. Ralston was a paragon of the Gilded Age, California style: a onetime Mississippi riverboat clerk who, since his arrival in San Francisco in 1854 (in between the masquerade balls he loved so well, the camaraderie of his amateur fire company, and racing the train in his horse-drawn trap down the Peninsula to Belmont, where he maintained an elaborate villa, the scene of yet more parties), had dedicated himself to making a fortune by providing San Francisco with what it needed: shipyards at Hunters Point on the southeastern edge of the city, the California Theater on Bush Street (Bret Harte, Leland Stanford, the Silver Kings, and Emperor Norton were in the audience on opening night in January 1869 for a play appropriately entitled *Money*), silk and woolen mills, the largest hotel in the Western Hemisphere (the Palace, opening in 1875), and the Bank of California itself, the premier financial institution in the Far West, as solid as the Comstock silver that backed it.

When that bank failed in August 1875, San Francisco experienced its own version of the Wall Street Panic of 1873. Ralston's agent in Virginia City, sitting atop the Comstock Lode, was his fellow Ohioan William Sharon. Throughout the second half of the 1860s, Ralston acquired increasing shares in Virginia City silver by lending Bank of California money to mining companies in exchange for shares or, in the case of foreclosures, for outright ownership. It was this Virginia City silver, pouring into the vaults of the Bank of California in San Francisco from the Consolidated Virginia Mine, that was making Ralston and Sharon so rich. The men who would eventually be known as the Silver Kings, however—Mackay, Fair, Flood, and O'Brien—financed a competitive scheme to dig even deeper into the Comstock Lode. A Prussian-born engineer by the name of Adolph Sutro had plans to sink a drainage and ventilation tunnel even deeper than all existing mines and hit even more pay dirt. With the help of the Silver Kings, the tunnel was completed in 1869, and from that time forward the Silver Kings began to surpass the Bank of California in revenues from Virginia City. Ralston countered with a stock-selling scheme based on the notion that the neighboring Ophir Mine, controlled by the Bank of California, was an even richer vein than the Consolidated Virginia. The bluff worked, and the price of stock in the Ophir soared.

Ralston, meanwhile, was secretly drawing upon Bank of California deposits to finance his many ventures. In January 1875, the Ophir scheme collapsed, and the Bank of California was left with a sheaf of worthless stock. Through various schemes, Ralston kept the Bank of California afloat, but finally, on August 26, 1875, panic broke out in the city and there was a run on the bank. Behind closed doors, major investors now learned just how extensively Ralston had depleted the resources of the bank, and they demanded his resignation. Going for his daily swim off the Larkin Street pier, Ralston either deliberately swam out too far, or he suffered a stroke or heart attack while fighting an adverse tide. His body was recovered shortly thereafter.

Taking down a number of other banks as well, the failure of the Bank of California drained San Francisco of capital for the rest of the decade, compounding the effects of the national depression that had brought some 154,000 impoverished migrants into California by 1875, including many Irishmen recently employed in building the Union Pacific. Over the next two years, San Francisco began to fill with unemployed and restless men. On July 23, 1877, some eight thousand showed up for a rally called by the Workingmen's Party, an American offshoot of the International Workingmen's Association. At this nighttime rally—so fearsome in its sheer size, with hundreds of men holding torches against the darkness—speakers denounced the capitalist system in general and the railroads in particular (the Great Railway Strike had broken out only six days earlier), with emphasis on the Chinese labor the railroad had imported. A group of young men beat up an unfortunate Chinese man who happened to be passing by the rally. "On to Chinatown!" came the cry after the beating, and a group of hoodlums (a term newly coined in San Francisco from the young men's war cry, "Huddle them! Huddle them!") proceeded to sack some twenty laundries in the Chinese quarter. The very next day, an alarmed oligarchy organized San Francisco's third vigilance committee, this one called the Committee of Public Safety, headed by businessman William Coleman, who had led the committees of 1851 and 1856. Coleman organized some four thousand vigilantes into patrolling brigades, each man armed with a hickory pickax handle attached to his wrist by a leather thong.

San Francisco was now divided into two armed camps, for the disgruntled unemployed men of the city were not intimidated by the pickax brigade. Far from it: a thousand of them rallied on the evening of July 24 and tried to sack a woolen mill employing Chinese workers, but they were prevented from doing so by armed state militia. The next evening, a similar crowd tried to take over the docks of the Pacific Mail Steamship Company, where Chinese immigrants arrived from the Far East. This time, pickax patrols from the Committee of Public Safety fought them off. Gunfire erupted, and the bodies of four rioting workingmen were left behind. In the days that followed, San Francisco seemed a city under military occupation as 252 policemen patrolled the city along with twelve hundred state militiamen and the four thousand vigilantes. In the Presidio army base, the army went on alert, and three navy gunboats took up positions offshore.

Among the men of the pickax brigade patrolling San Francisco in late July 1877 was thirty-year-old Denis Kearney. Born in County Cork, Ireland, Kearney had gone to sea as a youngster and had risen from cabin boy to first mate on American vessels before settling in San Francisco in 1872 and going into the drayage business. Bent on intellectual self-improvement as well as getting ahead, Kearney read extensively in the public library in his off-hours—politics, economics, Darwin, Spencer, current events—and dreamed of a political career. Something happened to Kearney in his time with the Committee of Public Safety as San Francisco came under internal siege. Kearney transferred his identification from the oligarchy to the workers, based on a recognition of his own class, or perhaps from mere opportunism, or a combination thereof. In any event, by September 1877, Kearney had changed sides and was addressing torchlit gatherings of the very same workers he had patrolled against two months earlier, telling them that the capitalists of the city were running them into the ground and the Chinese were taking their jobs. There is some suspicion that *Chronicle* reporter Chester Hall helped Kearney prepare the speeches he gave over the next few months, which always managed to appear verbatim in the next morning's *Chronicle.* They were ferocious in their revolutionary sentiment, including, in one speech, a threat to hang Charles Crocker. At another rally, a colleague of Kearney's pushed revolutionary rhetoric to its limits, threatening to seize Telegraph Hill, plant cannons there, and blow out of the water the Pacific Mail steamers that were bringing Chinese workers into San Francisco.

Was this street theater or real revolution or both? The leadership of the Chinese Six Companies took Kearney's harangues seriously and announced that any marauders coming into Chinatown would be met with volleys of rifle fire. So, too, did city officials go on alert, arresting Kearney and some of his followers in early November, although they were soon released by order of the superior court. At this point, the leaders of the Workingmen's Party of California found themselves at a moment of decision: should they continue down the pathway of torchlit rallies and incendiary rhetoric, or transform their movement into a political party? Under the influence of such figures as union activist Frank Roney and socialist Charles Beerstecher, the leadership chose to do the latter: get off the streets and instead devote their energies, through the ballot box, to promoting a rewriting of the state constitution.

Conventional politics—specifically, a statewide vote on September 5, 1877—authorized the election of delegates to a convention to be held in Sacramento in June 1878 to reconsider and revise the constitution of 1849. This in itself is important to recognize: that enough voting Californians, not just rioting workingmen in San Francisco, were sufficiently discontent that year to call for a time-out and restructuring of the state. The railroad, most voters recognized, was overly controlling; banks and corporations were unregulated; land was in the hands of too few; and there were next to no provisions in state law to deal with public utilities in an urbanizing state. While intensified by depression, the failure of the Bank of California, and the San Francisco disturbances, the call for a rewriting of the state constitution had the support of farmers, small business owners, and others concerned that California was bifurcating itself into polarities of rich and poor, landed and landless, corporations and a working class.

All told, the Workingmen's Party captured only a third of the 152 delegates convening in Sacramento. There were even eleven Republicans on hand. Most Workingmen's Party delegates were from San Francisco, where their candidate, the flamboyant Baptist preacher Isaac Kalloch, had been elected mayor, along with Workingmen's Party candidates for sheriff, auditor, tax collector, treasurer, and district attorney—the only such broad victory by the Workingmen's Party in the state. At the convention, Workingmen's Party delegates exercised some influence but were in general outmaneuvered by the dominant nonpartisan bloc (78 of the 152 delegates) who wanted reform, not revolution.

The very length of the constitution these delegates drafted (it was several times longer than the Constitution of the United States) attested to the contradictory impulses they were attempting to harmonize. On the one hand, Spanish was dropped as the second legal language and a strong anti-Chinese immigration statement was adopted; but these were practically the only explicit references to the sentiments of the San Francisco riots of July 1877 and the sandlot rallies that had followed. A proposal to banish the Chinese entirely from all forms of employment and trade failed to pass, as did a proposed unicameral legislature. The other major provisions of the new constitution—the regulation of corporations, especially in their issuance of stock; the regulation of the newly emergent public utilities; and, most dramatically, the establishment of a state Railroad Commission (San Francisco socialist Beerstecher was given a seat)—were more broadly based in their support. Workingmen and Grangers actually joined Republicans in drafting a ringing defense of property rights in the new constitution, although each might see the issue from a different perspective. Farmers were worried about having their farms sold out from under them by foreclosing banks, but large landowners were equally concerned about having their properties broken up, even confiscated, by the state. Thus a forceful condemnation of land monopoly was made acceptable to conservatives by a statement that the breakup of such monopolies could occur only in ways that were consistent with the rights of private property.

Little wonder, then, that economist and reformer Henry George considered the 1879 constitution—passed statewide in May by a majority of only 11,000 out of 145,000 total votes—a failure in its refusal to take up the issue of land monopoly, which George had been decrying throughout the decade as the original sin of American California. Take a look at California, George argued in his pamphlet *Our Land and Land Policy, National and State* (1871) and in his later masterpiece *Progress and Poverty* (1879), one of the landmark economic treatises of the nineteenth century (two million copies sold by 1900). California was, for all practical purposes, empty. Larger than Great Britain, Holland, Belgium, Denmark, and Greece combined, the state did not contain the population of even a third-rank modern city. Where were the flourishing cities and townships, the family farms, the signs of human progress and civility? Instead, one saw only endless steppes, planted in wheat or supporting cattle, with only an occasional shack here and there housing alien labor. Why was this so? Because so very few people owned most of the land in the state, George charged; and land, he argued, the ultimate sustainer of life, was also the ultimate source of wealth.

No, indeed, the revolution would not begin in California; and in 1880, Henry George moved to New York City. By 1881 the Workingmen's Party of California had faded from the scene, with most of its supporters shifting their allegiance to the rising Democratic Party machine being organized in San Francisco by old-fashioned political boss Chris Buckley, and there it stayed until the rise of the Union Labor Party in the early 1900s. After all the fuss and bother, the riots and sandlot rallies, the incendiary rhetoric and pickax brigades, the marches and countermarches of state militia and demonstrators, the fistfights and gunfire, the four dead bodies, and the overhauling of the state constitution, California entered the 1880s as a state in which railroads, corporations, and large landowners continued to call the shots.

6

THE HIGHER PROVINCIALISM

American Life in an Emergent Region

John Muir in later life

CALIFORNIA STATE LIBRARY

In 1908 Josiah Royce, then at the height of his career, published *Race Questions, Provincialism, and Other American Problems.* The theoretical core of Royce's book was the essay "Provincialism," in which the Harvard philosopher extolled regional life as something profoundly serving the human need for community. Provincial loyalties, Royce argued, fostered community by providing Americans with an appropriate human scale. Americans needed such a personalized connection more than ever, now that the United States was becoming an international empire. Provincial identity, moreover, enlivened arts and literature, and loyalty to province upgraded the moral significance of local life. Americans, indeed, could best discover what it meant to be an American when they discovered their American identity in a localized context. Such an identification, Royce argued, such service to the social order in its local context, constituted a Higher Provincialism that countered the centralizing and alienating tendencies of mass society in the United States.

Josiah Royce's favorite province for analysis was, not surprisingly, California, the subject of another important essay in the book, "The Pacific Coast: A Psychological Study of the Relations of Climate and Civilization." The physical context of California, Royce argued, specifically its topography and climate, was in the process of fostering a Higher Provincial version of American civilization that promoted simultaneously an independence of mind, individualism, and open simplicity of manner that might justifiably be described as Homeric, together with a benevolent closeness to nature fostered by a mild and nurturing climate. Such factors, among others, were making California a distinctive instance of American civilization.

Thus Royce, born in the Mother Lode mining town of Grass Valley in 1855, subsumed into his theory of Higher Provincialism all that he had experienced of California as a boy in a mining camp, a student in San Francisco, an undergraduate at the University of California at Berkeley, a novelist, historian, philosopher, and faculty member at Berkeley and Harvard. Royce's life had spanned the development of California from a remote frontier to an American province of continuing promise and even some distinction. For Royce, California was not an afterthought of the nation, an isolated society cut off from the centers of power, money, and thought in the East. California was rather a prism through which the larger American identity, for better and for worse, could be glimpsed.

The story of how this identity was interpreted and assembled begins with writing—en route to literature—just before and during the Gold Rush. Middle-class Americans of the mid-1840s knew how to write clearly and effectively and seem to have loved doing so. Embarking for California in the 1830s and 1840s or during the Gold Rush years, they recorded their experiences in a profusion of letters, diaries, and journals—augmented in later years by memoirs—that constitutes a literature in and of itself. Knowing that what they were experiencing was important—for themselves primarily, but also from the perspective of history—the forty-niners and their successors in the waves of 1850 and 1851 wrote of what they saw and experienced. They wrote letters, thousands of them, many on illustrated letter sheets issued by the post office. Historians have mined these letters for the revealing nuggets they contain: moments of exhilaration, loneliness, hope, despair, sexual longing. So too did thousands of the gold seekers keep journals in that literate and reflective age; and in time this record as well—edited by scholars and put into historical context—has come to constitute a second layer of documentary evidence. In the 1880s, when a generation of once young miners had become aged pioneers, many of these journals would be transformed into formal memoirs or autobiographies, and these, too, would document the era.

Then there were the professionals—writers such as Bayard Taylor of the *New York Tribune* or the English travel writer Frank Marryat—who came to California not to seek gold but to report upon the epic event and thereby help lay the foundations of the Gold Rush as a literary Mother Lode. Taylor's *El Dorado: or Adventures in the Path of Empire* (1850) and Marryat's *Mountains and Molehills* (1855) can be considered the high points of contemporary nonfiction coverage, although one must also make reference to such other outstanding works as Hinton Rowan Helper's *The Land of Gold: Reality Versus Fiction* (1855), J. Douglas Borthwick's *Three Years in California* (1857), and J.D.B. Stillman's *Seeking the Golden Fleece* (1876). These and many of the other nonfiction accounts of the Gold Rush, whether on-the-scene observations or later memoirs, not only reported on events but refashioned them imaginatively as well. The Gold Rush novel, on the other hand, would be another generation and more in making its appearance, although with typical insouciance, Alexandre Dumas wrote two Gold Rush novels without bothering to leave Paris.

A physician's wife with the improbable name of Louise Amelia Knapp Smith Clapp accompanied her husband to Rich Bar and Indian Bar on the Feather River. Her descriptive letters home written in 1851 and 1852, later published under the *nom de plume* "Dame Shirley" in *The Pioneer,* San Francisco's first literary journal, inspired at least one short story by Bret Harte and must be considered the formal beginning of literature in the Golden State. Using the epistolary format—and as such her work must be considered in the context of the hundreds of thousands of unpublished letters actually written by the emigrants—Dame Shirley reported on life in the mines with telling detail. One account, describing the death of a woman in childbirth and the plight of her surviving child, inspired Bret Harte to write one of his best-known short stories, "The Luck of Roaring Camp."

Then there were the humorists, as represented by Alonzo Delano, George Horatio Derby, and Prentice Mulford. Just exactly why humor, especially burlesque humor, should have been such a popular genre during the Gold Rush most likely relates to the earlier flourishing of this same genre on previous American frontiers. In each instance, predominantly male communities, by turns good-humored or violent, beyond the reach of society, encouraged humor as a way of dealing with novelty, uncertainty, debauchery, and violence. A onetime Wells Fargo agent in Grass Valley, Alonzo Delano voiced his observations in *Pen-Knife Sketches* (1853) and *Old Block's Sketch Book* (1856) through a proto–Will Rogers figure called "Old Block," with pioneer artist Charles Nahl providing appropriate illustrations. A West Point–trained army officer, George Horatio Derby adopted the Washington Irving–like persona of "John Phoenix"—a skeptical but bemused figure, defending himself through satire—in *Phoenixiana: or Sketches and Burlesques* (1855), together with the fugitive pieces later gathered as *Squibob Papers* (1865). A miner and sometime schoolteacher, Prentice Mulford wrote as "Dogberry," romping and roguish, in the humorous sketches he published in local newspapers, later gathered as *California Sketches* (1935). In the late 1860s, an ex-Missourian by the name of Samuel Clemens, working in San Francisco as a newspaper reporter, would reinvent himself as Mark Twain—canny, observant as to social types and distinctions, writing from a mixed insider/outsider point of view—and bring this genre to near-perfection.

Humor, however, was not what was on the mind of San

Francisco–based poet and journalist John Rollin Ridge, a half-Cherokee from Georgia writing under his Indian name of Yellow Bird, when he produced the early bestseller *Life and Adventures of Joaquín Murieta* (1854), based on the life and career of the Hispanic bandit recently run to ground by Captain Harry Love. Ridge transformed Murieta into a Robin Hood–like figure who turns to banditry only after his fiancée is raped and he is beaten by American miners, embellishments added by Ridge to the Murieta story, possibly based on a scene in one of Dame Shirley's letters in which a handsome young Hispanic is put to the lash for a trivial offense. Ridge also depicts Murieta as a freedom fighter dedicated to the liberation of his people from American bondage. A blend of fact and fiction, Ridge's nonfiction novel, as it might be called—published in the *Police Gazette* and given wide circulation in the East as a dime novel—entered the histories of Hubert Howe Bancroft and Theodore Hittell as fact, thereby further establishing the historicity of a folkloric figure embodying Latino resistance to the American order.

Already, by the mid-1850s, San Francisco was supporting something resembling a literary culture. In 1854 Ferdinand Ewer, a Harvard-trained civil engineer turned Anglo-Catholic clergyman, established *The Pioneer,* a literary monthly modeled on *The Knickerbocker* of New York. The very next year, three San Francisco–based journalists—Frank Soulé, James Nesbit, and physician John Gihon—gathered five years of contributions to the *Californian,* the *California Star,* the *Alta California,* and the *Herald* and produced a remarkable year-by-year history of the city from 1846 to 1854: the *Annals of San Francisco* (1855), a protean, sui generis sort of book, eight hundred pages long, part history, part epic, part fantasy, part promotional journalism, published by a New York firm, D. Appleton and Company, and remaining the Ur-text of the city in its founding era. The sheer lavishness of the *Annals,* not to mention the many newspapers and periodicals in which these sketches appeared, testified to the vitality of San Francisco as a rising urban center poised on the western edge of a near-empty continent, re-creating as rapidly as possible the forms and institutions of urbanism.

Through the 1860s, San Francisco continued to flourish as a solitary Pacific Coast epicenter of urbanism and artistic creativity. In 1860 the German-born San Francisco bookseller Anton Roman established a publishing house. Among its early books was *Outcroppings* (1865), a collection of poetry by Francis Bret Harte, a onetime typesetter on *The Golden Era* and now a functionary at the U.S. Mint, whose work had already been published by *The Atlantic Monthly.* Roman also published the work of another *Golden Era* poet, Charles Warren Stoddard, issuing his *Poems* in 1867. In 1868, on the advice of Stoddard, who would later foster the California and South Pacific career of Robert Louis Stevenson, Roman named Harte editor of his newly founded *Overland Monthly,* which published Harte's early short stories, together with contributions in the years that followed by such diverse Californians as travel writer J. Ross Browne, poet Ina Coolbrith, mountaineer Clarence King, art critic Benjamin Avery, and essayist Ambrose Bierce. The survivor of fierce combat with the Union army during the Civil War, in which he rose to lieutenant colonel, Bierce arrived in San Francisco following the conflict while still in uniform and began his literary career with mordantly satirical sketches submitted to *The Golden Era,* the *News Letter,* and the *Overland Monthly* before leaving in 1872 for a three-year residence in England and France.

Also arriving in San Francisco in 1868 was the Scottish-born naturalist John Muir, who proceeded almost directly to the Yosemite Valley. Across the next fifty years Muir would establish an enduring reputation as a nature writer through a series of books celebrating, among other landscapes, the Yosemite Valley, the mountains of California, and the glacial formations of Alaska. San Francisco bookseller Hubert Howe Bancroft, meanwhile, a former Ohioan who came to California via Buffalo, New York, was assembling the beginnings of a research library that would over the next two decades support the publication of a multivolume history of the Pacific Coast.

Fleeing the Civil War, in which he had served briefly as a Confederate irregular, Samuel Clemens, a former Mississippi riverboat pilot from Hannibal, Missouri, joined his pro-Union brother Orion, secretary to the territorial governor of Nevada, in Carson City in the summer of 1861, one of thousands of young men grateful to be escaping the battlefields of the East. Moving to Virginia City, Clemens began writing local color columns for the *Territorial Enterprise* under the name of Mark Twain, which was either a riverboat term or Virginia City saloon lingo for two free drinks, depending upon which authority one is following. In May 1864 Clemens moved to San Francisco, where he joined the staff of the *Call* for a short stint and began contributing local color articles to the *Californian,* a literary newspaper, coached in the development of his narrative style by Bret Harte. From this period came Clemens's breakthrough 1865 story "Jim Smiley and His Jumping Frog," which led to the eastern publication of *The Celebrated Jumping Frog of Calaveras County and Other Sketches* (1867). The success of this book turned Twain into a national figure.

The literature of California in the 1850s was characterized by humor, history, and memoir; in the 1860s, by local color, literary journalism, and poetry. The 1870s witnessed a continuation of these genres, with an added emphasis on nature writing, closely connected to geology, together with the economic essay as practiced by Henry George and at least one instance of investigative reporting. In the late 1870s and 1880s there ensued an efflorescence of historical writing, promotional literature, and the first instances of long fiction, as opposed to the sketch or short story.

Mark Twain's *The Innocents Abroad* (1869), an account of

Twain's travels in Europe and the Middle East, consolidated his national reputation; but it was *Roughing It* (1872), Twain's account of his early life in Nevada and California, that gave the canon of frontier literature its most commanding classic. Pervading Twain's descriptions of camping on the shores of Lake Tahoe was a sense on the part of this Confederate deserter of being, literally and figuratively, reborn in the American West. This conviction of being reenergized in Eden, however, does not last. San Francisco defeats it. (There is some evidence that Clemens spent a night or two in a San Francisco jail.) Samuel Clemens never really liked San Francisco, or California for that matter, and would return there only once in his lifetime, en route to Japan.

Equally important that year, although less well known, was Clarence King's *Mountaineering in the Sierra Nevada* (1872), which represents a high point in the continuously flourishing frontier genre of geological description and the mountaineering memoir. Born in Newport, Rhode Island, to a well-connected family, King worked in the Comstock Lode in Nevada in 1863 after graduation from the Sheffield Scientific School at Yale. Within the year, geologist William Brewer, another Yale graduate, recruited King to join the California Geological Survey founded in 1860 by yet another Sheffield man, state geologist Josiah Whitney. King spent three years with the survey, followed by a stint with the Army Corps of Engineers exploring and mapping the deserts of Southern California. (In 1878 King, still in his thirties, would become the first director of the newly established U.S. Geological Survey, with the equivalent rank of major general.) The writings of Brewer, Whitney, King, and the other geologists of the California Geological Survey established a record of accurate and well-written scientific fact. In the expressly literary sketches written by King during this period, later gathered into the *Mountaineering* anthology, King—a disciple of the Scots geologist Sir Charles Lyell, who had argued for the creation of mountain ranges through catastrophic events—made connection to what can be described as the "cataclysmic sublime" of the history of the Sierra Nevada, focusing on its creation through catastrophe and its storage of geological time. As evoked by King, the very seas, convulsions, lava, and glaciers that created the Sierra in eons past still seemed imminent of release. Geologically, California remained in a process of becoming. In *Mountaineering in the Sierra Nevada,* King sought an imaginative connection with the archaic and continuing life of the continent itself.

This was history in geological terms. The 1870s also witnessed the initial five-volume outpouring—*The Native Races* (1874–75)—of the cascade of solidly researched human histories, eventually totaling thirty-nine, which were issued by Hubert Howe Bancroft under his own name, although actually written, with the exception of two volumes, by uncredited historians in Bancroft's employ. Seven of the volumes in this series—comprising the *History of California* (1886–90) written by Dartmouth graduate Henry Lebbeus Oak—remain, along with the histories of Theodore Hittell, the commanding authorities in their field. A Yale-trained lawyer from Ohio, semiretired from a successful land title practice, Hittell did his own writing and research, in contrast to Bancroft, for his four-volume *History of California* (1885–97), which equaled the Oak volumes in solidity and narrative skill.

Journalism and belles lettres received a boost when Ambrose Bierce—now a recognized writer with three books to his credit—returned to San Francisco from Europe in 1875 and resumed his local career. In 1877 Bierce joined the staff of the newly founded *Argonaut,* a gossipy and trenchant review that would last until 1958, where he pioneered the bylined column as a journalistic genre. He later took his "Prattle" column to the *Wasp,* which he edited with great success from 1881 to 1886, before going on to the *San Francisco Examiner,* published and edited by William Randolph Hearst, the scapegrace scion of mining millionaire George Hearst, a U.S. senator. As editor, Hearst pioneered journalistic techniques—featured writers, columns, crusading editorials backed by vivid cartoons, coverage of society, the demimonde, and the sporting world—that he would soon take national. In 1876 New York journalist B. E. Lloyd, having spent time in the Pacific Coast city, published *Lights and Shades in San Francisco,* an equally pioneering, almost undercover, work of investigative reporting and first-person journalism that caught the city as it proceeded through a decade of poverty and wealth, cultural achievement and political turmoil.

By this time Bret Harte, like Mark Twain, had left for the East, following the enormous success of *The Luck of Roaring Camp and Other Sketches* (1870). Harte would never return; indeed, after service in Prussia and Scotland as an American consul general, he settled into literary expatriation in London, while continuing occasionally to mine the California frontier for material. Twain shook the dust of San Francisco from his feet and attained national prominence. Harte, by contrast, never passed the success of his 1870 short story collection. With the exception of a novel, *Gabriel Conroy* (1876), set partially in San Francisco, Harte's material became increasingly thin, although he continued to write almost up to the time of his death in 1902.

The return of Ambrose Bierce and poet Joaquín Miller from England offered a countervailing statement to the departure of Twain and Harte, for each of these writers was, in Royce's term, a High Provincial to the core and would do his best work in regional circumstances. Joaquín Miller (real name Cincinnatus Hiner Miller) was a lifelong poseur and figment of his own imagination: a onetime miner turned poet and compulsive fabulist (no one has ever fully been able to disentangle truth from fiction in the stories he told about himself) who decamped for London, where his *Pacific Poems* (1870) and *Songs of the Sierras*

(1871) were privately published with some success, especially among the Pre-Raphaelites, and where Miller attended literary soirées dressed in miner's attire and otherwise played the frontier troubadour. Returning to San Francisco, Miller completed *Life Among the Modocs* (1873), a typical blend of fact and fiction, but a narrative, whether true or not, that cannot be dismissed owing to its vivid depictions of life with the Modoc people beneath the shadow of Mount Shasta. Taking a wife, so Miller tells us, he fathered a daughter, Cali-Shasta, who iconically embodied the spirit and value of a blended civilization.

RISING FROM ITS PLAIN, a Mount Olympus in Native American myth, Mount Shasta, along with Mount Tamalpais in Marin County, remained a favorite subject of the generation of accomplished painters who trickled into California during the Gold Rush, arrived in significant numbers in the early 1860s, and by the late 1870s had firmly established California as a center of landscape painting. Artists arrived in California as visitors in the pre-American period, many of them attached to scientific expeditions: Others came as miners during the Gold Rush; among these were John David Borthwick, a member of the Royal Academy; George Holbrook Baker, a student at the National Academy of Design in New York; German-born Charles Christian Nahl and his brother Hugo Wilhelm, with whom he often collaborated; and French-born Erneste Narjot. Deliberate, long-term Californians arrived in the 1860s and 1870s, including accomplished artists such as Juan Buckingham Wandesforde, William Keith, Virgil Williams, Frederick Whymper, Thomas Hill, Gideon Jacques Denny, William Hahn, Jules Tavernier, Edwin Deakin, Domenico Tojetti, Samuel Marsden Brookes, and Raymond Dabb Yelland. These same decades saw visits from such temporary but engaged sojourners as Albert Bierstadt, George Inness, and Emil Carlson. Later in the century, a generation of California-reared painters came of age, among them Julian Rix, Thaddeus Welch, Lorenzo Latimer, Tobias Rosenthal, Charles Rollo Peters, the pioneering African American artist Henry Alexander, Jules Pages, Theodore Wores, and Arthur Mathews and his wife, Lucia, many of them also spending time in France and Germany across the fin de siècle.

The fact is that California supported art from the frontier days onward. The San Francisco Art Union, an exhibition and auction house, opened its doors as early as 1851. By the 1860s, the well-developed hotel and saloon culture of the city featured numerous paintings. The 1870s witnessed art buying by the rising oligarchy; the establishment of two art academies, the San Francisco Art Association, incorporated in March 1871, and the California School of Design, opening in 1874; and the founding of the Bohemian Club of San Francisco in 1872 by artists, journalists, and businessmen who supported an ambitious program of exhibitions through the remainder of the nineteenth century. While the Nahl brothers and William Hahn practiced genre painting—which is to say, scenes of domestic life, a decided preference among German painters—the majority of painters working in California specialized in landscape. There was plenty to paint in California, and in the second half of the nineteenth century the artists of the state compiled a painterly gazetteer of California that left no major portion of the landscape uncelebrated, with an emphasis on such signature places as Mount Shasta, Mount Tamalpais, the Yosemite Valley, Clear Lake, the Napa Valley, and the oak-dotted hills of the East Bay.

Likewise did photography flourish in such figures as Carleton Watkins and Eadweard Muybridge, two of the outstanding American photographers of the nineteenth century. Taking up photography in Sacramento in 1854, Watkins, a former New Yorker, opened his Yosemite Art Gallery in San Francisco shortly thereafter and for the next half-century made his living through passport photographs, portraits, and a variety of commercial assignments that today astonish photo-historians with their sophisticated composition and technical mastery. No aspect of California—whether Yosemite, the wild rivers, mountains, farms, ranches, or lumber mills of the northern coast, the hydraulic mines of Nevada County, the wineries and ranches of southern and central California, shipwrecks beside the Golden Gate, sea lions on the Farallons, a solitary cypress on the Monterey coast—escaped Watkins's notice. He photographed each of them in the course of one or another commercial assignment. Watkins regarded himself not as an artist, which he was to a supreme degree, but as a mechanic, a workingman, stepping out of a poem by Walt Whitman extolling honest labor and a satisfying day's work. Like Whitman, Watkins was a great walker with a restless curiosity, and he roamed the fields, mountains, and settled places of California, cataloging and documenting the natural and man-made environment of this new American domain.

The English-born Eadweard Muybridge, by contrast, was a self-conscious artist, and, as historian Rebecca Solnit has shown, he was fully aware of the capacity of this recently invented medium to document, arrest, even rearrange motion, hence to capture time itself through depicting movement and also to release time, as Muybridge did in 1872 when through a series of photographs he proved on behalf of his client Leland Stanford that all four feet of a trotting horse were at certain points simultaneously off the ground. These photographs and the subsequently published *The Horse in Motion* (1882), with text by J.D.B. Stillman of Gold Rush fame, and *The Human Figure in Motion* (1901) stand as founding texts for the development of cinema, just as, more practically, Muybridge's Zoopraxiscope, which he invented, allowed him to project such photographic sequences onto a screen and thereby to effect a simulation of motion, of time stored and released. These and other experiments, Solnit argues, established Muybridge as an early avatar of the high-technology culture that in the twentieth century would bring into being Silicon Valley and the world it revolutionized.

Most of what Watkins and Muybridge photographed was in Northern or central California. Through the 1870s, Southern California remained relatively unsettled. In 1876, however, the railroad, tunneling through the Tehachapis, reached Los Angeles from San Francisco, and within the next twenty-five years Southern California joined Northern California in making the transition from frontier to province. In the 1870s, adobe gave way there to brick and wood; candles and kerosene were replaced by gaslight; streets were paved and tracks laid for horse-drawn streetcars; police and fire departments were organized; a lending library was established; and a city hall, county hospital, opera house, and four-hundred-seat theater opened, as Los Angeles made the transition from Mexican to American city. The opening in 1869 of the Pico House, the finest hotel in the Southwest, ushered in the decade, followed by the construction of the Baker Block commercial structure and the dedication in 1876 of an ambitious Roman Catholic cathedral, St. Vibiana's (still standing), modeled upon the great church of San Miguel in Barcelona. In 1865, St. Vincent's College, a Catholic institution, opened its doors, followed in 1880 by the Methodist-affiliated University of Southern California, the Presbyterian-affiliated Occidental College and Congregationalist-affiliated Pomona College in 1887, and the Quaker-affiliated Whittier College in 1891.

The opening of a direct transcontinental railroad route into Southern California by the Atchison, Topeka & Santa Fe—which reached San Bernardino in 1885, Los Angeles in 1887, and San Diego in 1888—precipitated the brief but transforming "Boom of the Eighties" that finalized the Americanization of Southern California. It was, first of all, a middle- and upper-middle-class migration, whether for reasons of health, tourism, winter sojourn, or permanent residence. The ravages of consumption in mid- to late nineteenth-century America cannot be exaggerated. Starting in the late 1870s, gaining in intensity in the 1880s, and continuing into the twentieth century, influxes of consumptive health seekers poured into Southern California in search of recovery. From San Diego to Santa Barbara, a sanitarium culture grew up along the Southern California coast. Sunshine and fresh air helped in the recovery of many. Journalist Charles Fletcher Lummis regained his health by walking to Southern California from Ohio. Harvard graduate Frederick Hastings Rindge of Cambridge, Massachusetts, fought back a lung complaint on the Rancho Topanga Malibu Sequit. Dartmouth junior Harry Chandler combated consumption by working shirtless under the hot sun in the orchards of the San Fernando Valley. Many, however, lost their struggle for health and succumbed, and this drama of hope and defeat conferred upon Southern California a certain interplay of healthfulness and morbidity that in various forms, including the hard-boiled detective story and film noir, would persist into the mid-twentieth century.

Allied to this influx of health seekers (indeed, the categories frequently overlapped) were winter residents and tourists. Wealthy Chicagoans favored wintering in Santa Barbara, arriving there in private railroad cars and staying at the Hotel Wentworth. Inland Pasadena, at the foot of the San Gabriel Mountains, was another favorite destination, with winter tourists staying at the Hotel Raymond, the Hotel Greene, or the Hotel Maryland. Long Beach featured the Hotel Virginia; San Diego, the Hotel del Coronado; and Riverside, the Mission Inn. Each of these hostelries was a utopia of a sort, intensifying the aesthetics of the region. Together with such later-established hostelries as the Huntington in Pasadena, the Ambassador on Wilshire Boulevard in Los Angeles, the Beverly Hills Hotel in Beverly Hills, and the Hotel in Bel Air, they also stimulated a desire for permanent residence on the part of wealthy Easterners first arriving as tourists. A number of Southern California communities can trace their origins to tourism and to the great hotels that in this period established an abiding resort metaphor for these Southern California cities.

Throughout this period, in fact, a search was on for just the right metaphor to guide and stimulate development in "the Southland." Subsidized by the railroad, journalist Charles Nordhoff initiated this process with his *California for Health, Wealth, and Residence* (1872), intended—before the Panic of 1873 and the ensuing depression—to persuade hundreds of thousands of middle-class Americans to move to California, where they could live the good life. A decade later, a New England visitor, Helen Hunt Jackson of Amherst, Massachusetts, in her bestselling novel *Ramona* (1884), advanced an interpretation of Southern California that would dominate the region through the 1920s. Intending to write an *Uncle Tom's Cabin* on behalf of oppressed Mission Indians, Jackson stumbled instead onto the Mission Myth—the perception of Southern California as an imagined Spanish place, shimmering and romantic—that conferred a usable metaphor, indeed a pseudohistory, upon the region, anchoring it in a mythic time and place that manifested itself in architecture (Mission followed by Spanish Revival), place names for developing townships, local festivals (the Ramona pageant at Hemet, for example), and, later, motion pictures and popular song.

This perception of Southern California as Spanish Colonial daydream of Arcadia helped establish an expanded metaphor of Mediterraneanism. Unlike the Ramona myth, the Mediterranean metaphor for Southern California was based on fact, for in terms of climate and terrain, Southern California offers many parallels to Mediterranean Europe. As early as the 1840s and 1850s, visitors to California were fond of making climate and terrain, flora and fauna comparisons to Spain, Italy, and Greece. In the same decade that Helen Hunt Jackson was perceiving Southern California as a romanticized Mexico, the Italian-born physician Peter Remondino, having recovered his health in San Diego, began to promote that region as a neo-Mediterranean littoral that was a naturally created health resort. In 1892 Remondino gathered his articles into *The Mediterranean Shores of America*. Following closely upon Charles Dudley Warner's *Our Italy* (1891), the physician's study broadcast the image of Southern California as a Mediterranean region of sparkling blue skies and water, sunshine, and health. For winter tourist Warner (Mark Twain's partner at the *Hartford Courant*), moreover, this Italian comparison suggested the type of society Southern California might develop in addition to its health-oriented one. Southern California, Warner speculated, emerging as a second Italy, might also promote in its lifestyle a certain civility and graciousness, a regard for nature and the arts, that would differentiate it from the gritty practicality of the industrialized East.

Charles Fletcher Lummis, meanwhile, was promoting the Spanish metaphor in his newly established (1895) magazine *Land of Sunshine*. Southern California, Lummis argued in numerous editorials, was the capital of the Spanish Southwest and the direct heir to its artistic past and traditions. Lummis himself—the author of many books, including *The Spanish Missions and the California Pioneers* (1893)—dressed in a green corduroy *charro* suit and with his own hands built his home, El Alisal, in the style of the Spanish frontier. A classmate of Theodore Roosevelt at Harvard, Lummis delighted in the projection of Southern California as a place to amalgamate the genteel tradition and the strenuous life.

This was the message as well of another promotional writer of this period, George Wharton James, a former Methodist minister, whose many books revolved around the benefits of desert living and the example of healthfulness provided by the Native Americans of California when living in their natural state. To this formula, James added a Southern California version of the genteel tradition, prizing the arts and literature of the region as they interacted and drew strength from the environment (James ranged as far north as Lake Tahoe, as far south as the Colorado Desert) and from Native American life, personal refinement, and Anglo-Protestant rectitude.

Such an interplay of metaphors helped Southern Californians develop their built environment in a manner akin to a stage set. Across the 1890s and early 1900s, the architects of the region turned increasingly to Mediterranean motifs. In 1914 a Spanish City dominated by Bertram Goodhue's California Building was created in Balboa Park, San Diego, for the Panama California International Exposition. After the destruction of Santa Barbara by earthquake in 1925, the entire city was rebuilt in the Spanish Revival style. Mediterranean, whether Spanish or Italian in inspiration, was the architecture of choice for most public buildings in Southern California throughout this period. In the field of domestic architecture, the only competition came from the Arts and Crafts tradition flourishing in Pasadena and elsewhere in the San Gabriel Valley.

AS FAR AS agriculture was concerned, Northern California witnessed the triumph of wheat in the 1870s and 1880s. California led the nation in wheat production until surpassed by Minnesota in the early 1890s. Dominating the vast expanses of the Sacramento and San Joaquin valleys, wheat ranching was agribusiness on a heroic scale, with gangs of hired men planting and harvesting across vast landscapes behind equipment drawn by mules or, after 1885, by steam-powered harvesters or, after 1904, by the track-belt-driven machine called the "tractor" invented by Fresno wagoneer Benjamin Holt. Wheat, however, did not create a neo-Mediterranean landscape that charmingly bespoke human cultivation. Wheat was remote, abstract, as were the cattle and sheep ranches of the Central Valley.

In Southern California, by contrast, citrus, vineyards, and

other forms of intensive agriculture (olives, deciduous fruits, date palms, honey-producing apiaries) brought to California a new kind of agriculturist—the intensive farmer, educated, middle class, capable of making a living on forty acres—and an aesthetic reshaping of the landscape. Thanks to the refrigerated rail car, California produce could by the 1890s reach Eastern markets within a week. Thus by the early 1900s a veritable sea of citrus groves—orange, lemon, grapefruit (although Texas would eventually dominate the grapefruit market)—ran from the interior counties of Riverside and San Bernardino into Los Angeles, heading for the coast. In contrast to the Central Valley, the agriculturists of Southern California were living on the land, as evident in innumerable farmhouse bungalows and the townships arising in the Southland. While these citrus ranches remained under individual ownership, growers did form cooperatives such as the Southern California Fruit Growers Association, established in 1895, for the harvesting, packaging, and marketing of their products. In 1905 a number of these associations formed the California Fruit Growers Exchange, whose "Sunkist" trade name became one of the best-known brand names in American marketing. Farther north, in Fresno County, the California Raisin Exchange was employing similar techniques for its "Sun Maid" brand, which in the form of a small red box of raisins selling for a nickel was soon making its appearance in the school lunch boxes of America.

Horticulturists, meanwhile, were planting the pervasively barren landscape of Southern California with trees of every sort, especially the eucalyptus, a blue gum tree from Australia. Abbot Kinney, the developer of Venice (a lagoon-laced Los Angeles suburb keyed to the Mediterranean metaphor), headed the Eucalyptus Crusade to transform Southern California through the wholesale planting of stands, lines, and groves of eucalyptus trees, growing rapidly to great heights, their leaves shimmering silver-green in the sunlight.

Thanks, then, to a number of factors—the surviving and refurbished missions (Charles Fletcher Lummis led this crusade), the construction of picturesque Arts and Crafts bungalows and neo-Mediterranean urban villas, the Eucalyptus Crusade, the rapid rise of a local gardening tradition (to include the Zen garden of Pasadena, set in place by immigrant Japanese gardeners), together with the preexisting natural beauty of hills, valleys, seashore, and sky—the artists of Southern California, most of them working in the plein air landscape tradition, had by the early 1900s more than enough subjects to paint. Over the next thirty years, through Impressionism and Postimpressionism (which remained the style of choice in Southern California until the 1930s), artists such as J. Bond Francisco, Guy Rose, Elmer and Marion Wachtel, Alson Skinner Clark, and Maurice Braun announced and promoted through their canvases a new American landscape: Southern California, Land of the Sun. To celebrate such sunshine, especially in January, when much of the nation was struggling with snowdrifts and windchill factors, the community of Pasadena in 1890 established a New Year's Day parade of chariots and floral floats in celebration of the Southern California climate and the winter-blooming gardens of the region. In 1902, a collegiate football game was added to the program. By the mid-1920s, this annual Tournament of Roses parade through the sunny winter streets of downtown Pasadena, followed by a postseason championship football match, had become a ritualized regional event, with its gridiron game being played in the Rose Bowl (1923), designed by Pasadena architect Myron Hunt.

High Provincial literature, meanwhile, was entering a golden age as a young generation of writers—among them Frank Norris, Jack London, and Robinson Jeffers—began their literary careers and such prior presences as Ambrose Bierce and John Muir went into high gear. The literature of California during this 1890–1915 period had three continuing preoccupations: nature, naturalism, and bohemia. Producing such works as *The Mountains of California* (1894), *My First Summer in the Sierra* (1911), and *The Yosemite* (1912), John Muir, president of the newly established (1892) Sierra Club, epitomized nature writing in this era. In April 2004, Governor Arnold Schwarzenegger chose an image of John Muir in the Yosemite, a California condor flying overhead, as the iconic image for the California quarter to be issued by the U.S. Mint. Schwarzenegger cited Muir, Yosemite, and the condor as symbols of the threatened but resilient environment of the state.

Other writers such as Malibu rancher Frederick Hastings Rindge, Inyo County vineyardist Mary Austin, educator J. Smeaton Chase, former Methodist minister George Wharton James, journalist Ernest Peixotto, English travel writer Horace Annesley Vachel, and Pasadena sportsman Charles Frederick Holder were also producing prose descriptions of the state which remain regional classics. These literary landscapes ran parallel to an equally vibrant third wave of plein air painting by a newly arrived generation of artists in their twenties and thirties—Charles Rollo Peters, Percy Grey, Gottardo Piazzoni, Xavier Martínez, and Francis McComas among them—who were busy taking an Impressionist and Postimpressionist look at the Bay Area and Monterey-Carmel, where a new bohemia was arising.

Visiting California in the process of courting his future wife—Fanny Osbourne of Oakland, whom he had met in France—Robert Louis Stevenson discovered Monterey as literary territory in 1879 before moving on to San Francisco, where he awaited Fanny's divorce from her philandering husband. Stevenson's sojourn in San Francisco, where he was invited into the Bohemian Club, can be said to have decisively shaped the bohemian movement in that city. Stevenson's friends—among them artists Virgil Williams (in 1880, Fanny and Robert honeymooned in a Napa cabin owned by Williams and his wife, Dora), artist Jules Tavernier, poet Charles Warren Stoddard, and fine printer Edward Bosqui, each of them a founding member of the Bohemian Club—had remained in San Francisco or the Bay Area expressly because the city and its hinterlands favored a genteelly bohemian lifestyle. So, too, did the visit of Oscar Wilde in March 1882 add to local lore. Wilde stepped off the train in Oakland wearing a Spanish sombrero, a velvet suit, a puce cravat, yellow gloves, and buckled shoes, and wended his way across the bay to the Bohemian Club, where he is reported to have drunk his hosts under the table.

By the turn of the century, bohemia centered on San Francisco poet George Sterling—whose best work anticipated the later achievement of Robinson Jeffers—and the artists and writers hanging out at Coppa's restaurant at 622 Montgomery Street, where they painted a four-walled mural in which locals were mixed with the immortals of art and literature. Bohemia became the subject as well, both positively and negatively, in novels by such diverse hands as Frank Norris, Jack London, Gertrude Atherton, Gelett Burgess, and Charles Tenney Jackson. Atherton's *Ancestors* (1907), Burgess's *The Heart Line* (1907), and Jackson's *Day of Souls* (1910) remain the best of this genre.

While Frank Norris covered bohemia for *The Wave,* a San Francisco talk-of-the-town magazine, his literary ambitions were heading in another direction: naturalism. As an undergraduate at Berkeley and a graduate student at Harvard, Norris had devoured the novels of Emile Zola in the original French, which Norris had mastered as an art student in Paris. Of upper-class background, moving in select circles, Norris—the Boy Zola, as he signed his letters—was nevertheless mesmerized by naturalism as a literary movement, with its emphasis upon chance, brute force, and crushed and bewildered antiheroes such as the self-taught dentist McTeague in Norris's 1899 novel of the same name or the ranchers and farmers in *The Octopus* (1901), broken by a dominating railroad. Presley, the poet protagonist of *The Octopus,* was loosely based upon Oakland schoolmaster-poet Edwin

Markham, whose tour de force poem of social protest, "The Man with the Hoe," published in the *San Francisco Examiner* on January 15, 1899, became an international sensation.

Coming of age in opposite social circumstances—the illegitimate son of a wandering astrologist, passed off to a failed stepfather, leaving Berkeley in 1897 after a few months as a freshman to join the Klondike gold rush—Jack London, like Frank Norris, was enamored of brute force and the underlife, except that London knew it from firsthand experience as an oyster pirate on San Francisco Bay, a Klondike miner, and an overworked wretch stoking the furnace in the basement of the same prep school in Belmont on the San Francisco peninsula that Norris had attended as a privileged student. There is no record that the two men ever met, despite their common Bay Area origins. The fact that they might once have been on the same ship to Cuba during the Spanish-American War only underscores a possible antagonism. Norris was a patrician conservative with an occasional interest in the underclass; London was a red-flag-waving socialist who signed his letters "Yours for the Revolution." Norris succumbed in 1902 to peritonitis at the age of thirty-two, leaving a great gap in American literature that Jack London did his best to fill. Between 1900, when his first book, *The Son of the Wolf,* appeared, and his premature death at the age of forty, sixteen years later, London poured forth a steady stream, nearly sixty titles, of short stories, novels, and nonfiction—*The Call of the Wild* (1903), *The Sea-Wolf* (1904), and *Martin Eden* (1909) being the best known—that kept him read and appreciated for the rest of the century.

As the twentieth century dawned, the population of California stood at 1,485,053—quite a small figure for such a vast state. Nearly half this population was living in the San Francisco Bay Area, with San Diego, its population slightly under

18,000, remaining a venerable but inconsiderable settlement, and Los Angeles barely passing the hundred thousand mark. Across the next decade, the interurban electric Big Red Cars of the Pacific Electric Railway, incorporated in 1901, would connect the City of Angels to most of the cities and towns on the Los Angeles plain, transforming Los Angeles into the hub of Southern California with a population of 319,198 by 1910.

By and large, the Big Red Cars possessed a benevolent image, as did the Atchison, Topeka & Santa Fe. This cannot be said, however, of the statewide network maintained by the Southern Pacific Railroad. The SP, as it was known, constituted the predominant public works infrastructure of California in the nineteenth century. The railroad linked the state, shipped the freight, owned and developed the land, founded the cities of the interior, and controlled the political machines of San Francisco and Los Angeles. The railroad was the primary fact and symbol of industrialism, hence the commanding icon of modern life. When in the spring of 1880 the Southern Pacific raised its promised selling price for land from $2.50 per acre to $17, then to $40, the tenant ranchers of the Mussel Slough area (near Hanford, on a branch of the Kings River in Kings County), who had improved their rental properties with a self-financed irrigation district on the promise that they would be able to buy their ranches at $2.50 per acre, organized the Grand Settlers League and went into open revolt. The railroad countered with evictions. A shoot-out on the morning of May 11, 1880, between twenty ranchers and a posse of U.S. marshals with eviction notices left seven men dead. The so-called Battle of Mussel Slough dominated the consciousness of the rest of the century as the example *par excellence* of railroad power in the state, hence a significant piece of unfinished business in politics and governance. Josiah Royce wrote his only novel on the topic, *The Feud of Oakfield Creek* (1887), and it provided Frank Norris with the bloody conclusion to *The Octopus.*

And so Higher Provincial California, as Royce described it, entered the twentieth century. The thirty-plus years since the arrival of the transcontinental railroad had seen California evolve into a distinctive American commonwealth: a railroad-served agricultural empire with a developed industrial base in and around San Francisco. In *The Octopus,* Norris allowed San Francisco industrialist Cedarquist, based upon the real-life figure of Irving Scott, founder of the southern San Francisco–based Union Iron Works, to speak on behalf of the industrial future of the state, centered in the Bay Area. Already in the 1880s, economic commentator John Shertzer Hittell, brother of the historian, was making similar predictions in *The Commerce and Industries of the Pacific Coast* (1882). By the mid-1880s, Union Iron Works was building ironclad ships of the line for the United States Navy, some seventy-five warships in all, including the battleship *Oregon* and the cruiser *Olympia,* which would serve as Admiral Dewey's flagship at Manila Bay.

Already, sentiment was building for a better governance of this emergent society. The constitution of 1879 had effected some reform, but most observers would agree with the observation of David Starr Jordan, the founding president of Stanford University, that California continued to require a makeover of its public culture, especially its politics. If California as a society were to be worthy of its natural resources, Jordan argued in a November 1898 *Atlantic Monthly* essay (issued separately as *California and the Californians* in 1899), it would have to embark upon an ambitious program of reforming its architecture, town planning, business culture, and politics. The next decade proved that Jordan was not alone in this belief as a generation of pre-Progressive and Progressive reformers once again set about the business of trying to make California worthy of its geographical grandeur.

Jordan's own university, Stanford, represented one step in this program of reform. No tuition was required (at least initially), and women were admitted on an equal basis, as had been the case since 1868 at the University of California at Berkeley (then also in the process of upgrading its faculty, physical plant, and programs, thanks to the patronage of Phoebe Apperson Hearst and the academic leadership of Theodore Roosevelt's friend, classicist Benjamin Ide Wheeler, appointed president in 1899). At Stanford, Jordan encouraged students to practice high thinking and the strenuous life. At Berkeley, President Wheeler and Professor Joseph LeConte—like Jordan, a physician, natural scientist, and student of Louis Agassiz—encouraged their students (who included undergraduates Jack London, Frank Norris, and Franklin K. Lane, later secretary of the interior under Woodrow Wilson) to pursue an equally high-minded, evolution-friendly theism whose matrix and primary symbol was California as natural place.

Feminist Sarah Cooper of San Francisco, meanwhile, since the 1870s, had been playing a major role in the female emancipation movement, as had Caroline Seymour Severance of Los Angeles. They, together with Kate Douglas Smith of Santa Barbara and Phoebe Apperson Hearst of San Francisco, were especially convinced that the kindergarten movement pioneered in Germany offered a promising way for youngsters, especially girls, to develop self-esteem at an early age, together with a capacity for further education. Incorporated in San Francisco in 1884, the Golden Gate Kindergarten Association pioneered the effort to bring what would later be called Early Childhood Education to the United States. By 1894 it is estimated that 235 free public kindergartens had been established in the United States and abroad on the Golden Gate model.

When it came to the politics of California, the pre-Progressive reformers had their work cut out for them, for despite the reforms of 1879, the political bureau of the Southern

Pacific Railroad continued to exercise decisive influence on the politics of the state. Stacked with genial publicists and men of letters in search of an income, the three-man railroad commission established by the 1879 constitution was waggishly known as the Southern Pacific Literary Bureau. In San Francisco, the SP initially exercised its influence through Christopher Buckley, a blind saloonkeeper turned political boss. When Buckley fled the state in 1891 to avoid indictment, the SP, after some searching, turned to Abraham Ruef, a dapper University of California–trained lawyer who had begun his career as a pre-Progressive reformer before going over to the dark side of the Force and becoming a lobbyist and bagman extraordinary. Matters in Los Angeles were handled for the SP by land agent and lobbyist Walter Parker, a Ragtime political boss from central casting. Portly, mustachioed, by turns ruthless or genial depending upon whether or not he was getting his way, Parker surveyed life through a haze of cigar smoke, which did not prevent him from keeping a close eye on the city council, which he stacked with his own retainers.

Throughout the 1890s and into the early twentieth century, reformist sentiment tried to consolidate itself. In Southern California, reformers—the good-government crowd, derided as "goo-goos" by their opponents—tended to come from a distinctive sector of wealthy Fabian Socialists. Developer H. Gaylord Wilshire, for example, espoused nationalism, based on ideas extracted from Edward Bellamy's reformist novel *Looking Backward: 2000–1887,* published in 1888. John Randolph Haynes, another millionaire developer holding M.D. and Ph.D. degrees from the University of Pennsylvania, founded the Christian Socialist Economic League of Los Angeles. The city of Pasadena was vibrant with Fabian Socialists of equally comfortable backgrounds—plumbing heiress Kate Crane Gartz, oil heiress Aline Barnsdall, razor blade magnate King Gillette—anxious to see California reform itself.

The socialists of Northern California, by contrast, tended to be anchored in the labor movement and were, many of them, Reds, as opposed to the Fabian *haute bourgeoisie* of the Southland. In the *San Francisco Examiner* of January 15, 1899, Oakland schoolmaster Edwin Markham provided in "The Man with the Hoe" a poetic *J'accuse!* on behalf of exploited workers that galvanized the Left throughout the English-speaking world. In 1907 another Oakland socialist, Jack London, published *The Iron Heel,* predicting a forthcoming cycle of revolution and oligarchic repression in the United States if working conditions did not improve.

Across the Bay in San Francisco, meanwhile, the very same oligarchy that London so feared was dividing over the issue of corruption and reform. A significant part of the San Francisco establishment, especially those bidding for streetcar and public utilities contracts, were happy to let Abe Ruef conduct business via discreetly delivered envelopes stuffed with cash. Other oligarchs, however—sugar heir Rudolph Spreckels, for example, together with former mayor James Duval Phelan and his colleagues in the Association for the Adornment and Beautification of San Francisco—were interested in reform. Spreckels personally financed a series of investigations that would ultimately snare lobbyist Ruef and, as the dapper Ruef noted upon his sentencing, force him to exchange his pinstripes for the zebra stripes of a San Quentin convict. The graft trials of late 1906 that eventually sent the scapegoat Ruef to "Q" constitute the grand saga of political reform prior to the Progressive takeover of the state in 1910. Among other events, the prosecutor was shot in court, his assailant was found dead in his cell under suspicious circumstances, and the police chief of San Francisco met a watery end in the Bay under equally mysterious conditions. In the course of the trials, half of the San Francisco establishment turned on the other half, revealing a network of corporate bribery for which, crusading editor Fremont Older complained, only Abe Ruef was required to take the rap. Affronted by Ruef's solo conviction while his bribers sank into their leather chairs in their posh clubs, cigars in hand, whiskeys at elbow, Older reversed course and successfully campaigned for the early parole of the onetime bagman. A free man after serving four years and seven months of his fourteen-year sentence, Ruef returned to San Francisco and, continuing to tell no tales, prospered in real estate.

Revisionist historian Philip Fradkin sees Ruef as the victim of the entire graft investigation. Of French-Jewish descent, Ruef was, he argues, the Alfred Dreyfus of San Francisco—that is, a Jew persecuted by an anti-Semitic coterie of Progressive reformers led by Spreckels and Phelan, who were anxious to find a scapegoat that would give them a pretext to seize power in San Francisco from the Union Labor Party administration being advised by Ruef. Chief investigator William J. Burns virtually kidnapped Ruef with the approval of a complaisant judge and submitted him to psychological torture. While Abe Ruef was no angel, he was certainly not the Darth Vader who was vilified, brought to trial, and sent to San Quentin by the Progressives.

By April 1906, as the case against Ruef and his colleagues was being prepared, photographs of San Francisco revealed an articulated cityscape of multistoried office buildings along Market Street; a grand city hall near Market Street and Van Ness Avenue; cable cars running up and down hills past ornate Italianate residences; warehouses and factories in the South of Market district; the looming Palace Hotel at Market and New Montgomery, a new hotel, the St. Francis, facing Union Square, and the nearly completed Fairmont Hotel atop Nob Hill; the spires of churches and synagogues everywhere; a grand ferry terminal at the foot of Market Street surmounted by a tower based on the Giralda Tower of Seville; streetcars serving the major streets; block upon block of newly constructed homes in the Castro, Eureka Valley, and Western Addition neighborhoods; gardens and statuary and a great glass conservatory in Golden Gate Park; and steamships and square-riggers crowding the Embarcadero waterfront. Truly, this was the realization of Higher Provincialism as Royce had envisioned it: not the predominant city in the United States, to be sure, but a ranking American city complete in each aspect of its urbanism, filled with a talented and diverse population, served by four major newspapers, with the great Enrico Caruso even then appearing in *Carmen* at the Mission Opera House. The morning edition of the *Chronicle* had already appeared late on the evening of the seventeenth of April. After the opera and the other entertainments let out, the lights continued to burn at such restaurants and resorts as Jack's, Zinkand's, the Savoy Tivoli, Coppa's, the Fior d'Italia, Mayes' Oyster House, the Poodle Dog, and the drinking establishments along the Cocktail Route on Kearny Street before the city went fully to sleep.

At 5:12:05 on the morning of Wednesday, April 18, 1906, the Pacific and North American tectonic plates suddenly sprang over and from nine to twenty-one feet past each other along the 290 miles of the San Andreas fault. Shock waves sped across the terrain at 7,000 miles per hour. The first quake to hit San Francisco (8.3 on the Richter scale, it would later be estimated) shook the city in two phases for forty-five seconds. Within the hour, there would be seventeen serious aftershocks. City Hall and numerous other unreinforced brick buildings, together with many crowded tenements south of Market Street, collapsed instantly. Façades fell from homes, revealing the furniture within. Less sturdy homes crumpled completely.

What followed during the next three days remains obscure in many of its details. Fire Chief Dennis Sullivan had been mortally wounded in his home on Bush Street. Innumerable water mains were broken, and this impeded firefighting on the first day of the disaster. Then came a second wave of fires, most likely originating from an overturned cookstove, which compounded the growing conflagration. All this was exacerbated by a political impasse as reform elements opposed the leadership of Mayor Eugene Schmitz; army troops under the command of Brigadier General Frederick Funston assumed control of the city, despite the lack of any clear mandate to do so. How did the politics of the graft trials and continuing investigations then under way fracture the leadership of the city during the crisis? Who exactly authorized the Army to assume control? Was it Mayor Schmitz, or did he merely bend to the inevitable? Whom exactly did the army troops shoot as looters? Were they mostly minorities, and were all those shootings necessary? Was it necessary, moreover, to dynamite so many downtown buildings to halt the fire, or was the dynamiting the real cause of most of the destruction? Once again, Philip Fradkin has come up with bold and revisionist answers. Martial law was never officially declared, he proves. Army assistance was requested by the mayor, he asserts, and General Funston never considered that he had sole control of the city. Mayor Schmitz gave the order that looters should be shot on sight, despite the fact that there was no evidence of widespread looting. Far from impeding the fire, the inept dynamiting of buildings created the firestorms that destroyed the city.

In any event, within three days, the central and northeastern quadrants of San Francisco lay smoldering in ruins. More than three hundred people had died, it was initially reported—a figure increased tenfold by later researchers. Anxious to save the reputation of the city, the oligarchs downplayed the extent of the crisis. The destruction of central and downtown San Francisco, together with the damage caused to neighboring communities—most notably to the newly constructed campus of Stanford University in Palo Alto—brought to a standstill the comforting certainties of Higher Provincial California in its Bay Area manifestations. Buried beneath the smoking ruins was more than thirty years of nineteenth- and early twentieth-century effort on the part of a city that, as historian Gray

Brechin has shown, drove the development of the state—as a financial and political power, as intellectual center, as primary consumer and arbiter of taste—before the rise of Los Angeles. In 1869 the arrival of the railroad had ended the splendid isolation of the frontier. Now, the Great Earthquake and Fire of April 1906 had ended the second phase of California's development, its High Provincial years of regional achievement and contentment. Ahead lay the challenge and task for the next era: the creation of an infrastructure that would make possible a mega-state.

7

GREAT EXPECTATIONS

Creating the Infrastructure of a Mega-State

Golden Gate Bridge shortly after its dedication

CALIFORNIA STATE LIBRARY

The first forty years of statehood saw California organize its political and socioeconomic structures and lay the foundations of its built environment. In its second forty years as a state—the twentieth century, with some activity beginning in the 1890s—the public works infrastructure of California was established. The dams, aqueducts, reservoirs, power plants, industrial sites, bridges, roadways, public buildings, and stadiums created during this second phase served the growing population of the state. They also foretold and empowered the mega-state to come.

It began with water, the sine qua non of any civilization. In California, two thirds of the annual precipitation falls in the northern third of the state. Much of Southern California is desert terrain. Despite its two great rivers, the Sacramento and the San Joaquin, the Great Central Valley is itself a semiarid steppe, with soil baked by the sun to such hardness that it frequently had to be broken with dynamite. For California to become inhabitable and productive in its entirety would require a statewide water system of heroic magnitude. Californians recognized this almost immediately. In 1878 the legislature passed the Drainage Act, creating the position of state engineer and appropriating $100,000 for irrigation, drainage, and navigation studies. Over the next ten years, state engineer William Hammond Hall researched and published a series of studies that laid out a comprehensive program for the development of California through water projects. Hall's published reports—among them *The Improvement of the Sacramento River* (1880), *Report on Irriga-*

tion (1884), *Irrigation Questions* (1886), *Irrigation Development* (1886), and *Irrigation in California* (*Southern*) (1888)—not only bristled with specific recommendations integrated into an overall plan, but also put California into the historical context of irrigated civilizations of ancient and modern times.

From this perspective, William Hammond Hall envisioned modern California through water and must therefore be considered a founder of the state. Even as Hall was winding up his research, moreover, a long-standing water lawsuit—*Lux v. Haggin,* filed in 1877—was also drawing to a close. The suit, which pitted land barons Henry Miller and Charles Lux against the Kern County Land and Water Company regarding riparian rights (the right to draw flowing river water upstream from another's property), had so exhausted both sides that a compromise was reached in July 1888 between the Kern County Land and Water Company and thirty-one water ditch companies. The agreement, which allowed each side to draw water at stated intervals, immediately emerged as a model for cooperation between competing water interests. State senator C. C. Wright of Modesto, meanwhile, was shepherding through the legislature the Wright Act of 1887, which empowered local communities to form irrigation districts that could tax, issue revenue bonds, acquire land by eminent domain, and divert river water to dry lands for irrigation and/or flood control. The Wright Act and the resolution of *Lux v. Haggin* thus established the legal and political framework for hundreds of irrigation districts that would in the decades to come bring water to previously arid land and, in short order, transform the Central Valley and portions of Southern California into an agricultural empire.

But where was this water to come from in the southern portions of the state that were beyond the reach of the Sacramento or San Joaquin rivers? From the mighty Colorado River, argued state engineer Hall and other engineers in the field, including Canadian-born George Chaffey, who had already developed Ontario and Etiwanda in western San Bernardino County as irrigation-based townships, and Charles Robinson Rockwood, an irrigation engineer who had already made extensive studies of bringing the water of the Colorado into Southern California. A mere sixty miles, they pointed out—all of it downhill—lay between the Colorado River and the lowlands of the Salton Sink. Why not build a gravity canal, tap the Colorado River, let its waters flow westward, and turn the Salton Sink into a reservoir for the use of southeastern California? It took ten years and three trips to Europe for Rockwood and Chaffey to organize and capitalize the California Development Company, but a mere five months to dig the canal once construction had started. Late in the morning of May 14, 1901, George Chaffey ordered the last headgate to be lifted, and water from the Colorado flowed into the Salton Sink, now renamed the Imperial Valley: imperial as in empire, for millions of acres of arable land would soon be reclaimed from the desert.

The successor to the California Development Company, although it was called the Imperial Land Company, was really selling not so much land as water. The acreage in the valley was free or available at nominal cost for the asking under a succession of federal laws—the Homestead Act of 1862, the Desert Land Act of 1877, the Carey Land Act of 1894—intended to settle and irrigate desert lands. Settlers bought shares in the Imperial Land Company, which in turn saw them through the land claims process. To serve as advertising manager of the company, Chaffey appointed publicist L. M. Holt. In the previous decade, Holt had used the Mediterranean metaphor to package the emergent citrus belt of San Bernardino and Riverside counties as a healthful sanatorium where Americans might regain their vitality by going back to the land. He now promoted the Imperial Valley as the Egyptian delta of the United States, with the Colorado River serving as its Nile. Skillfully, Holt advanced a biblical scenario. Going down to the Imperial Valley, Americans were reenacting the going down into the Egypt of Joseph and his brethren, called by the Lord to a life of missionary improvement, in this case the irrigation and cultivation of a million acres of desert.

The master publicist of such imagery was William Ellsworth Smythe. At the very time that George Chaffee was organizing the construction of his canal, Smythe was arguing in *The Conquest of Arid America* (1900) that a new civilization was rising in Southern California—Ultimate California, Smythe called it—based on irrigation, the joint-stock company, and the New England town meeting. As in the case of Holland, each square foot reclaimed through irrigation would be cherished. In time, Southern California would develop into a landscape of irrigated fields, vineyards, orchards, and orange groves; townships planted in trees; comfortable homes awash in vines and flowers; and a people living a healthful and high-minded life based on irrigation. Disciples of Christ minister Harold Bell Wright employed such themes—the mysticism and transcendence of the desert, the biblical resonances of making the desert bloom—in his novel *The Winning of Barbara Worth* (1911), which sold 175,000 copies in its first two years of publication.

Irrigation, however, was a reorganization of nature, and all such reorderings have their risks. In October 1904, the California Development Company cut a second canal from the western bank of the Colorado across northern Mexico into the Imperial Valley. Done illegally and on the cheap, the second cut was a disaster waiting to happen. In the spring of 1905, there occurred a shift of titanic proportions: a westward wrenching of the Colorado River, as if seeking its ancient destination. Gorged by spring rains, the Colorado River was now running at a level of twenty-five to two hundred feet above the rim of the Imperial Valley, and it overwhelmed the second canal. The Colorado River began to pour into the valley at a rate, at its most intense, of 360 million cubic feet of water per hour. For a while, it looked as if Southern California would once again be drowned beneath a vast inland sea. It took seven attempts by Southern Pacific—the only civil engineering entity capable of dealing with a catastrophe of this proportion—to stanch the flooding by pouring some 2,500 carloads of rock, gravel, and clay into the break until by February 10, 1907, an eight-foot-high levee stretched for fifteen miles on both sides of the original rupture, and held. Fifteen hundred men had been pressed into service. President Theodore Roosevelt had promised Southern Pacific president E. H. Harriman that the federal government would compensate the railroad for, in effect, preventing much of Southern California from being turned into WaterWorld. Congress, however, refused to pay, and all that SP got for its efforts was ownership of the now-bankrupt California Development Company.

The technology developed in the Gold Rush for moving water across land had led to the technology of irrigation. This same technology would also enlarge and stabilize the metropolitan infrastructure of San Francisco and Los Angeles. By 1900—when 40 percent of the 1.5 million population of the state lived either in the Bay Area or Greater Los Angeles—each city knew that it would need more water to serve its present population and support desired growth. Each city established an administrative board—the appointed Board of Public Works (1898) in San Francisco and the popularly elected Board of Water Commissioners (1903) in Los Angeles—to develop water plans and programs. In each city, a talented city engineer—William Mulholland of Los Angeles and Michael O'Shaughnessy of San Francisco—pushed a major water project to a successful conclusion by tapping, in each case, a river—the Owens for Los Angeles, the Tuolumne for San Francisco—and bringing its water to the city through a system of dams, reservoirs, and aqueducts that took years to construct. Each project involved its own long and intricate political and financial history, from first filing of water claims to finished construction.

It took more than six years to construct the Los Angeles

Aqueduct—235 miles of canals, conduits, tunnels, flumes, penstocks, tailraces, and siphons—from its intake point twelve miles above the town of Independence on the Owens River in Inyo County on the eastern side of the Sierra Nevada, to its last spillway in the San Fernando Valley, where the water at long last arrived on the morning of Wednesday, November 5, 1913, welcomed by a crowd of thirty to forty thousand, many of whom had brought along tin cups to take their first drink.

On July 7, 1923, San Francisco mayor James "Sunny Jim" Rolph dedicated the O'Shaughnessy Dam, named in honor of the city engineer; it took another eleven years (and ninety lives) to complete the four dams, the five reservoirs, the hydroelectric power plant, the nearly one hundred miles of pipeline, and the sixty-six miles of tunnel needed to conduct the waters of the Tuolumne to San Francisco.

In each instance, the water and hydroelectricity thus obtained enabled each city to serve as many as four million residents, hence to metropolitanize the Bay Area and to allow Los Angeles to expand to 441.7 square miles by 1930, its population of 1,238,048 making it the fifth largest city in the nation.

In each instance, too, the water system involved almost equally monumental damage to the environment: in the case of San Francisco, the loss of the magnificent Hetch Hetchy Valley near Yosemite when the Tuolumne River was dammed and the valley filled to create a reservoir, and in the case of Los Angeles, the desiccation and devastation of the once-fertile Owens Valley when the Owens River was siphoned off to Los Angeles. Each project, moreover, was plagued by claims of deception, double-dealing, and conflict of interest that became the subject of many histories, novels, and films—to include the Oscar-winning *Chinatown* (1974)—in the decades to come.

In each instance as well, these water projects were part of an even larger upgrading and enhancement of the built environment. At the same time that the oligarchy of San Francisco was turning its attention to its water future, it was also upgrading the architecture of the city and its environs. Prior to the 1890s, visitors to San Francisco—the novelist Anthony Trollope, for example—frequently noted the disparity between the ramshackle architecture of the city and its spectacular site. The 1890s witnessed a concerted effort on behalf of the San Francisco oligarchy to sponsor an entirely new level of architecture in a deliberate effort to celebrate and memorialize the coming of age of the city as capital of the Far West. Both the money and the architectural talent were available for this effort. A new generation of architects, many of them trained at the Ecole des Beaux Arts in Paris, were establishing studios in the city. Miraculously, many of the buildings they designed survived the earthquake and fire of April 1906. These architects, moreover, were on hand for the rebuilding of the city between 1906 and 1909, and thus the architectural standards of the pre-quake city were observed. These very same architects, so capable of working on large-scale projects, were also fashioning for the Bay Area an engaging tradition of domestic design for the middle, upper middle, and upper classes. South of San Francisco, in the townships of Burlingame, San Mateo, Menlo Park, Atherton, and Woodside, the Italianate or neo-Gothic villas of the nineteenth century had been succeeded by a second generation of estates designed in the Beaux Arts style for the elegant rustication of Bay Area elites. These stately homes—for which architect Willis Polk's "Filoli" (1916) in San Mateo County, designed for mining and water company heir William Bowers Bourn II, can easily serve as a summation and concluding paradigm—more than fulfilled Bayard Taylor's predictions in 1850 that the peninsula south of San Francisco was destined to develop as a Tuscan landscape of villas, cypresses, lawns, flowers, and fountains.

Mediterranean Revival style was also characteristic of the newly developing neighborhoods of San Francisco—St. Francis Wood, Presidio Terrace, Seacliff—and the upscale community of Piedmont in the Oakland hills. At the same time Bernard Maybeck and other architects were transforming domestic Berkeley into a wonderland of redwood bungalows, rustic without, gleaming in polished wood within, inspired by an amalgam of Swedenborgian naturalism, the Arts and Crafts movement, and ideas put forth by Berkeley poet Charles Augustus Keeler in his treatise *The Simple Home* (1904). Unfortunately, fire would destroy many of these homes in September 1923. Those that survived, however, remained as picturesque affirmations of a style Lewis Mumford would later describe as Bay Region.

The university culture of the Bay Area, meanwhile, was being enhanced by the construction and continuing development of the Leland Stanford, Jr., University in Palo Alto and the University of California at Berkeley. To design the Quadrangle (1891) of the privately endowed Stanford University, Senator and Mrs. Stanford selected Henry Hobson Richardson of Boston, preeminent practitioner of American Romanesque. When Richardson died suddenly in 1896, the successor firm of Shepley, Rutan, and Coolidge amplified Richardson's preliminary sketches for a campus of thirteen one-story buildings of highly textured yellow sandstone with red tile roofs, built around a quadrangle and connected by arcades. The young architects enlivened Richardson's Romanesque with restrained but effective suggestions of Mission Revival, a style only then gaining ground. No less an architect than the great Frederick Law Olmsted designed the landscape for the campus, dispatching his partner H. S. Codman to Spain and North Africa to search out trees and plants appropriate to the dry Mediterranean garden he was planning. When construction and landscaping were complete, Stanford University emerged on its opening day in the fall of 1891 as an idealized garden of the West as well as one of the most vivid implementations of the Mediterranean metaphor in the state.

This in turn inspired an equally dramatic effort to upgrade

the campus of the University of California at Berkeley. Its first woman regent and generous patron, Phoebe Apperson Hearst—widow of the ultrawealthy mining engineer and U.S. senator, George, and mother of the innovative publisher of the *San Francisco Examiner,* William Randolph—was challenged by what was being accomplished by Jane Stanford—widow (since 1893) of the former governor, senator, and Big Four railroad magnate—and wished to do likewise. Frederick Law Olmsted had surveyed the Berkeley campus in 1866 and submitted a preliminary master plan, but as of the late 1890s it remained undeveloped. In 1896, in a letter to the regents, Mrs. Hearst offered to sponsor an international architectural competition on behalf of the campus in honor of her late husband. In 1900, following numerous submissions, the sketches of Emile Bernard, professor at the Ecole des Beaux Arts, were chosen. Three years later, Beaux Arts–trained architect John Galen Howard of Massachusetts was appointed as university architect to implement Bernard's plan in light of Olmsted's earlier suggestions. In the decades to come, under Howard's supervision, the Berkeley campus steadily developed as a Beaux Arts city of learning. Classical Revival buildings including a campanile, a stadium, and an outdoor Greek theater (softened and enlivened in many cases with California touches) lined plazas and eucalyptus-girded pathways in a bold and unambiguous assertion that high university culture and purpose now reigned supreme on a university campus that alumna Joan Didion would later describe as California's best idea of itself.

So strong was this taste for neoclassical order in the Bay Area that the Association for the Improvement and Adornment of San Francisco, formed in 1904 under the presidency of former mayor James Duval Phelan, extended that year a formal invitation to the renowned architect and planner Daniel Hudson Burnham of Chicago—already familiar to San Franciscans as the designer of the Mills Building (1891) and the Merchants Exchange (1903)—to create a comprehensive master plan for the city. With his plan for the Chicago World's Fair of 1893, Burnham had launched the City Beautiful movement, which envisioned the transformation of American cities into neo-Baroque orchestrations of boulevards, plazas, fountains, statues, and Classical Revival structures. Working with local architect Edward Bennett out of a studio atop Twin Peaks with a commanding view of the city, Burnham called for the transformation of San Francisco along City Beautiful lines. Ironically, the Burnham Report was formally filed in City Hall just a day before the earthquake of 1906. Notified by telegraph in Paris that most of San Francisco lay in ruins, Burnham left immediately for California in hopes that his plan could now be implemented immediately and on an unprecedented scale. Such a reorganization of Jasper O'Farrell's grid of 1847, followed by sixty years of further development, would take years, however, even with the clearance afforded by the earthquake and fire; and so, while there was some support for implementing the Burnham Plan in the immediate aftermath of the catastrophe, *Chronicle* editor Michael H. de Young, speaking for the oligarchy, launched a successful campaign to have San Francisco rebuilt on its prior grid as quickly as possible so that the city would suffer no loss of momentum. While aspects of the Burnham Plan were realized—the Great Highway along Ocean Beach, the ambitious Civic Center, a streetcar tunnel beneath Twin Peaks—San Francisco was rebuilt within three years on its 1847 grid.

San Francisco further implemented the Burnham Plan, however, in the idealized idiom of festival architecture when the Panama Pacific International Exposition was opened on February 20, 1915. For ten months, San Francisco enjoyed an idealized version of itself, master-planned by Edward Bennett, Burnham's colleague of 1904, in the colorful dream city of Harbor View on the northern edge of the city, facing the Golden Gate. So, too, did San Diego indulge that year in an equally idealized vision of itself through its parallel Panama-California Exposition, which reprised the 1908 plan developed for San Diego by the noted city planner and landscape architect John Nolen of Cambridge, Massachusetts. While the Burnham Plan envisioned San Francisco in neoclassical grandeur, the Nolen Plan envisioned San Diego as the Naples, the Rio de Janeiro, of the Northern Hemisphere: a harborside city embellished by Italian and Spanish buildings, palm-lined avenues, and sunny plazas, set against a neo-Mediterranean setting of hills, sea, and sky. New York architect and planner Bertram Grosvenor Goodhue, master of Spanish Revival, oversaw the creation of the Panama California International Exposition as an idealized Spanish city expressing San Diego's deepest conception of itself.

Thus, as Europe plunged itself into war, San Francisco and San Diego, through dream cities created by the most notable architects of that generation, established architectural and planning paradigms that would inspire and guide the development of the built environment in Northern and Southern California for decades to come. In this regard, the Panama California International Exposition in Balboa Park, San Diego, was the more effective, in that it was preserved almost in its entirety, with Goodhue's California Building serving as a master icon for the development of Southern California for the next two decades. In San Francisco, only Bernard Maybeck's Palace of Fine Arts was preserved; yet this structure as well—a romantic orchestration of dome, column, colonnade, and lagoon—continued to speak across the rest of the century to the city that was lost in April 1906 and to a world at war that would never be the same.

The population of California, meanwhile, continued its steady growth, reaching 2.3 million by 1910, 3.4 million by 1920, 5.6 million by 1930, 6.9 million by 1940. Yet given the land mass of the state, this could still be considered a small population. In the first decade of the twentieth century, more than half this population lived in the San Francisco Bay Area. Los Angeles entered the century with a paltry population of

102,479. In the first three decades of the twentieth century, however, more than a million people would settle in the City of Angels, bringing its population to 1,238,048 by 1930, a feat of growth surpassing even the rise of San Francisco in the nineteenth century. Southern California as a whole was taking in another two-million-plus citizens. The decades from 1900 to 1930, then, witnessed this overnight creation of metropolitan Los Angeles, San Diego, and Southern California as new American places.

The majority of these newcomers to Southern California were white people from the Midwest. Nine tenths of Los Angelenos by 1926, for example, were of European descent. On the other hand, the city also supported challenged but persistent Japanese American, Mexican American, and African American communities. Between 1910 and 1924, thanks to an agreement between Japan and the United States, some thirty thousand Japanese women migrated to the United States, most of them for marriages arranged according to ancient Japanese custom to *issei,* first-generation immigrants, from their local regions. The arrival of these young women, followed by their marriages and childbearing, saved the Japanese from following in the footsteps of the Chinese in the nineteenth century after further immigration was prohibited by the Exclusion Acts of 1882, 1892, and 1902, which is to say, remaining a population of isolated and aging men. Circumscribed by the Alien Land Act of 1913 (augmented in 1920), which prohibited *issei* from owning property, the Japanese of California, centered in Japantowns in Los Angeles, San Francisco, Sacramento, and San José, nevertheless Americanized at a rapid rate, especially in the American-born *nisei* generation, born in the 1920s and raised in a world of public schools, sandlot baseball, and Boy Scouts.

Between 1920 and 1930, the Mexican American population of the city of Los Angeles, the single largest minority group in the city, tripled from 33,644 to 97,116. Los Angeles thus surpassed San Antonio, Texas, as the leading Mexican American community in the United States. Los Angeles County had a Mexican American population of 167,000 by 1930, more than in all but a few large cities in Mexico. Most of this growth came from children born in the United States; nearly half of the Mexican American families of the region had five or more children. Blue-collar labor in metropolitan Los Angeles in meatpacking, tire manufacture, auto assembly, and other manual jobs was significantly Mexican American. Despite the overwhelmingly American nature of this community, however, millions of Mexican immigrants, including their American-born children, were forcibly repatriated to Mexico during the early 1930s by the federal government in a program that can only be described as ethnic cleansing. The spectacle of thousands of Mexican people being assembled at local stations with their luggage and hastily wrapped belongings prior to being stuffed into crowded trains for shipment back to Mexico would prompt chilling comparisons with the even more ominous deportations of Europe soon to begin, and it foreshadowed the removal from the Pacific Coast in early 1942 of all people of Japanese ancestry, citizen and noncitizen alike.

The African American population of Los Angeles was small (approximately five thousand) and prosperous, and tended to vote Republican. By the 1920s, the black community was coalescing in and around the Watts subdivision in south central Los Angeles, annexed to Los Angeles in 1926. As the number of African Americans in Los Angeles grew, however, they lost their quasi-protected status (*Los Angeles Times* editor Harrison Gray Otis was an ardent champion of the black community) and came up against the hardening of racial attitudes and more explicit color line characteristic of the rest of the United States. Housing restrictions led to de facto segregation in schools. Jim Crow practices, cruel and insulting, were everywhere. In the city of Los Angeles, for example, blacks were allowed to swim in public swimming pools only on the day before the pool was scheduled to be drained. Yet like the other minority communities, African Americans in Los Angeles showed resilience and a desire for a better life. This was the community, after all, that was even then in the process of nurturing the talents of future Nobel Prize winner Ralph Bunche, architect Paul Williams, and mayor Tom Bradley.

The white majority of Southern California, Los Angeles especially, could be divided into three categories: Oligarchs, Babbitts, and Folks. The Oligarchs consisted of older Southern California families (Banning, Bixby, Patton, Hellman, Newmark), now in their second or third generation of wealth, or, in the case of oilmen Edward Doheny and George Getty, enjoying first-generation wealth of great magnitude. Oil, in fact, created the industrial infrastructure of Southern California beginning in the 1890s. By the 1920s, oilmen such as Doheny and Getty and the corporations they formed were presiding over a vast industrial infrastructure producing millions of barrels each year. The Los Angeles Basin alone in 1924 produced 230 million barrels of crude oil and 300 billion cubic feet of natural gas. Pumps and derricks were everywhere, extending into the ocean itself. Southern California even had its oil scandals, including the indictment and trial of Doheny in 1930 on bribery charges. (Doheny was acquitted of offering the $100,000 cash bribe that Interior Secretary Albert B. Fall was convicted of taking.) Already, however, despite his acquittal, Doheny was a broken man, having lost his son Edward Jr. to murder in February 1929, a watershed event in the social history of the city. "Oildorado," as it was called, even had its own Ponzi scheme, perpetrated by salesman Chauncey C. Julian, a onetime Texas oil field roustabout, who bilked some forty thousand investors before fleeing to Shanghai, where he committed suicide. A smaller subsector of Oligarchs—entrepreneur Abbot Kinney, for example, developer H. Gaylord Wilshire, and banker Joseph Sartori—were known as the "New Men," as were such young lawyers on the rise as Jackson Graves and Henry O'Melveny.

The Babbitts represented the newly arrived middle classes: the corporation executives, the bankers and lawyers, the doctors, the real estate developers, the automobile dealers such as Earl C. Anthony, whose Packard dealership first brought neon light to Los Angeles in 1922 and sold a way of life to its middle-class clientele along with each shiny new automobile. That middle-class way of life was centered on clubs: city clubs (the Los Angeles telephone directory listed two hundred of them by 1927), golf and tennis clubs, and more than fifteen beach clubs between Malibu and Venice.

Farther down the socioeconomic ladder but predominant in numbers were the Folks: white Anglo-Saxon Protestants from the Midwest, American Gothic in background and style, many of them in late middle age, most of them from rural or small-town backgrounds, undergoing urbanization for the first time. Once a year they would gather for the state association picnics sponsored by the Federation of State Societies of Los Angeles and the All-States Society of Long Beach that would bring thousands of ex-Midwesterners (the Iowa Society averaged 125,000 attendance for its picnics) for daylong festivals of reunion and reminiscence accompanied by fried chicken, potato salad, and hard-boiled eggs. Evangelical and fundamentalist in their religious preferences, the Folks flocked to church on Sunday, and after 1926, when religious radio station KGEF went on the air, were wont to listen to the Reverend Robert Shuler, the Savonarola of the Southland, as he scolded sinners and errant politicians.

The epicenter of religiosity for the Folks was the new (as of January 1923) $1.5 million Angelus Temple on the northwest edge of Echo Park in Los Angeles. There, of a Sunday morning, evangelist Aimee Semple McPherson—a charismatic preacher given to flamboyant theatricality—preached to congregations of four thousand and more Folks (the temple seated 4,300) her "Foursquare Gospel" of evangelical healing and hope. Weekly sermons were announced from an electric marquee over the temple entrance, as in a motion picture palace. Entering the temple on a motorcycle in a policeman's uniform, McPherson placed sin under arrest and urged her audience not to speed to ruin. Prodding him with a pitchfork, she chased the Devil from the stage. Dressed as a USC football player, she urged her congregation to carry the ball for Christ. Dressed as a nurse, she prayed over the sick. McPherson's healing ministry, in fact, was at the core of her success, since so many of the Folks had come to Southern California in late middle or old age in the hope of regaining lost health. By the late 1920s, a special display area at the temple featured the canes, crutches, and braces that so many of the Folks, now healed, no longer found necessary.

It was easy to make a living in this booming economy. The construction of the Los Angeles Aqueduct kept thousands employed between 1907 and 1913. Agriculture and related activities (packing, shipping, canning, food processing) continued to offer seasonal and regular employment, as did transportation and shipping via two railroads, two large streetcar companies, and the fourth busiest port in the nation. With home building constant across three decades, there was an expanding job sector in the building trades. The oil industry was producing 106 million barrels a year by 1920, a quarter of a million barrels of it coming from Signal Hill south of Los Angeles. More tires were manufactured in Greater Los Angeles than in any place other than Akron, Ohio. More automobiles were being assembled than in any city other than Detroit. The hotel and tourist industry gained even further strength, along with two new economic sectors, aviation and motion pictures. An ambitious fishing industry grew up among the Portuguese in San Diego and the Japanese in San Pedro. Consciously designing itself as the Gibraltar of the Pacific, the city of San Diego wooed and secured the large and permanent presence of the Navy and the Marine Corps. So, too, did the Port of Long Beach become an important naval installation. Numerous colleges and universities, dominated by a rapidly expanding University of Southern California and the newly established University of California at Los Angeles, sustained large payrolls.

These were the late teens and 1920s, after all, a time of prosperity and well-being across the nation in general and Southern California in particular. Nowhere was this more evident than in the ambitious construction projects of the era, not only in the housing tracts initiated by such mega-developers as Harry Culver and Alphonso Bell, but also in such ambitious structures as Myron Hunt's nine-hundred-room Ambassador Hotel (1919) on Wilshire Boulevard, with its wildly popular Cocoanut Grove nightclub; the Coliseum and Rose Bowl stadiums (1921); the Biltmore Hotel (1923) at Fifth and Olive facing Pershing Square in the downtown sector, designed in opulent Italian and Spanish Revival motifs by the firm Schultze and Weaver; the Central Library of Los Angeles designed by Bertram Goodhue and Carleton Winslow (1926); Robert Farquhar's California Club (1929); and the new and expanding university campuses.

By 1929, then, Southern California had emerged into the sunlight as both an imagined and a fully materialized American place. It had been a rapid rise, resembling the construction of a set at a motion picture studio; indeed, the set for the film *Intolerance* (1916) between Sunset and Hollywood boulevards might very well stand as a paradigm for the interconnection of the nascent film industry and the rising region. Intended to depict the essence of the city of Babylon at the height of its power, the three-hundred-foot-high set—inspired by the Tower of Jewels at the Panama Pacific International Exposition—functioned, like the expositions recently concluded in San Francisco and San Diego, as a dream city referencing the past and suggesting the future. Not surprisingly, it was left intact for more than a decade after director D. W. Griffith finished filming his epic spectacle. No sooner was it dismantled than Los Angeles erected a second monument to its emergent identity as Babylon on the Pacific: its new City Hall (1928), designed by the firm of Parkinson, Martin, and Austin, topped by a Halicarnassan ziggurat. In raising the ancient temple, a symbol of power and wealth, above its skyline, Los Angeles suggested the sheer influx of people and capital that had brought the region into being over the past thirty years.

Far from retarding such growth, the Great Depression of the 1930s witnessed the continuing creation of a statewide infrastructure as the state and federal governments sponsored ambitious programs of public works that, in effect, completed California. The dangers of reordering California through public works, however, became painfully apparent on the night of March 12, 1928, when the St. Francis Dam near the town of Saugus in Los Angeles County, part of the Los Angeles water system, catastrophically collapsed. The tidal wave released killed some four hundred people and devastated everything in its path as it swept down to the sea.

Still, for there to be a modern California—extensive in population, its people and economy served by water and electricity—work on the infrastructure had to continue, whatever the risks. Thanks to the sponsorship of President Herbert Hoover, a Californian, the monumental Boulder Dam (later named in his honor)—the most formidable dam up to that time in human history—was constructed between 1931 and 1935 on the Colorado River at the Nevada-Arizona border. Water from Lake Mead, created by the Hoover Dam, together with the hydroelectricity generated by the dam's turbines, arrived in Southern California in the late 1930s, thanks to an equally impressive delivery system built by the Metropolitan Water District, and formed the water and electrical basis for the preeminence of

Southern California as a defense manufacturing center during the Second World War.

Central California would be equally served by the Central Valley Project, first envisioned in 1919, on which the federal Bureau of Reclamation began construction in 1935. Based on reservoirs created by four enormous dams—Shasta (1944) and Keswick (1950) on the Sacramento River, Folsom (1955) on the American, and Friant (1949) on the San Joaquin—the Central Valley Project would eventually organize the interior of California into one fully integrated system of dams, reservoirs, canals, pumping stations, and power plants.

So, too, would state and county roadways be necessary for a population increasingly wedded to the private automobile. By the end of 1924, approximately 310,000 automobiles—more than the total number of automobiles registered in the state of New York—were daily entering Los Angeles, where the corner of Adams and Figueroa, passed by 69,797 cars a day, was the busiest intersection in the United States. By 1933, streetcar usage in Los Angeles had halved since its peak year of 1924. By 1935 it had halved once again. Metropolitan Los Angeles was an integrated plain, hence amenable to automobile traffic via the great boulevards—Figueroa, Pico, Western, Olympic, Wilshire, Sunset—that were either inaugurated or expanded in the 1920s. In March 1938, construction began on the Arroyo Seco Parkway linking Pasadena and downtown Los Angeles on a continuously moving basis, with no intersections. Dedicated on December 30, 1940, just two days before the annual Tournament of Roses, the parkway anticipated the freeway system of post–World War II California. In Northern California, the Caldecott Tunnel, punched with much difficulty through the Contra Costa Range in 1937, likewise linked to automotive traffic the Bay Area and the spacious plain of Contra Costa.

The Bay Area comprised a series of land masses separated by

water. By the mid-1920s some fifty thousand commuters were entering and leaving the city of San Francisco each day via ferry, making the San Francisco Ferry Building the busiest terminal in the world outside Charing Cross Station in London. The growing automobile culture, however, was creating pressure to unify the Bay Area through bridges. As early as 1853, San Franciscans had been talking about the possibility of a bridge linking their city to Oakland on the East Bay shore. The completion of the railroad in 1869 intensified such talk, since the city of San Francisco could be approached by rail only from San José via the San Francisco peninsula. Already in 1906, the Southern Pacific had spanned the southern portion of San Francisco Bay with a low-level trestle across the shoals and mudflats between Dumbarton Point and Palo Alto. A parallel span for automobiles was added in 1927. Also completed in 1927 was a bridge across the Carquinez Strait in the North Bay, followed in 1929 by a low-level trestle between San Mateo and Hayward. Already, as the secretary of commerce in the Harding and Coolidge administrations, Herbert Hoover, a Stanford-trained engineer, was spearheading discussions regarding a great bridge linking Oakland and San Francisco. As president, Hoover directed the Reconstruction Finance Corporation to purchase $62 million in state bonds from the California Toll Bridge Authority toward the construction of such a bridge. The federal Public Works Authority authorized another $15.2 million in loans and grants, bringing the total budget for the bridge to $77.2 million, which made the San Francisco–Oakland Bay Bridge, dedicated in November 1936, one of the most expensive public works projects in American history.

As if this bridge were not enough, the counties surrounding San Francisco Bay, joined by Del Norte County on the Oregon border (eager to bring automotive tourists into the Redwood Empire), organized the Golden Gate Bridge and Highway District in 1923 to realize yet another persistent Bay Area ambition:

a bridge across the Golden Gate Strait between San Francisco and Marin County, thereby linking the Bay Area directly to the North Coast. For many years prior, engineer Joseph Strauss had been advocating such a span. In November 1930, voters in the district authorized the issuance of $35 million in bonds to construct a bridge across the Golden Gate, with Strauss serving as chief engineer. Strauss had in hand a stunning design by Charles Alton Ellis, professor of engineering at the University of Illinois. A theoretical mathematician turned structural engineer (and in his spare time a student of classical Greek), Ellis designed a suspension system that, combined with the architectural stylizations of San Francisco architect Irving Morrow and a color scheme based on international orange, resulted in a bridge—built between January 1933 and April 1937—that not only linked the San Francisco peninsula to the North Coast but created a masterpiece of art and engineering that ranks, so its historian John van der Zee has justifiably claimed, with the Parthenon as a harmonization of site and structure, nature and public work. Soon the Golden Gate Bridge, like the Brooklyn Bridge, asserted itself as an icon of American civilization.

The financing of the Golden Gate Bridge by the Bank of America, which bought the district's bonds, underscores the importance of banking during this period. Thanks to the Bank of America and to the Security Pacific Bank of Southern California, California enjoyed the ability to raise the capital necessary for the public and private works of this era.

As a boy, Amadeo Peter Giannini witnessed his father, a San José rancher, being shot to death by a disgruntled employee over a disputed sum of less than two dollars. Small sums could mean everything to little people, as young Giannini had learned in the most tragic way possible. Entering the family produce business at the age of twelve, Giannini became a financial success before he was thirty. In 1904 he opened the Bank of Italy in San Francisco. In May 1908 Giannini attended a speech in Pasadena by

Princeton president Woodrow Wilson in which Wilson complained that American banks restricted their services to the affluent. Inspired by Wilson's remarks, Giannini toured western Canada, where a system of branch banking was in operation. In 1909 Giannini established the first Bank of Italy branch outside San Francisco, in San José. Another branch, in San Mateo, followed in 1912. By 1922, the Bank of Italy had a total of sixty-two branches extending from Chico to San Diego. Giannini believed, correctly, that he could build large concentrations of capital from the small deposits of ordinary Californians. At his insistence, shares in the Bank of Italy were sold to as many investors as possible, with no one being allowed to acquire a dominant interest. Giannini also believed in making loans, provided that the recipient be a man or woman of proven character (not necessarily great assets) and be willing, in the case of a business, to accept the bank's advice as to its development.

Thus the Bank of Italy helped reverse the prevailing notion that a bank loan was a privilege. Giannini's philosophy was adhered to as well by another Italian American banker, Joseph F. Sartori, the founder (in 1888) of the Security Savings Bank of Los Angeles, who also went into branch banking and lending with equal gusto. Thus, the Bank of America, as the Bank of Italy became in 1930, and Sartori's Security and Trust Savings were on hand for the first three decades of the twentieth century to finance the construction of homes, hotels, office buildings, and regulated public utilities in the private sector, and—especially in the case of the Bank of America—to back publicly issued bonds for construction projects such as the Golden Gate Bridge. Owing to Giannini's background in agriculture, the Bank of Italy/America was especially active in financing the rise of California agriculture, as well as the rise of Hollywood in the same period. During the Depression, an active loan program by the bank enabled innumerable farmers to keep their properties and an even larger number of Californians to refinance their homes. Because of the Bank of Italy/America, the Security Trust, and the other banks of the state (among them Wells Fargo, the Bank of California, the Anglo-California Bank, and the Crocker Bank), California escaped becoming an economic colony of the East or the property of offshore investors through most of the twentieth century.

The completion of the two great bridges gave rise to the idea of an exposition to be built on the protruding shoals and mudflats adjacent to Yerba Buena Island in San Francisco Bay, which would then serve as an airport for land-based and sea-based aircraft. It took eighteen months, from February 1936 to August 1937, to create Treasure Island atop the shoals, and another two years to build there the ambitious Golden Gate International Exposition celebrating Latin America and the Asia-Pacific Basin and the developing relationship of California with these regions. Like the 1915 expositions, it was a City Beautiful stage set featuring rectilinearly orchestrated courts, exhibition halls, open spaces, and promenades, dominated by architect Timothy Pflueger's "Court of Pacifica" from which rose sculptor Ralph Stackpole's eighty-foot-high statue of that name, intended to be placed after the exposition closed on a promontory overlooking the Bay as a westward-oriented Statue of Liberty. Unfortunately, Pearl Harbor necessitated a change in plans. The Navy commandeered Treasure Island when the United States declared war on Japan, and in 1942, with no other alternative possible at the time, the statue was demolished.

Whatever California was to become could nonetheless be glimpsed in the paradigms and prophetic patterns discernible as by night a river of headlights flowed down the Arroyo Seco Parkway linking Pasadena and Los Angeles, and as midway up the coast an illumined Golden Gate International Exposition radiated color and light from Treasure Island, a dream city, an Atlantis recalled from the sea.

8

MAKING IT HAPPEN

Labor Through the Great Depression and Beyond

Preparing citrus for shipment, the early 1930s

CALIFORNIA STATE LIBRARY

The Great Depression came late to California, and it came more subtly because the California economy was diversified into agricultural, industrial, entertainment, tourist, and service sectors; hence it could not be crippled as completely as was the case in many of the industrialized states of the Northeast, so dependent upon manufacture, or Midwestern states whose economy was based on agriculture. Nevertheless, the Depression did come to California by the early 1930s, and the resulting social strife was compounded by the structural instability of the agricultural workforce; a militant labor movement in the San Francisco Bay Area; a labor-resistant oligarchy, especially in Southern California; and, among working people, a radical tradition going back to the nineteenth century.

The sandlot riots in San Francisco in the 1870s and the brief influence of the Workingmen's Party leading up to the second constitutional convention underscored the foundations of California in labor. The Gold Rush was an epic of personal labor in which men of every social background sought their fortunes through the work of their hands. In the Mother Lode, it was no disgrace to do physical work, and this inserted a labor-oriented egalitarianism into the California formula. Those who remained in the service economy during this period, meanwhile, were doing extremely well through the work of their hands. A carpenter could make as much as $14 a day as of 1849. An unskilled laborer could make up to $8, and a skilled washerwoman could charge up to $20 to do a load of laundry. Since labor for hire in the cities and towns was scarce—most people preferring to be in the mines—the workers of California organized themselves almost immediately. The carpenters and joiners of San Francisco, for example, struck for $16 a day in November 1849 and received something approaching that compensation. By 1859, the topographers and teamsters of San Francisco had organized the first two labor unions in the state. As the manufacturing sector developed—stimulated by the rise of, among other enterprises, the Union Iron Works of San Francisco—so, too, did the union movement keep pace. By 1863, San Francisco had the Trade Union Council representing fifteen labor organizations and as many as three thousand workers. Even Chinese workers, who later bore the brunt of white trade unionist resentment, organized. In June 1867 the Chinese struck the Central Pacific, demanding twelve-hour days and $40 a month. The demand by organized labor for an eight-hour day was pioneered in the mid-1860s in San Francisco. As a political force, the eight-hour crusade helped send Irish-born Eugene Casserly, a Democrat, to the U.S. Senate in 1869.

The developing strength of the unionist movement in San Francisco during the 1860s set the stage for the violence and turmoil of the 1870s when a nationwide depression destroyed the local economy and San Francisco was already filled with former railroad construction workers, now the angry unemployed. The Chinese were seen as a special threat. They, too, could make bricks, do road work, do joining and carpentry, and otherwise compete. Already, the Chinese were in the process of constructing a series of levees throughout the lower Sacramento Valley and Delta region that constituted a reclamation project of great ambition. Without the levees then being built by the Chinese, agriculture could not have been established on such an extensive basis in the Sacramento Valley.

While a number of family farms had been developed prior to 1870—especially in Northern California on the Santa Cruz peninsula and in Marin, Sonoma, and Napa counties—the great wheat ranches developed in the 1870s, vast acreages worked by phalanxes of seasonal labor, constituted a more predominant model. Wheat king Hugh James Glenn, a dentist from Missouri, was by 1880 producing more than half a million bushels of wheat per year on fifty-five thousand acres in Colusa County. So enormous were his holdings that an entire new county was carved out of Colusa in 1891, nine years after Glenn's death, and named in his memory. The creation of irrigation districts in the 1880s and 1890s, together with the introduction of the refrigerated railroad car during the latter part of this period, accelerated the development of California as an agricultural state.

The problem was that these great fields of grain, these vineyards and hop ranches, these orchards and citrus groves, these fields teeming with potatoes, lettuce, and every variety of vegetable, these cotton fields in the southern San Joaquin, each required intense seasonal labor at planting and harvesttime and only small cadres of permanent workers in between. Thus a pattern of migratory labor grew up in California—starting with the wheat ranches—in which large numbers of migrant workers would converge on an area at harvesttime, perform the work, then move on to another crop. It was a world of single men, bunking in barracks while on the job, then shoving off, their belongings and bedrolls slung across their shoulders. Photographs from the 1880s and 1890s reveal these men to be predominantly whites and Chinese. Photographs from the early 1900s show that Japanese and East Indian workers were now in the fields. Photographs from the 1920s show even further diversification: Filipinos, especially on the Monterey Peninsula; African Americans in the southern San Joaquin; Mexicans throughout Southern California, including the newly irrigated Imperial Valley.

In cities and fields alike, as well as in ports and on the sea, there was agitation and strife as working people sought to better their lot. Under the leadership of Frank Roney of the Moulders

Union, the San Francisco Trades Assembly was revitalized in 1881, gathering fifty unions into concerted action. By 1885 the Federated Trades and Labor Council had absorbed the assembly into an even larger federation. Himself a workingman, Roney—the Samuel Gompers of California, a non-ideologue—rejected the Marxist-Socialist theories then coming into vogue in favor of more practical negotiation of working conditions and contracts. Roney's contemporary Burnette Haskell, by contrast—a lawyer and a journalist by profession, not a workingman—preferred more radical solutions such as those proposed by the International Workingmen's Association, a study club for socialist and anarchist theory that Haskell organized in San Francisco in June 1884. Secretly, if we are to judge from his notebooks, Haskell was ever daydreaming of a worker insurrection leading to the seizure of power by labor. Across the nation, in fact, violence and the threat of violence were in the air, as was vividly evident when a bomb exploded, thrown perhaps by an *agent provocateur,* in Haymarket Square in Chicago on May 4, 1886, during a rally for an eight-hour workday. Seven policemen and four demonstrators were killed, and more than one hundred demonstrators were wounded. Eight anarchist leaders were tried and convicted on no evidence whatsoever. Four were hanged, and one committed suicide; the remaining three served seven years in prison before being pardoned. This was in Chicago, true; but it reflected the temper of the times in the Bay Area as well, as Haskell and an undetermined number of his colleagues discussed violent action.

In his more practical moments, Haskell did effective legal work on behalf of the Coast Seamen's Union, organized in San Francisco in 1885 in an effort to secure better rights for ship's crews who were still working under eighteenth-century conditions, including semi-sanctioned floggings at sea. Joining the Coast Seamen's Union in June 1885, Andrew Furuseth, a Norwegian-born seaman and labor activist, brought that organization new strength, amalgamating it with the Steamship Sailors Union in July 1891 to form the Sailors Union of the Pacific, one of the most successful unions of its kind and size in the country. Thanks to Furuseth and his union, President Woodrow Wilson in March 1915 signed the Seamen's Act, intended to remove the last vestiges of forced servitude from life before the mast.

Another member of the Coast Seamen's Union, the German-born sailor Alfred Fuhrman—who had begun his union career as a disciple of Burnette Haskell—qualified for the bar but remained in the union movement. Fuhrman turned his attention to the bakers and brewers of San Francisco, the industrial serfs of the city. Bakers worked fourteen hours a day, seven days a week, and were required to live in cramped dormitories at or near their work sites. Brewers worked similar hours in similar conditions for $15 a week. Employers encouraged them to drink beer during the day to keep up their strength, which resulted in a pervasive temptation to drunkenness. Organizing some two hundred of the estimated eight hundred brewery workers in the city into the Brewers and Maltsters Union of the Pacific Coast, Fuhrman led a strike in May 1887 that got the members of his union a raise from $15 to $17 per six-day week, together with the right to live outside the dormitories.

A depression struck the nation in 1893, as it had in 1873, and like the 1870s, the 1890s represented a setback for the labor movement throughout the nation and in California. A citywide San Francisco labor council was organized in December 1892, but it lost just about every strike it sponsored throughout the decade. Most working San Franciscans continued to work a twelve-hour day, and the bakers of the city did not secure a six-day week until 1900. A citywide strike led by the newly formed Teamsters Union raged throughout the summer and fall of 1901. Two hundred ships stood idle in the Bay. An equal number of special police, hired by Mayor James Duval Phelan, escorted nonstriking teamsters around the city. Five workers lost their lives in violent clashes, and there were more than 250 serious assaults. The Reverend Peter Yorke, an Irish-born Roman Catholic priest with intense pro-union sentiments, did his best to upbraid the nominally Catholic Phelan for his suppression of the strike. Yorke based his arguments on the rights of labor as set forth by Pope Leo XIII in his 1891 encyclical *Rerum Novarum*. Appealing directly to Governor Henry Gage, Yorke and the strike leaders brought the governor in to enforce a settlement. Phelan was humiliated and did not run for reelection.

The momentum created by the General Strike of 1901, as it came to be called, led to the formation of the Union Labor Party in San Francisco, which held power through the tenure of two mayors elected from their ranks: orchestra leader Eugene "Handsome Gene" Schmitz, president of the Musicians' Union, followed by the County Limerick–born Patrick Henry "Pin Head" McCarthy, president of the Building Trades Council. Schmitz was removed from office in 1907 for corruption, a conviction that was later overturned on appeal, allowing the genial musician to return to public life as a city supervisor. McCarthy (despite the nickname that plagued him throughout his life) did a more than creditable job as mayor until he left office in 1912 to prosper in construction and investments and to build for himself an imposing redwood mansion in the Ashbury Heights section of the city. McCarthy's successor as mayor, the flamboyant James "Sunny Jim" Rolph, Jr., a self-made shipping millionaire, although a Republican, maintained excellent relations with the unions of San Francisco during the next two decades.

In this as in other things, San Francisco contrasted greatly with Los Angeles, where *Los Angeles Times* publisher Harrison Gray Otis, the dominant force in the city, was a vociferous opponent of unions. In the course of a strike by the metal trades, the headquarters of the *Times* was bombed on the morning of October 1, 1910. Twenty employees were killed and seventeen injured. Mayor George Alexander called in the well-known private detective William J. Burns, who soon fingered three culprits: Ortie McManigal, a radical with a taste for dynamite; James McNamara; and McNamara's brother John, an official of the Bridge and Structural Iron Workers Union. The McNamara brothers protested their innocence, claiming a frame-up, and many believed them, including their lawyer, Clarence Darrow, until the brothers abruptly confessed. When it was over, McManigal and the McNamara brothers were serving life sentences and some thirty-three union members were convicted of various degrees of complicity in the crime. In many ways, the *Times* bombing severely impeded the union movement in Los Angeles for the next quarter of a century.

Two years later, in 1912, San Diego found itself in an equally bitter dock strike spearheaded by the Industrial Workers of the World (IWW), a loose federation of anarchists (hence a very loosely organized movement indeed) founded in Chicago in 1905. Energized by a theoretically hazy but psychologically potent amalgam of romantic anarchism, Marxist socialism, and a distinctly American distrust of big shots, the IWW movement looked to the workers of the United States eventually to seize the state and establish an industrial utopia. Their quasi-pacifism, moreover, did not discourage members from resorting to violence to achieve such ends; and it was this capacity for violence—in fact as well as in rhetoric—that gave the IWW its dreaded reputation. By 1909, there were IWW locals in San Francisco, Los Angeles, Redlands, and Holtville in the Imperial Valley. Now dubbed "the Wobblies" by the *Los Angeles Times,* the IWW favored free-speech confrontations and strike actions. Between April 1910 and March 1911, Wobblies flooded Fresno, demonstrating continuously and filling the jails to capacity.

In 1912, the Wobblies took on San Diego, then in the course of a dock strike. Alarmed by what had happened in Fresno, the San Diego oligarchy was more than ready for the Wobblies, and throughout February and March 1912 the otherwise serene city of San Diego resembled a real-life version of Sergei Eisenstein's later film *Potemkin* (1925) as cops and vigilantes pulled incoming Wobblies off trains, took them into custody, and roughed them up, forcing them to run violent gauntlets. When a crowd of five thousand protesters gathered outside the city jail, high-pressure fire hoses were used to disperse the crowd. At least one detainee was beaten to death. On May 4, 1912, two San Diego police officers shot and killed an IWW member in front of the IWW headquarters. At the height of the tension, Emma Goldman, the Russian-born high priestess of anarchy, and her lover, Ben Reitman, arrived in San Diego on a lecture tour. A hostile mob gathered outside the U.S. Grant Hotel where they were staying. That night, Reitman was kidnapped, tortured, forced to kiss the American flag and sing "The Star-Spangled Banner," tarred and feathered, then put back on the same 2:45 owl train on which Goldman was also forcibly boarded.

The very next year, on August 13, 1913, a deadly riot in the hopfields of Wheatland in southern Yuba County in the Sacramento Valley created yet another IWW scare. Given the seasonal nature of harvest work in California, living conditions for migrant workers were by and large appalling. Nowhere was this more true than on the Ralph Durst hop ranch outside Wheatland. In the early summer of 1913, Durst had spread circulars throughout California, southern Oregon, and northwestern Nevada advertising harvest work on his ranch. By late July some 2,800 men, women, and children—approximately one third of them people of color—had flooded onto the Durst ranch in search of work. Living conditions were more horrible than usual (there were as few as eight toilet sheds for the entire workforce), and wages averaged $1.50 a day, with workers expected to pay for their own food and water (temperatures frequently soared to 120 degrees) from Durst-owned concessions. With the help of IWW activists, a strike action was organized. Ralph

Durst called in the sheriff, a posse of sheriff's deputies, and the district attorney of Yuba County. When this group confronted a crowd of workers listening to IWW activist Richard "Blackie" Ford, a bench on which some workers were standing collapsed, startling the crowd. Scuffling ensued, which led to fistfights. Someone began swinging a two-by-four as a club. A deputy fired a shotgun into the air, trying, as he later said, to sober the crowd into cooperation. Instead, more gunfire broke out, some twenty shots in all, this time from within the mêlée. The deputies fought their way back to their automobiles and sped off. When the crowd dispersed, five prostrate forms were revealed on the ground: the sheriff, clubbed into unconsciousness but still alive, together with the dead bodies of the district attorney, a sheriff's deputy, and two unidentified workers. The IWW fled the scene, leaving the impression that they were responsible for the violence. A manhunt ensued, with the usual round of arrests and beatings. Eventually, two IWW activists, Blackie Ford and Herman Suhr, were tried, convicted, and sentenced to life in prison.

The scene was set for another six years of growing tensions. On July 22, 1916, a bomb went off on lower Market Street in San Francisco in the course of a Preparedness Day parade intended to display the American readiness for war, if and when war should come. Ten people were killed and more than forty injured. Historian Curt Gentry makes a good case that a German *agent provocateur* most likely set off the bomb, but the evidence Gentry cites never surfaced in the days following the explosion, nor was there any suspicion of German involvement. Instead, a radical socialist leader by the name of Tom Mooney and his associate Warren Knox Billings were arrested, charged, and put through a near–kangaroo trial in which District Attorney Charles Fickert used fabricated and altered evidence, together with perjured testimony, to win death for Mooney, life for Billings. Even though Mooney's sentence was later commuted to life, the Mooney/Billings convictions remained the Dreyfus case of California for the next twenty-plus years: a rallying point for the left and those offended by the obvious railroading of the two, which no doubt played a role in the decision of Governor William Stephens to commute Mooney's sentence to life.

On the other hand, Stephens was also willing to sign into law on April 30, 1919, the Criminal Syndicalism Act just passed by the legislature. The act declared it a felony, punishable by one to fourteen years in prison, to advocate or in any other way to promulgate violence as a means of "accomplishing a change in industrial ownership or control or effecting any political changes." Merely to belong to an organization advocating such doctrines constituted a felony. Passed at the height of the nationwide anti-Red hysteria following World War I, the California Criminal Syndicalism Act was a draconian measure specifically directed against the IWW. By 1921 forty Wobblies were doing time in San Quentin, convicted under this act, which lasted on the books until 1968, when the Ninth Circuit of the U.S. Court of Appeals declared it unconstitutional.

Thus the stage was set for violent confrontations between capital and labor during the 1930s. For all its seeming amiability, its self-propagated and self-authenticated image of itself as a free and easy society, California had at the center of its complexity a tendency toward the hard right, evident as early as the San Francisco vigilance committees of 1851, 1856, and 1877. This was a state, after all, in which a hard-nosed corporation, the Southern Pacific, exercised significant political and economic control into the early twentieth century. It was also an agricultural state in which farming was conducted on a quasi-industrial basis and most big farmers were living close to the edge. It was also—outside San Francisco and Los Angeles—a suburban and small-town state, characterized by conservative political values. On the other hand, it was also a left-wing state, with a militant labor union tradition that, like the vigilance committees, dated back to the 1850s. In the 1870s, again in San Francisco, it had nurtured a workers' radicalism that Lord James Bryce, writing in *The American Commonwealth* (1888), would later describe as a form of Marxism running out ahead of Karl Marx himself. The IWW had found a receptive environment in California, and so in the 1930s would the Communist Party.

California entered the Great Depression with a pervasively moderate Republican orientation, tinged by reformist Progressivism. To the right could be found hard-nosed corporate oligarchs, busy perfecting a number of merchants' and manufacturers' associations, a cadre of ultraconservative ranchers, many of them of Southern ancestry, and the usual assortment of nuts. To the left could be found not the mainstream unions, for Samuel Gompers and the American Federation of Labor kept such unions oriented to the center, but old-fashioned socialists (especially in Oakland, Berkeley, and Los Angeles), remnants of the IWW, utopian radicals of various persuasions, disciplined and dedicated Communists . . . and the usual assortment of nuts. Thus the stage was set for a dramatic confrontation between left and right that mirrored the larger struggle between fascism and communism in Europe.

In 1927 the improbable happened. Mexican American field workers—most of them living in Jim Crow conditions on the margins of society—organized the pioneering Confederación de Uniones Obreras Mexicanas, or the Confederation of Mexican Workers, with twenty locals throughout Southern California. In the Imperial Valley, 2,746 Mexican workers, with the assistance of the Mexican consul general in Calexico, formed a local that initially called itself the Imperial Valley Workers Union but backed off that designation as being too confrontational, calling itself instead the Mexican Mutual Aid Society of Imperial Valley. Whatever its name, it was a union; and in May 1928, just before the start of the cantaloupe harvest, the organization submitted a list of demands for wages and working conditions.

Once again, the local sheriff plunged into action, arresting union leaders on the flimsiest of charges. The Red Scare was immediately launched. The union protested directly to the president of Mexico, who protested to the president of the United States, who sent a state department official to the Imperial Valley to investigate. Despite such official resistance, the sheer magnitude of what had been accomplished—the organization of a Mexican agricultural workers' union—was not lost on either the growers or the workers of California.

DURING THE GREAT DEPRESSION, California was flooded with more than three hundred thousand agricultural workers—not Asians or Mexicans this time, but white Americans from the Great Plains and the Southwest, the drought and Depression–stricken dust bowls of Texas, Arkansas, Kansas, Missouri, and, most dramatically, Oklahoma, whence the generic pejorative epithet for all such people, "Okies," was derived. By the middle of 1934, there were 142 agricultural workers in California for every one hundred jobs. Wages plummeted by more than fifty percent. In May 1928, for example, Mexican workers in the Imperial Valley were receiving seventy-five cents an hour for picking cantaloupes. Between April and June 1933, many of them were working for as little as fifteen cents an hour.

Enter the Communists, specifically the Cannery and Agricultural Workers Industrial Union (CAWIU), founded by the Trade Union Unity League, a national organization chaired by William Zebulon Foster, the Communist Party candidate for president in 1924 and 1928. When eight thousand Mexican, Filipino, Chinese, Japanese, and Sikh workers—led by the Mexican Mutual Aid Society—went out on strike in the Imperial Valley in January 1930, organizers from the CAWIU hastened to their assistance. Their key contributions were the automobile and the mimeograph machine. The CAWIU activists cranked out thousands of leaflets—in English, Spanish, Chinese, Japanese, Tagalog, and Slavonian—together with a Spanish-language newsletter, and spread them via automobile throughout the Imperial Valley, provoking further organization and strike action. Empowered by the Criminal Syndicalism Act, police, sheriff's deputies, American Legion vigilantes, the district attorney, and the courts launched what by now had become the almost standard counteroffensive of Red Scare roundups, arrests, harassments, indictments, and trials. Nine union leaders were convicted of criminal syndicalism. Five of them, including a Japanese American, were sentenced to three to forty-two years in Folsom or San Quentin; a Filipino defendant was given twenty-eight years; and three Mexican defendants were ordered deported. These were Communists in conspiracy to destroy the economy of the Imperial Valley, superior court judge Von Thompson stated from the bench upon sentencing, and anything short of a life sentence should be considered too lenient. When two of the defendants were released on parole in early 1933, they were ordered deported to the Soviet Union.

In late July and early August 1931, the CAWIU organized a strike by two thousand cannery workers, the majority of them women, in the Santa Clara Valley south of San Francisco. Once again the local sheriff went into action, rounding up the usual suspects. Once again an assembly of strikers—this time in St. James Park in downtown San José—was assaulted by squads of police who waded into the crowd with blackjacks and nightsticks. Once again the crowd was dispersed with water cannonades from high-pressure hoses. This time, however, there was a further escalation: the emplacement of Army surplus machine guns at a cannery. Once again, a Red Scare ensued, with the usual results. In late November 1932, CAWIU organizers turned their attention to Vacaville in Solano County, with the same scenario of confrontation, Red Scare, and arrests going into effect. All in all, the CAWIU played leadership roles in twenty-four agricultural strikes in 1933: pea pickers in Santa Clara and Alameda counties demanding hourly wages of seventeen to twenty cents, a beet strike in Ventura County, peach strikes in Fresno and Merced counties, a grape strike in Merced, a cherry and pear pickers strike in the Santa Clara Valley.

Then came the largest single agricultural strike in the history of the nation: a cotton pickers strike in the San Joaquin Valley with ten thousand strikers across a five-hundred-mile front, led in part by such CAWIU organizers as Patrick Chambers, Sam Darcy, and twenty-one-year-old Caroline Decker, executive secretary of the union, astute in her organizational skills, charismatic in her fiery oratory, a "La Pasionaria" for California (as the Spanish Communist orator Dolores Ibarruri was called). Now, truly, were the fields of California witnessing a confrontation international in its magnitude and its showcasing of the battle between left and right: a violent succession of clashes, arrests (three hundred strikers in jail by early October), the cooperation of local government with the growers (the sheriff of Madera County urged growers to pour castor oil down the throat of any organizer coming onto their ranch), and a brilliantly organized resistance. Antistriker vigilantism had always been characteristic of these confrontations, but in the cotton strike of 1933, it reached new dimensions and was fully legitimized. The sheriff of Kern County deputized more than three hundred growers to confer legality on their efforts to break the strike. On the afternoon of Tuesday, October 10, 1933, an automobile caravan of forty armed vigilantes drove into the small Tulare County town of Pixley as CAWIU organizer Pat Chambers stood speaking to a gathering of strikers. Leaving their automobiles, the vigilantes approached the crowd with drawn pistols and rifles. Delfino Dávila, a fifty-eight-year-old part-time consular representative of Mexico in nearby Visalia, approached an armed vigilante and pushed his rifle to the ground. A nearby vigilante clubbed Dávila to the ground, then shot him to death. "Let them have it, boys!" one of the vigilantes yelled as he and the others fired into the crowd. Another striker, fifty-year-old Dolores Hernández, was killed and eight others were wounded.

The Cotton Strike of 1933 ended inconclusively. It did show, however, a decided tilt to the right on the part of California. Over the next half-decade, California Highway Patrol cars were in evidence during a myriad of new strike actions. The American Legion became an almost permanently mobilized vigilante group. The Associated Farmers of California, Inc., became a potent force both in the suppression of local strikes and in the state legislature, where it blocked any proposed pro-striker legislation. Its magazine, *Associated Farmer,* continued to fan the Red Scare. Extensive spy networks were established. In July 1934, at the height of the dock strike in San Francisco, Sacramento police raided the CAWIU state headquarters, arresting twenty-four. Seventeen defendants, including Pat Chambers and Caroline Decker, were brought to trial on six counts of criminal syndicalism. The Sacramento Conspiracy Trial, as it came to be known, represented the most powerful courtroom counterattack to date by the California right. The city of Sacramento went into a de facto condition of martial law, with a National Guard colonel placed in charge of the police and five hundred businessmen sworn in as deputies. When the entire charade was over—the hostile judge, the intimidated jury, the denied motions by defense attorney Leo Gallagher, the rising hysteria of the community—it was perhaps a miracle that four defendants were acquitted and that two of the convicted were recommended for probation. Eight of the convicted, including Caroline Decker, were sentenced to one to fourteen years in state prison, where they languished until, after long and tortuous arguments, the Third District Court of Appeal of the State of California on September 28, 1937, reversed the verdict and ordered the remaining defendants released.

EVEN AS THE SACRAMENTO CONSPIRACY TRIAL was being conducted, national guardsmen were patrolling the Embarcadero waterfront of San Francisco with rifles and fixed bayonets or manning machine gun emplacements at strategic locations or sweeping through the area in tanks. What had brought about this extraordinary display of insurrection and repression, this acting out of left versus right? Nothing less than the largest maritime strike up to this point in American history, by the International Longshoremen's Association (ILA), protesting employer domination of hiring halls through a shape-up system of spot-hiring and the issuance of a company-controlled blue book allowing an individual longshoreman to be chosen for work. The longshoremen walked out in early May 1934, joined by other locals in Seattle, Tacoma, Portland, San Pedro (Los Angeles), and San Diego. Then the San Francisco Teamsters Union, Local 85, went out, followed by the boilermakers and machinists, followed by the Sailors Union of the Pacific; the Pacific Union; the Ship Clerks Coast Marine Firemen; the Oilers, Watertenders, and Wipers Association; the Marine Cooks and Stewards Association; the International Seamen's Association; the Marine Engineers Beneficial Association; and the Masters, Mates, and Pilots Association. The Waterfront Employers Union, meanwhile, launched plans to bring in up to twenty-five hundred strikebreakers, to be housed in two ships offshore so as to avoid the necessity of their crossing picket lines to get to the docks.

At the center of resistance and counter-resistance were two charismatic San Franciscans, left and right. Roger Dearborn Lapham, the fifty-one-year-old president of the American Steamship Company, was the absolute paragon of establishment values—prep school, Harvard, the Bohemian and Pacific Union clubs, poker, duck hunting, golf, a sultanic appetite for the good life. Leading the strikers was Australian-born Alfred Renton "Harry" Bridges, thirty-four, thin, sharp-featured, terse, and sardonic, a look of feral distrust in his narrowed eyes, long suspected of Communist affiliation. The fleshy Lapham wore double-breasted suits, cuff-linked white shirts, old school ties. Bridges wore blue denim shirts, a flat white longshoreman's cap, and heavy black canvas pants with a cargo hook hanging from the back pocket. Whether or not Bridges was a Communist (and in the mid-1990s, when certain Soviet archives were opened, many held evidence claiming that he was a high-ranking agent), he openly welcomed Communist participation in the strike, which soon erupted into violence. The day before the longshoremen went on strike, San Francisco police chief William Quinn organized an antistrike task force of patrolmen, mounted policemen, and radio cars. A few days later, the police clashed with five hundred longshoremen near the waterfront, prompting Chief Quinn to purchase a cache of tear gas bombs. Throughout the rest of May, police and strikers clashed frequently. By June 18, 1934, employers were telegraphing President Roosevelt, claiming that Communists were taking over the ports of the Pacific Coast and indirectly suggesting that Roosevelt send in federal troops as President Hayes had done in the Great Railway Strike of 1877. On July 3, 1934, five thousand longshoremen and their sympathizers gathered on the Embarcadero to prevent the exit of trucks from Pier 38. Later that day, at approximately one-thirty in the afternoon, police and strikers clashed at Second and Townsend streets. The police fired into the crowd, and a striker later died from a fractured skull.

Two days later, July 5, 1934—"Bloody Thursday," as it came to be called—police and strikers spent the morning in a full pitched battle atop Rincon Hill near the waterfront. It was almost a classic military confrontation, with a line of mounted police advancing up the hill behind a covering barrage of rifle and pistol fire, and longshoremen on the heights resisting with two-by-fours and bricks and, in one instance, an oversized slingshot capable of propelling missiles at a high velocity for distances up to four hundred feet. That afternoon, during a lunchtime lull in the confrontation, a phalanx of police converged on the ILA headquarters on Steuart Street, where downtown San Francisco ran into the Embarcadero. Once again tear gas and guns were fired; two strikers lay dead on the street, thirty others suffered gunshot wounds, and forty-three others were clubbed, gassed, or hit by projectiles. At this point, Governor Frank Merriam sent in 4,600 national guardsmen under the command of Major General David Prescott Barrows, former president of the University of California. The response was a general strike on July 15, 1934, which virtually shut down the city. At this point, with government and the strikers in a condition of total confrontation, the private sector intervened, in the form of a newspaper publisher–dominated group led by John Francis Neylan, a respected Progressive serving as Pacific Coast counsel to William Randolph Hearst. Neylan organized a mediation, and on July 18, 1934, the Strike Strategy Committee, over the strong objections of Harry Bridges, voted 191 to 174 to end the general strike the following day and to submit the entire dispute to the National Longshoremen's Board for arbitration.

The sheer drama of the San Francisco waterfront strike—its capacity to stimulate such a panorama of open insurrection and suppression—underscored the volatility of California, battered as it was by powerful forces on both the left and the right. Where else in the United States, for example, could a socialist writer such as Upton Sinclair, author of the muckraking exposé *The Jungle* (1906)—a health faddist, a radical whose novels and tracts had offended just about every sector of the establishment, a three-time candidate for Congress and the governorship on the Socialist ticket—almost on a whim change his registration to

Democrat in September 1933 and win that party's nomination for governor in the 1934 primary? Sinclair's program, End Poverty in California (EPIC), was based on the notion of production for use, not profit. It also incorporated a number of programs from the utopian socialist soup stock, a blend of the utopia described by Sir Thomas More with the doctrines of Charles Fourier and Karl Marx stirred into the persistent utopianism of avant-garde America as expressed by Robert Dale Owen and the New Harmony colony, the New England Transcendentalists and Brook Farm, and the United States of the year 2000 as imagined by Edward Bellamy in the futurist novel *Looking Backward* (1888). Characteristically, Sinclair sat down at his typewriter and developed his political platform even further in the form of a Bellamyesque social-science-fiction tract titled *I, Governor of California, and How I Ended Poverty: A True Story of the Future* (1934).

When it looked as if Sinclair was about to win the governorship, a panicked establishment went into high gear, aided by Hollywood, which produced bogus newsreels depicting hobos and various Bolshevik types speaking into the camera in heavy Russian accents about how they were going to California to help make the Revolution happen. Toward the conclusion of the campaign, Sinclair suffered something like a nervous breakdown, although whether this was because he thought he was going to lose or to win is unclear. In any event, the voters sent to Sacramento Republican Frank Merriam of Long Beach, a man whom George Creel (the well-known former official in the Woodrow Wilson administration whom Sinclair had defeated in the Democratic primary) with some justification described as "reactionary to the point of medievalism." Interestingly enough, a number of Sinclair's proposals made it into Franklin Delano Roosevelt's New Deal (old-age pensions of $50 a month, for example, reappearing as Social Security), despite the fact that Roosevelt had refused to come out for Sinclair in the runoff.

EPIC had plausibility because it spoke to a certain millenarian tendency that surfaced in California during these stress-laden years. The very month that Sinclair registered as a Democrat, a Long Beach physician by the name of Francis Everett Townsend began to argue that the way out of the Depression was the immediate granting of monthly pensions of $150 to fifteen or twenty million Americans over the age of sixty, the money to be raised from a national sales tax with the requirement that it be spent within the month so as to recharge the stalled economy. Townsend was aware that because of modern longevity, a new type of American was on the scene: people of advanced age who in a previous era would have been long gone. By the early 1930s, roughly one third of the 150,000 residents of Long Beach were over the age of sixty. Never before in human history had there been so many elderly people in one place at one time vis-à-vis the total population. By January 1935 the Townsendites of Southern California had their own man in Congress, and half a million Americans belonged to Townsend Clubs. By the end of 1936, the figure had jumped to 2.2 million, each member paying dues and subscribing to the *Townsend National Weekly* newspaper, which was raking in nearly a quarter of a million dollars a year in advertising.

In 1937 the Townsend movement spun off the California Pension Plan Association spearheaded by two Hollywood publicists, the brothers Willis and Lawrence Allen, assisted by radio commentator Sherman Bainbridge and aspiring Democratic politician Sheridan Downey. As outlined in a campaign booklet, *Ham 'n' Eggs for Californians,* the program called for a constitutional amendment granting $30 in warrants every Thursday to every unemployed Californian over the age of fifty. The proposal got on the statewide ballot in 1938, and Ham 'n' Eggs rallies were held up and down the state at which audiences cried "Ham 'n' Eggs! Ham 'n' Eggs!" at the top of their lungs—which liberal commentator Carey McWilliams said disconcertingly resembled the *Sieg Heil!* of comparable rallies in Germany. The movement even had its own Horst Wessel, a counterpart to the famous Nazi martyr, by the name of Archie Price, an unemployed sixty-two-year-old who had committed suicide in July 1938 in San Diego after his life savings had been destroyed by the Depression; Price left a note in his pocket, "Too young to receive an old-age pension, and too old to find work." Although Ham 'n' Eggs went down in defeat in the election of November 1938, support for the measure played an important role in electing Sheridan Downey to the U.S. Senate as a Democrat and Culbert Olson, a liberal Democrat, to the governorship.

Carey McWilliams could not decide whether the Ham and Eggers were on the right or on the left. They can be seen as incorporating both extremes. Throughout the second half of the 1930s—despite the election of Culbert Olson in 1937—the right was gaining as much strength as the left. The Salinas lettuce strike of September–October 1936, for example, represented a triumph for the Associated Farmers of California, Inc. It was actually more of a lockout than a strike. Hearing rumors of a strike, growers took preemptive action, including the mobilization of local police and sheriff's deputies, the Highway Patrol (140 officers in all), and even a local Boy Scout troop. By the time the lettuce workers were locked out of the packing sheds and a large strikebreaking workforce was brought in, the entire city—indeed, the entire antistrike effort—had come under the control of Henry Sanborn, a colonel of infantry in the Army Reserve, who coordinated the resistance of the growers with military precision. *San Francisco Chronicle* reporter Paul Smith covered the strike and was shocked by the militarized nature of the resistance. Smith wrote four articles for the *Chronicle,* December 23 to 26, 1936, entitled "It Did Happen in Salinas," a takeoff on Sinclair Lewis's bestselling novel of fascism in America, *It Can't Happen Here* (1935). The Salinas strike ended on November 3, 1936, with the complete victory of the vegetable growers and shippers association and the intricate network of organizations behind it, led by the Associated Farmers of Monterey County. A similar strategy—a preemptive lockout coordinating the efforts of government and nongovernment groups—repeated this scenario the following year in Stockton. In the case of both Salinas and Stockton, a Red Scare was an essential tactic. What the strikers faced can best be described as a form of syndicalism or parafascism in which the public and private sectors coalesced in resistance, with the private sector calling (and sometimes firing) the shots.

Two books from this period—*The Grapes of Wrath* (1939) by John Steinbeck and *Factories in the Field: The Story of Migratory Farm Labor in California* (1939) by Carey McWilliams—constituted a form of counterattack. Steinbeck had reported on conditions in the field for the *San Francisco News.* While he was not formally on the left, his depiction of vigilante action against Dust Bowl migrants, most dramatically the nighttime burning of a migrant encampment ("Hoovervilles," such encampments were called), certainly positioned his protagonists, the Joad family of Oklahoma, against a sea of troubles caused by the hostile growers of the San Joaquin Valley. Because *The Grapes of Wrath* was so successful as a documentary novel, it was taken as literal truth. Even FDR referred to the Joads in one of his Fireside Chats as though they were actual people. On the other hand, Steinbeck outraged Oklahomans as well as Kern County growers with his depiction of the Joads and was denounced in the House of Representatives by a congressman from Oklahoma.

Carey McWilliams was a brilliant and committed activist on the left: a lawyer who had turned to activism and investigative reporting and was in 1938 appointed commissioner of immigration and housing in the Democratic administration of Governor Culbert Olson. *Factories in the Field* offered a powerful indictment of the way farm labor had been treated in California for most of the twentieth century. The book concluded with a depiction of Colonel Sanborn's mysterious parafascist governance of Salinas during the lettuce strike.

When he was running for governor, Culbert Olson vowed that if elected, he would free Tom Mooney, who was still serving a life sentence in San Quentin for the 1916 Preparedness Day bombing he did not commit. Olson kept his word. Early on the morning of January 7, 1939, Mooney was driven to Sacramento for a ten o'clock meeting with the governor. A half-hour later, on the floor of the Assembly, over a live nationwide radio hookup, Olson gave Mooney a full and unconditional pardon, restoring to him all civil rights and privileges. Stepping to the microphone, an unbowed Mooney, a free man after twenty-six years of imprisonment, gave a speech in which he compared the war on unions to the repressions of Fascist Germany and Italy. Later that day, Mooney marched at the head of a great parade in San Francisco, with Harry Bridges at his side. Governor Olson, meanwhile, left his office that afternoon for an event at the California State Fairgrounds, where he collapsed from exhaustion.

Some claim that Olson never recovered his momentum following the humiliating collapse. Republican Earl Warren, the attorney general, successfully ran against Olson in 1942. Warren promised that the first thing he would do as governor would be to fire Carey McWilliams. Keeping his word, as Olson had kept his in the Mooney case, on his first day in office Warren fired McWilliams. As World War II progressed, California found itself short of agricultural workers, as opposed to the oversupply of the 1930s, and turned to a federally sponsored *braceros* ("strong-armed ones") program that brought Mexican workers into California by train during the harvest season. The program lasted until 1964. The very next year, Arizona-born César Chávez, who had founded the National Farm Workers Union in 1962, joined Filipino grape pickers led by Larry Itliong in a resistance against grape growers in the San Joaquin, Imperial, and Coachella valleys. In 1966 the unions coalesced to form the United Farm Workers. The *huelga* (strike) launched by this organization included a nationwide boycott of California-grown table grapes.

As César Chávez orchestrated the *huelga,* however, it was more than a short-term strike action. It was a crusade, vital with religious and moral power, insisting upon the intrinsic dignity of work in the fields and the men and women who performed it. Chávez had himself performed such work all of his life, with the exception of the time he spent in the Navy during World War II. Like Gandhi, whom he admired, or Mother Teresa, whom he resembled in religious commitment, César Chávez, shrewd and competent though he was as a labor organizer, was not a figure fully of this world. He was, rather, a kind of saint, bespeaking the essential dignity of labor. For one hundred years, California had sustained a tendency to take such labor for granted: to pay and house its workers as cheaply as possible, to move them on to other places as quickly as possible, to abandon them in their old age. César Chávez and the *huelga* he led could not, did not, end this tendency. It did, however, suggest a better way. Far from being a discardable resource, the agricultural workers of California had by their stooped and backbreaking labor played a crucial role in bringing California into existence and into prominence. They had a right to a decent and dignified life in the state they had helped to create, to sustain, and to enrich.

9

WAR AND PEACE

Garrison State and Suburban Growth

Aircraft worker, Los Angeles, late 1944

REGIONAL HISTORY COLLECTION
UNIVERSITY OF SOUTHERN CALIFORNIA

Seized as an act of war in 1846, governed by the military until 1850, California remained closely connected to the military through the rest of the nineteenth century. From 1854 the Navy maintained an important ship repair facility on Mare Island in San Francisco Bay. The Union Iron Works shipyard south of San Francisco built ships of the line for the American fleet. At the Presidio in San Francisco, the Army maintained its Pacific Coast headquarters. Starting in 1891, the 4th Cavalry had responsibility for patrolling the Yosemite Valley. As the United States moved in the direction of becoming a global military power—especially a sea power, as was being advised by naval theoretician Alfred Thayer Mahan—the military importance of California increased. The Spanish-American War of 1898 formally established the United States as an Asia-Pacific power. A number of the ironclad ships of war sailing into Manila Bay that year under the command of Admiral Dewey had been constructed by Union Iron Works, and the 1st California Volunteers fought as infantry in the Philippines. During the San Francisco earthquake and fire of 1906, Brigadier General Frederick Funston helped to police San Francisco in ambiguous circumstances that nevertheless testified to the strong presence of the military establishment at the Presidio. In April 1908, the Great White Fleet visited California in the course of its around-the-world cruise intended to demonstrate the United States as a two-ocean naval power. Tragically, the admiral of this fleet, Robert "Fighting Bob" Evans, fell ill in Santa Barbara and died shortly thereafter.

In 1914 the Navy established its Pacific Fleet, supported by a growing naval presence in San Diego. During the First World War, California contributed its fair share of troops, including a number of locally raised regiments whose soldiers entered the trenches bonded to each other by local association and civic pride. Professor George Ellery Hale of the Mount Wilson Observatory in Pasadena also played a key role in organizing the national scientific establishment on behalf of the war effort. In the 1920s, the oligarchy of San Diego, operating through Congressman William Kettner, deliberately recruited a major naval and Marine Corps presence to that city, transforming San Diego into a kind of Gibraltar on the Pacific, complete with a Marine Corps training depot designed in Spanish Revival by Bertram Goodhue, architect of the California Building at the Panama California International Exposition. The Army, meanwhile, was expanding its presence through a series of forts and installations in the San Francisco Bay Area, including Hamilton Field Air Station in Marin County. In 1931, the naval air service established Moffett Field, an important lighter-than-air facility, at the border between Sunnyvale and Mountain View on the San Francisco peninsula, centered on an airship hangar of such monumental proportions that it created its own interior weather zones. Californians, meanwhile, such as Chester Nimitz, Henry "Hap" Arnold, Jimmy Doolittle, and George S. Patton had earned, or were in the process of earning, distinguished military reputations that would propel them into leadership roles in the conflict to come. The San Francisco Bay Area and metropolitan Los Angeles had each finally developed important port and ship repair facilities, both military and civilian, and secured the sources of water and hydroelectricity necessary for an expanded defense-industrial capacity.

The Second World War formally began on September 1, 1939, when Germany invaded Poland. In the Pacific, however, it could be seen to have begun even earlier with the Japanese invasion of Manchuria in 1931. From 1939 to December 1941, as the Japanese expanded their Co-Prosperity Sphere in Asia and Nazi Germany occupied most of the Continent, leaving only Great Britain and Greece in resistance, the United States struggled with the question: was this—or did it have to become—an American war as well? Californians in support of the "America First" movement, dedicated to keeping the United States out of war, included publisher William Randolph Hearst, novelist Kathleen Norris, film and stage star Lillian Gish, and Stanford University president Ray Lyman Wilbur. On the evening of June 20, 1941, more than thirty thousand people filled the Hollywood Bowl for an America First rally, which was repeated eleven nights later at the Civic Auditorium in San Francisco to a full house of twelve thousand. The author of the bestselling novel *Mother* (1911), Kathleen Norris spoke most effectively at each of these rallies. Did the mothers of America, she asked, wish to see their sons killed or maimed in a foreign war, if it could be avoided? The Carmel-based poet Robinson Jeffers presented an even more apocalyptic vision in a series of antiwar poems and a lecture he gave at Harvard. Jeffers was joined in this effort by California's best-known writer, William Saroyan, and San Francisco poet Kenneth Rexroth, among others.

The attack on Pearl Harbor on the morning of December 7, 1941, took all the force from the America First movement, already reeling from the anti-Semitic direction it had taken in certain speeches by former Californian Charles Lindbergh. Even before Pearl Harbor, however, the War Department had been increasing its presence in California, upgrading its installations, purchasing property, commissioning (this by FDR in May 1940) the construction of fifty thousand war planes in an effort to make the United States the "Arsenal of Democracy." In early 1940, the Army Air Corps established a number of pilot and mechanic training programs in California through contracts to private companies. Major General Henry Arnold, chief of the

Army Air Corps, visited these facilities in April 1940 and reconnoitered various sites in Riverside County for bombardier and bomber crew training programs.

The attack on Pearl Harbor threw California, indeed the entire Pacific Coast, into a panic—a state compounded on February 23, 1942, when Submarine I-17 of the Japanese Imperial Navy, under Commander Kozo Nishino, surfaced in the Santa Barbara Channel and fired twenty-five five-inch shells across the Pacific Coast Highway into oil storage tanks at Elwood, causing minor damage but effecting a psychological blow of some magnitude. Sailing brazenly out of the channel into the Pacific, Nishino sank two American cargo ships off the California coast before heading back across the Pacific to his home port of Yokosuka. All of California went on alert. An erroneous report from either the Western Defense Command or the 4th Interceptor Command, most likely leaked by midlevel sources, stated that unidentified aircraft had been sighted over Los Angeles. At 3:12 on Thursday morning, February 26, 1942, the antiaircraft units of the Los Angeles–based 37th Coast Artillery Brigade fired a total of 1,430 shells at unidentified aircraft alleged to be over the city. The barrage lasted an hour. Searchlights swept the inky horizon, sirens wailed, yellow tracer bullets pierced the darkness, and antiaircraft barrages exploded overhead in fiery orange bursts of shrapnel. The next day, FBI agents began rounding up people suspected of subversion. Twenty of the thirty arrested were Japanese.

Ever since the early 1900s, a sector of California had been at war with the state's Japanese immigrants. This California-Japanese War, as Carey McWilliams described it, was part of a larger "Yellow Peril" movement that brought with it a virulent "White California" crusade led by former San Francisco mayor James Duval Phelan, who was elected to the U.S. Senate in 1914. Upper-class Californians such as Phelan and *San Francisco Chronicle* publisher Michael H. de Young scapegoated the Japanese to please the masses. Politicians such as Phelan, in turn, took a hard line against the Japanese to please de Young and the *Chronicle.* In early 1905 the *Chronicle* led a campaign to segregate Japanese children in the public schools of San Francisco through a series of virulently racist editorials that one dare not even quote. When the school board and Mayor Schmitz put this segregation into effect in October 1906, President Theodore Roosevelt went ballistic. How dare San Francisco, Roosevelt fumed, so grossly insult the proud people of Japan, the Yankees of the Pacific, long-standing American friends? Summoning Schmitz and the president of the school board to the White House, Roosevelt brokered the so-called Gentlemen's Agreement with Japan, put into effect in 1908, in which the Japanese government promised not to issue any further passports to laborers seeking to emigrate to the United States in exchange for the withdrawal of the offensive San Francisco ordinance. Roosevelt was further embarrassed in 1908 when, just as the Great White Fleet was sailing into Yokohama Harbor, the California legislature began to discuss the statewide segregation of Japanese children in public schools and a ban on Japanese ownership of land. Roosevelt took his case directly to Governor James Gillett, protesting California's contravention of national policy. The next year, 1909, saw the publication of *The Valor of Ignorance* by the Los Angeles–based soldier of fortune Homer Lea, who outlined in great detail a future Japanese invasion and occupation of the Pacific Coast.

The White California movement was gaining strength, and in 1913 the legislature passed the Alien Land Act prohibiting Japanese immigrants from owning land in the state. This time, President Woodrow Wilson sent Secretary of State William Jennings Bryan to Sacramento to plead the case against passing this bill. Governor Hiram Johnson, however, rallied the anti-Japanese lobby, and the bill became law. In April 1919—as Japan sat with the other victorious allies at Versailles—California once again embarrassed the Department of State by an expansion (passed in 1920) of the Alien Land Act of 1913, a re-discussion of segregation, and a series of viciously anti-Japanese speeches given in the U.S. Senate by Phelan. The fact that Governor Johnson and Senator Phelan, a Progressive Republican and a Progressive Democrat, otherwise involved in the reform and upgrading of California, were so determinedly anti-Japanese underscores the disquieting fact that Progressivism itself sustained a strong anti-Japanese message that was based, when all was said and done, on a toxic level of racism that refrained from no argument, however base and vile, against the Japanese.

This toxicity, this racism, while not universal in California, nevertheless tainted a portion of the population, including elements of the Progressive upper middle class, through the 1930s, despite the fact that in other ways Californians admired Japan and—in architecture and landscape design especially—were doing their best to assimilate its culture. Bay Area artist Theodore Wores spent much of the 1890s in Japan painting its scenery and was decorated by the Japanese government for his efforts. In 1894 the Japanese Pavilion from the Columbian Exposition in Chicago was permanently installed in Golden Gate Park in San Francisco, where it became an instantly popular teahouse and public garden. The San Francisco department store Gump's did a thriving trade in Japanese furniture and art. Bay Area architects such as Bernard Maybeck redeployed the Japanese wood-building tradition using Northern California redwood. In Southern California a generation of Japanese gardeners helped shape the horticultural aesthetics of that region. David Starr Jordan, the founding president of Stanford and an ardent Nipponophile, traveled to Japan in 1900 and 1911 to recruit Japanese students. Thanks to Jordan's efforts, Stanford ranked second only to Harvard as the university of choice for Meiji-era students eager to sharpen their professional and technical skills. In October 1905, Jordan joined San Mateo attorney

Henry Pike Bowie to form the Japan Society of Northern California. Fluent in Japanese, married to a highly placed Japanese woman attached to the Imperial Court, and a skilled painter in the Japanese style, Bowie devoted his considerable energies to promulgating the strength and beauty of Japanese culture. Even more boldly, he erected a memorial gate on his San Mateo estate to honor the valor of Japanese soldiers and sailors during the Russo-Japanese War.

The White California movement, in short, represented the common, even vulgar, side of the California identity, however highly placed its leadership. It was, moreover, a racism based on envy. Japanese immigrants to California did well. They worked effectively as agricultural laborers, skillfully brokering their contracts through appointed leaders. With their savings, they rented land and started profitable farms. In thc carly 1920s, Japanese women were allowed to enter the United States as "picture brides," so called because their marriages were brokered in home villages sight unseen, according to Japanese custom. The marriages and family formation resulting from the arrival of these women created a baby boom of American-born *nisei,* who were citizens and grew up fully American in the 1920s and 1930s. The window for such immigration was brief, however, and the Immigration Act of 1924 prohibited the Japanese from immigrating to the United States. Perceived as an insult in Japan, the act provoked demonstrations of protest and further poisoned the relationship between the two nations.

Even before Pearl Harbor, *Newsweek* ran an article, on October 14, 1940, warning of the threat posed by Japanese living around military installations in Hawaii and California. On the day of Pearl Harbor itself, the FBI, assisted by sheriff's deputies, began rounding up suspected Japanese aliens in Los Angeles County. By December 9, 1941, some five hundred *issei* (Japanese noncitizens) were in federal custody on Terminal Island in Los Angeles Harbor. On February 19, 1942, President Roosevelt signed Executive Order 9066 allowing the War Department to remove suspicious or possibly dangerous people from military areas. Even with this, most Japanese Americans in California believed that they did not fall into this category and continued to live their lives. In late February 1942, following the shelling at Santa Barbara and the phony air invasion of Los Angeles, the *Los Angeles Times* began running a series of articles calling for the removal of the Japanese from the coast. From February 2 to March 2, 1942, the House Committee on Defense Migration, chaired by Congressman John Tolan of Alameda County, held hearings on the question. Tolan was a well-known liberal, and the Japanese American community and such sympathizers as Carey McWilliams initially welcomed his committee to California, believing that it would take testimony that would counter the pro-evacuation argument. In sessions in San Francisco and Los Angeles, the exact opposite occurred. On opening day of the hearings in San Francisco, California attorney general Earl Warren argued for the evacuation of all Japanese, including American citizens.

Lieutenant General John L. DeWitt, head of the Western Defense Command, had already made up his mind that the Japanese should be evacuated. Since the entire West Coast had been declared a theater of war, DeWitt possessed proconsular authority, which had remained latent in his dealings with civilian officials but now came to the fore as DeWitt acted out of his own instincts and reluctance to become another Admiral John Kimmel, demoted following Pearl Harbor. The Japanese were a threat, DeWitt had earlier told a congressional committee, whether they were citizens or not. "A Jap's a Jap" was the way the general put it. "They are a dangerous element, whether loyal or not." DeWitt was also influenced by the fact that what he called the "best people" in California—the governor, the attorney general, the two U.S. senators, the mayors of San Francisco and Los Angeles, the entire California membership of the

House of Representatives, the publishers and editors of the leading newspapers—were advocating evacuation.

On March 1, 1942, DeWitt issued Proclamation Number One designating the western half of California, Oregon, and Washington and the southern third of Arizona as military zones from which all Japanese were to be removed. On March 11, one day before the Tolan hearings concluded, DeWitt established the Wartime Civil Control Administration, headquartered in the Whitcomb Hotel on Market Street, with Lieutenant Colonel Karl Bendetsen in command, to carry out the evacuation program being planned since January. On March 18, on the advice of the Tolan Committee, Roosevelt issued Executive Order 9102 creating the Civilian War Relocation Authority, headed by Milton Eisenhower, brother of the general, to establish and administer the relocation camps. Four months later, some 110,000 Japanese aliens and Japanese Americans were behind barbed wire, where they would remain for the next three years and more, except for those young *nisei* who volunteered for the draft in 1943 and, assigned to the 100th Infantry Battalion and the 442nd Regimental Combat Team, fought their way up the Italian peninsula in 1944 and early 1945, emerging as the most decorated combat units of the war.

Training for that war, as of April 1942, was very much on the mind of Major General George Smith Patton, Jr., of the Desert Training Center, a military reserve almost the size of Pennsylvania bestriding sections of California, Nevada, and Arizona. Throughout the spring of 1942, Patton, a third-generation Californian, drove his men through exhaustive maneuvers with tanks and motorized infantry and artillery, seeking to instill in his troops the flair and mobility of the Afrika Corps commanded by Field Marshal Erwin Rommel, whom Patton longed to meet on the field of battle. That very same month, another Californian, Lieutenant Colonel Jimmy Doolittle, a 1922 graduate of the University of California, was sailing across the Pacific with sixteen normally land-based B-25 twin-engine bombers and their crews aboard the aircraft carrier USS *Hornet.* On April 18, Doolittle took his bombers in low over Tokyo in a surprise raid that warned Japan of things to come. Seven months later, Rear Admiral Daniel Judson Callaghan, former naval aide to FDR, was leading five cruisers and six destroyers through the channel off Savo Island north of Guadalcanal. Born in San Francisco, raised in Oakland, educated at St. Ignatius High School in San Francisco and the U.S. Naval Academy (Class of 1911), Callaghan had spent half a year on the staff of Vice Admiral William Halsey before being given his own command. At 1:41 on the morning of Friday, November 13, 1942, Callaghan's section ran head-on into a fast-approaching Japanese naval force. What ensued were perhaps the last ship-to-ship naval engagements in military history. A salvo from a Japanese battleship smashed the bridge of Callaghan's flagship, the USS *San Francisco,* killing him and his staff. Altogether, one hundred officers and men were lost that night aboard the *San Francisco.* Two surviving officers were awarded the Medal of Honor.

As 1942 edged into 1943, the San Francisco Bay Area was emerging as the premier military command center and port of embarkation and supply on the Pacific Coast. Shipping experts such as Roger Lapham lent their expertise to the military. Approximately two hundred thousand military vehicles—jeeps, trucks, half-tracks, tanks—were given precombat checkouts and prepared for shipment overseas at the Ordnance Automotive Shop in Emeryville near Berkeley, where a hundred or more vehicles per day (the record was 360) were prepared for combat in the Pacific. By the Battle of Okinawa toward the end of the war, whole blood was reaching combat troops within forty-eight hours of being donated in California. Forty miles northeast of San Francisco near the city of Pittsburg was the thousand-acre Camp Stoneman, named in honor of Civil War general George Stoneman, the fifteenth governor of California, where one million soldiers were processed between May 1942 and August 1945 for service in the Pacific. A Women's Army Corps band serenaded the troops as they embarked from Fort Mason in San Francisco, and Red Cross volunteers handed out coffee and doughnuts. As the tempo of the war increased, the shipment of troops reached staggering proportions.

There was also traffic in the other direction. By late 1943, George Patton had gotten his wish to meet Rommel on the field of battle in North Africa, and members of the Afrika Corps were arriving in San Francisco by the hundreds for processing to POW camps in the interior. More than twenty-two hundred German prisoners remained permanently in detention camps at nearby Camp Stillman, with another three hundred remaining at Fort McDowell for KP and other assignments. When Italy surrendered in 1943 and became a cobelligerent with the United States, Italian POWs were given the option of joining Italian Service Units, which performed noncombat duty for the Army. Many Italians who volunteered had relatives in the North Beach and Excelsior districts of San Francisco whom they visited on leave. By 1945 the Italians were moving freely throughout San Francisco wearing United States Army uniforms with an ITALY patch on the left shoulder.

In general, the Bay Area was Army country, while Southern California belonged to the Navy and Marine Corps. Still, the Navy maintained air stations in Alameda and Sunnyvale, an administrative headquarters on Treasure Island, ship repair facilities on Hunters Point at the southern edge of San Francisco and on Mare Island in the North Bay, naval hospitals on Mare Island and in Oakland, and a preflight school on the campus of St. Mary's College in Moraga. In Southern California, the Navy had long maintained a strong presence in Long Beach and San Diego, which it now augmented. The Marines had an existing recruitment depot in San Diego, and in 1942 the War Department purchased for use as an advanced Marine Corps training center the sprawling 122,798-acre Rancho Santa Margarita y Las Flores on eighteen miles of shoreline in northern San Diego County, designating it Camp Pendleton in honor of the recently deceased Marine Corps major general, Joseph Pendleton, who had played a key role in the 1920s in enlarging the Marine presence in San Diego. The Marine Corps air service, meanwhile, established stations at El Toro near Santa Ana, at Goleta near Santa Barbara, at El Centro in the Imperial Valley, and in the Mojave Desert. There were also naval air stations at Santa Ana and on the Salton Sea in Imperial County. The navy construction corps (Seabees) had its Pacific Coast headquarters at Port Hueneme in Ventura County. Some twenty thousand air cadets went through preflight training at the Army Air Forces West Coast Training Center at the Santa Ana Army Air Base before being sent on for pilot, bombardier, or navigator instruction at the nearby Victorville Army Flying School, the Army Air Forces Advanced Flying School at Mather Field in Sacramento, or elsewhere throughout the West.

All this is to suggest the ubiquitous presence of uniformed men and women in California during the war years. On any weekend at the height of the war, as many as twenty thousand military personnel might be on leave in metropolitan Los Angeles. San Diego was equally teeming with sailors and marines. San Francisco gained a reputation as the best leave town on the coast. A certain egalitarianism in the psychology of San Francisco, the legacy perhaps of its hundred-year vitality as a port city, made it especially hospitable to enlisted men. Visiting columnist Lucius Beebe reported with glee the spectacle of the maître d' at the Garden Court of the Palace Hotel waving a group of enlisted sailors to their table while a four-striper captain stood glumly in line with his lady guest. Throughout the war, thousands of young men on leave flocked to the USO Hospitality House at the Civic Center for a shave, a shower, a game of pool or Ping-Pong, conversation with a young lady from one or another support organization, and other chaperoned social events. Later in the war, the city of San Francisco held an open house in Civic Center Auditorium for ten thousand men in uniform and an equal number of invited young women. It was the largest USO dance during the conflict. For the more rebellious—young sailors especially—a score of tattoo parlors lined Market and Kearny streets, and there were plenty of bars in the Tenderloin district, an increasing number of them placed off limits by the Shore Patrol as the war progressed. Officers favored the Patent Leather Lounge in the St. Francis Hotel and the Top of the Mark bar of the Mark Hopkins Hotel atop Nob Hill, where it became the custom to leave a signed dollar bill, to be claimed upon return. All told, more than 1.6 million military personnel passed through San Francisco en route to the Pacific during the war years.

Leave patterns in Southern California lacked the geographical concentration of the Bay Area, although the Biltmore Hotel on Pershing Square in downtown Los Angeles became a popular spot for air cadets on leave. Just down from the Biltmore extended a zone of honky-tonk bars, burlesque theaters, cheap movie houses, dance halls, and tattoo parlors, most of it centered on Main Street. Each weekend, thousands of sailors in uniform could be seen on the streets of Los Angeles, Long Beach, and Wilmington–San Pedro. Military police and the Shore Patrol patrolled constantly. Each weekend as well, San Diego filled with thousands of sailors and marines on pass. The young marines, novelist Leon Uris would later note in *Battle Cry* (1953), had what he called the "boot camp stare" of boys away from home who had just been put through the transformative experience of basic training.

To accommodate such lads, at least those on leave in Los Angeles, film stars Bette Davis and John Garfield led an effort to transform a well-known but temporarily abandoned building on Cahuenga Boulevard just off Sunset into a USO center staffed by Hollywood celebrities. By October 1942, the Hollywood Canteen, as it was called, was open for business. An estimated three million servicemen and women would pass through the Hollywood Canteen during the war, drinking coffee and dancing with the likes of Hedy Lamarr, Marlene Dietrich, Rita Hayworth, and Betty Grable. The Hollywood Canteen had a paid staff of only nine; hundreds of volunteers, celebrities and ordinary citizens alike, did the bulk of the work necessary to keep the program going.

Which was a good thing, given the volatility of the situation. Here were hundreds of thousands of young men, the majority of them draftees or enlisted because of the draft, taken from their homes, forced into rigid conformity, knowing that they would soon be in harm's way. Many could not take the pressure and cracked. Others misbehaved as a result of stress. The miracle was that the vast majority behaved so well under such trying circumstances. An exception to this rule was the so-called Zoot Suit Riots of early June 1943, which arose out of conflict between young (mostly teenage) servicemen and young (mostly teenage) Mexican Americans not yet in uniform and were exacerbated by Mexican American baiting by Los Angeles newspapers.

Like logs piled atop one another to create a fire, motivations behind the riots moved from the subconscious, to the conscious, to the stereotyped. First of all, when the war broke out there was some suggestion by the intelligence unit of the Los Angeles sheriff's department that the Mexican population of Southern California might contain pro-Axis elements. This suggestion had no basis in fact, but it must have become part of the buzz, as a later era would put it, given the prejudice against Mexican Americans evident in the Jim Crow City of Angels. Then there was the general belief that Mexican American young men were by their very nature prone to violence, a belief that in August 1942 led to the arrest, kangaroo trial, conviction, and sentencing to long terms in San Quentin of members of the 38th Street group (police insisted on calling it a gang) charged with the murder of one José Diaz near a gravel-pit swimming hole in East Los Angeles (which an enterprising reporter dubbed "Sleepy Lagoon" after a popular song of that name). Although the Sleepy Lagoon convictions were reversed two years later by the Second District Court of Appeal, irreversible damage had been done to the lives of seventeen young men, and Anglo-American Los Angeles, a good portion of it at least, had sent an unambiguous message: with the Japanese Americans now in camps, Mexican Americans could henceforth be treated as the enemy within.

Mexican American teenagers in Los Angeles, meanwhile, were featuring the zoot suit and the *pachuco* style. As a style, *pachuquismo* represented a sartorial form of late adolescent rebellion. The zoot suit—a long frock jacket with wide lapels and exaggerated shoulder pads plus pleated trousers, high-waisted and pegged at the cuff—worn with triple-soled shoes, an overlong watch or key chain, and a wide-brimmed hat, marked the *pachuco* or zoot-suiter as a stylized outsider/insider, going his own way. The zoot-suiters of Los Angeles were also enjoying the company of glamorous *pachucas,* Mexican American teenage girls in sheer blouses and high pompadours, where, according to certain press reports, they secreted knives. All this was ridiculous, certainly harmless, except for the fact that the slightly older teenagers in uniform—their heads shaved, in contrast to the zoot-suiters' ducktail haircuts, forced into severe uniforms so different from the insouciant drape of the zoot suit, denied the pleasant company of the abundance of cute Mexican American girls throughout L.A.—began seriously to resent the Mexican American kids just a few years younger than they were but free of military constraint.

All these forces came together on June 3, 1943, when two sailors made moves on two Mexican American girls at a dance in the seaside Venice district of Los Angeles and provoked a full-scale brawl between sailors and Mexican American youths, some of them in zoot suits. That same evening, eleven sailors got into a fight with a group of Mexican American young men in the downtown. The press luridly reported the alleged beatings of the sailors by the zoot-suiters, and rumors of a full-scale counterattack by zoot-suiters swept the city. On the evening of Friday, June 4, a caravan of twenty-nine taxicabs took some two hundred sailors and marines through the city. Upon sighting a zoot-suiter, the sailors and marines would stop the caravan, pour out into the street, and surround the hapless victim. Pulling off his pants, they would proceed to rough up their captive and, if possible, hack away at his ducktail haircut. The rioting continued through the weekend, fanned by screaming headlines and sensational press reports that five hundred zoot-suiters were organizing a counterattack. By this time, naval officials knew that they had a problem on their hands, a riot that could evolve into mutiny. They put an end to the riot in short order by threatening to court-martial any serviceman who did not return immediately to his unit. When it was all over—the rioting, the rumors, the fistfights—no one, neither serviceman nor zoot-suiter, had been killed. What the servicemen wanted, argued Mauricio Mazón, a psychoanalyst as well as a historian, was the symbolic annihilation of the zoot-suiter, the suppression of his insolent freedom, not his actual murder.

Still, it remained difficult to be a minority in wartime Los Angeles, as African American novelist Chester Himes discovered through personal experience and chronicled in *If He Hollers Let Him Go* (1945), the story of a black shipyard worker in an industrial culture based on segregation, which was the norm in the armed forces as well. Black Navy stevedores, for example, were loading ammunition at Port Chicago on the south shore of Suisun Bay north of San Francisco when on the night of Monday, July 17, 1944, shortly after ten o'clock, two Liberty ships, a fire barge, and a loading pier, disappeared in an explosion of ammunition equivalent to five kilotons of TNT, which is to say, an explosion comparable to that of the atom bomb that would be dropped on Hiroshima thirteen months later. Three hundred and twenty men—202 of them black enlisted stevedores—lost their lives in an instant, and another 390 military and civilian personnel, including 233 black enlisted men, suffered injuries. When more than two hundred black enlisted men balked at returning to work until the disaster could be investigated, fifty alleged ringleaders were charged with and found guilty of mutiny, and were sentenced to fifteen years in prison and dishonorable discharges. They were not released from prison and returned to the fleet, given the seagoing assignments most of them had wanted in the first place, until January 1946.

During World War II, California witnessed the triumphs of industrial culture and, simultaneously, the deep fissures—the barriers of race, class, and gender—that divided American society. Industrialist Henry J. Kaiser of Oakland achieved the near-impossible, which is to say, the overnight establishment of shipbuilding facilities virtually from scratch in California, Oregon, and Washington. As the labor pool was necessarily limited to an aging and unhealthy population of draft rejects, Kaiser hired physician Sydney Garfield to devise a comprehensive health plan, based on prepayment, that foreshadowed the HMO movement of a later era. Within five years, Kaiser built 1,490 ships for a total cost of $4 billion: 822 Liberty ships (small, fast 10,000-ton freighters); 219 Victory ships, a larger version of the Liberty; fifty small escort carriers; and an assortment of tankers, tenders, and other craft. All told, the Kaiser shipyards built thirty percent of American wartime shipping vessels. In one instance, the shipyard at Richmond in the East Bay produced a ship in four days, fifteen hours, and twenty-six minutes from keel-laying to launch. It was as much a human as an industrial challenge, for the Kaiser shipbuilders were forced to employ, almost en masse, a workforce as deeply divided against itself as was the larger United States. More than 150,000 African Americans, for example, most of them recent immigrants to the West Coast, were working in the Kaiser shipyards: this in an industry that at the beginning of the war was either overtly or de facto closed to African Americans. As the draft began to dig deep into the male population, women workers—subsequently folklorized as "Rosie the Riveter"—became increasingly crucial to the shipbuilding effort. White workers, male and female alike, included a high number of Dust Bowl migrants, still despised as "Okies" by many Californians. All this gave rise to a social experiment fraught with tension and indicative of the unfinished social business of the United States that would preoccupy the postwar era.

In this context, the overall success of the aircraft industry in Southern California during these war years is all the more remarkable. This period saw the creation of an industrial culture that represented a great leap forward for American labor, for women, and for efficient and socially responsible management. Even more than at the shipyards, women came into the aviation workforce, taking their place on the line at one or another of the three eight-hour shifts at Douglas, Lockheed, Vega, Northrop, North American, or Convair. What is particularly impressive is not only the extraordinary production of warplanes, but the social sophistication of aviation culture: the pooled transportation programs, the day care centers for children, the growing equality of women on the line and in middle management, the support services—medical care, food service (the cafeteria at Lockheed served a well-prepared lunch each day to six thousand workers at nominal cost), the banking and postal outlets, the social programs including big band dances and concerts—integrated into factory culture. An entire generation of women came into new identities as they mastered the intricacies of airplane manufacture and, starting around 1944, assumed supervisory positions. By the end of the war, young and attractive aircraft workers such as Norma Jean Baker Dougherty (soon to be better known as Marilyn Monroe) had been granted, almost en masse, starlet status, in contrast to the more robust Rosie the Riveter image of women workers in the shipyards. Aviation production had a kind of glamor; indeed, the parallel between the aircraft factories and the film studios was frequently cited.

And so the war ended in May 1945 as Germany, followed by Japan in August, unconditionally surrendered; and thirty-three months of mobilization and feverish and expectant living began to wind down. For millions of men and women in uniform, as well as for Rosie the Riveter and the aviation starlets, life after the war would never be the same; nor would it ever be the same for California, now that it had played such an important role as Arsenal of Democracy, training camp, and port of embarkation. The federal government had spent more than $35 billion in California during these war years (a sum exceeded only in New York and Michigan), and this in turn had multiplied the manufacturing economy of the state by a factor of 2.5 and tripled the average personal income. Approximately 1.6 million Americans had moved to California, and millions of others had received military training there or passed through or gone on leave there before being shipped to the Pacific. Sailing out through the Golden Gate, many of them had vowed to return to California and make their lives in California, if they survived the conflict. Many kept their word, and the postwar era represented a boom that would propel California into becoming, by 1962, the most populous state in the nation.

In 1944 Bing Crosby had been singing a popular song by Gordon Jenkins about making the San Fernando Valley his home. Between 1945 and 1960, the San Fernando Valley—acquired by the City of Los Angeles in 1915 as a kind of local Louisiana Purchase, doubling the area of the city—was transformed from a landscape of ranches, farms, and small towns into a near-continuous suburbia of tract housing, swimming pools, boulevards, and shopping centers. Between V-J Day (August 14, 1945) and November 1946, the urbanized portions of the San Fernando Valley saw the subdivision of 10,514 housing lots. Nearly ten thousand new homes were completed in 1947 alone, with a total of 24,858 building permits issued. In partnership with developer Fritz Burns, industrialist Henry J. Kaiser had, even before the war was over, turned to the mass production of housing on the 411-acre Panorama Ranch between the cities of Van Nuys and San Fernando, fifteen miles from downtown Los Angeles. Kaiser Community Homes sold at $4,000 to $5,000 each, with a mere $150 down. Various veterans' loan programs, federal and state, took care of the financing; and an entire generation of new Californians, now suburbanites, entered into their version of the California dream in such places as Panorama City in the San Fernando Valley; Westchester in West Los Angeles; Lakewood near Long Beach; San Diego, Riverside, San Bernardino, and Orange counties; and, in the north, the Westlake annex to Daly City south of San Francisco, Sunnyvale a little farther south, San Lorenzo Village across the Bay in Alameda County, and, eventually, metropolitan Sacramento. Developed between 1950 and 1953, the community of Lakewood in southeast Los Angeles County east of Long Beach—57,000 residents by 1954, living in 17,500 houses on 3,500 acres—equaled the scale and extent of the comparable community of Levittown on Long Island. Photographed from the air, the newly laid out and constructed streets and houses of Lakewood, gleaming in the sun, surrounded by open fields that were still under cultivation, offered the very portrait of the changes that were coming to California.

Between 1940 and 1950, the state population grew from 6.9 million to 10.6 million, a gain of 53 percent. Between July 1945 and July 1947 alone, more than a million people migrated to California, which created a housing shortage of monumental proportions. It also made driving the overburdened highways a special danger. In 1946, California traffic deaths—thirty-eight hundred of them—outstripped the combined total for New York and Pennsylvania, despite the fact that these two states had three times the population. It took time to alleviate the crisis. By August 1948 it was estimated that 900,000 new homes were still needed, *yesterday,* if Californians were to be properly housed. Writing in *The Saturday Evening Post* for August 7, 1948, Governor Earl Warren frankly confessed that the entire physical and social infrastructure of California was being overwhelmed by the influx. State government was doing what it could to meet the crisis, Warren wrote: $55 million in state aid to schools, representing ten times that on the local level; comparable sums for public health, higher education, and the expansion and upgrading of the state park and recreation system; and, most dramatically, $1 billion over a ten-year period for highways. Even as Warren announced these programs, however, another 850,000 veterans were in the process of moving to California.

Such massive development demanded anchorage in time, place, and theme. Disneyland helped to do this. In the rise of Southern California, hotels, resorts, and expositions played a founding role. These institutions, it must be remembered, were utopian statements. In the fin de siècle, the great hotels of the Southland upgraded and stylized regional experience. These hotels often expanded into larger resorts that represented idealizing statements regarding the possibilities of life in Southern California. Opening in July 1955, Disneyland was likewise a utopian statement: a species of city planning that set up a paradigm of value for Orange County and the rest of Southern California. Disneyland suggested that complex urban environments could be deliberately created and orchestrated to incorporate regional and related cultural values. In the case of Disneyland, a permanent exposition and resort assured a newly suburbanizing generation that the values of a more intimate America—small-town America—need not be lost, as was being feared, in the creation of the suburban developments of the postwar era.

Disneyland perfectly expressed this sustaining mythology of small-town life and identity via the schematized intensity of a theme park that was a metaphorical landscape for the new cities being developed across the American West. Walt Disney intended Disneyland to be, literally, the happiest place on earth. Again and again, he stressed to his executives and employees that the fundamental purpose of Disneyland was to promote human happiness. If Disneyland is to be considered as a new community (it might, in fact, be the archetypal new community), then Walt Disney was its developer and chief imagineer, as Disneyspeak would put it. As in the case of the new suburban communities, Disneyland was family oriented and child centered.

Disneyland was definitely not Coney Island, which is to say, raucous, demotic, spontaneous, alive with the fleshy exuberance of a Reginald Marsh painting, taking its vitality from the big city. It was, rather, a controlled development, orderly and restrictive, staffed by well-trained and polite middle-class employees, attuned to an equally middle-class and well-behaved clientele. The very concept of the theme park, Walt Disney stated, derived from his musings on Saturdays when he would take his two daughters to a merry-go-round in a nearby park; while they rode, he sat on a bench eating peanuts and imagining a more complete place shaped by the themes and peopled by the characters he was creating in his studio.

At the entrance to Disneyland was Main Street USA: that mythologized small town fixed forever in the American imagination (sometimes for better, other times for worse), which was now being transferred West and reimposed onto the new developments. Like these new developments, Disneyland was based on a mythologized reverence for the past, Main Street USA, and the related values of the adjacent Frontierland, which anchored Main Street in the larger myth of the West. Like the new communities, Disneyland could be fun. Adventureland proved that. And it could also nurture the imagination, as Fantasyland indicated. But it was faith in the future, centered on Tomorrowland, that projected Frontierland and Main Street USA forward into a gloriously unfolding history of technology, prosperity, and social order.

As science fiction writer and urbanologist Ray Bradbury was quick to recognize, Disneyland constituted a probe into the urban future, most notably in its monorail, but also in its conception of the city as planned and controlled environment, as opposed to the spontaneous product of site and historical circumstances. Disneyland can legitimately be seen, then, as a kind of city planning paradigm for Orange County. Between 1950 and 1961, Orange County (population 220,000 in 1950, and 704,000 by 1960) witnessed the construction of 2,500 housing tracts containing 144,000 building lots. Developers transformed Newport Beach from a yachting resort into a residential city and augmented cities such as Orange, Santa Ana, Anaheim, and Fullerton with housing developments. Eight new cities—Buena Park, Costa Mesa, La Palma, Cypress, Stanton, Westminster, Fountain Valley—were incorporated in the 1950s alone. By the early 1960s Disneyland was the epicenter of a residential area triangulated by Harbor Boulevard, the Santa Ana Freeway, and Katella Avenue. In a manner that would later be described as postsuburban, the residential developments of coastal and southern Orange County, no matter how they were affiliated in terms of local government, tended to meld their identities into a continuous suburban region.

It is no accident, finally, that one of the greatest science fiction writers to be produced by Southern California, Ray Bradbury, is also among the region's most astute city planners and urban theorists. Like Bradbury's *The Martian Chronicles* (1950), Tomorrowland at Disney, together with Frontierland, constituted a displaced narrative about values and social structures in transition in Orange County, California, and postwar America. To use the recent language of literary criticism, Disneyland is a text through which we can look back and reexperience the hopes and fears, the beliefs and illusions, of a postwar generation in the throes of creating the place we know as suburban Southern California.

The public history of California between 1945 and 1960 is almost exclusively driven by the saga of postwar development. No sooner had California welcomed and housed incoming veterans and their families than the Cold War, followed by the Korean War, broke out. The defense-related economy of California, which had been in the process of closing down in the late 1940s (with talk of aviation factories producing refrigerators), flared once again into incandescence; and California remained a garrison state—Fortress California, as historian Roger Lotchin describes it—for the next half-century. Indeed, as Lotchin has shown, suburban development in these years was centered on the defense industries that were driving California's economic engine. San Diego, for example, economically tied to the Navy and the Marine Corps since the 1920s, having experienced a boom during the war as the result of defense spending, now saw its economy dominated by General Dynamics and the production of the Atlas missile. Numerous communities throughout the state paced their economic development to the local military base or defense factory. As aviation evolved into electronics and aerospace, Los Angeles County alone found itself by the mid-1950s with more than forty percent of all aerospace contracts in the nation. California-based organizations such as the Rand Corporation of Santa Monica were performing the bulk of defense-related research on various Cold War campuses.

California had become a much more sophisticated place, and no one understood this better than Clark Kerr, chancellor of the University of California at Berkeley since 1952, and, after 1958, president of the multicampus UC system. The war had brought to California many of the finest scientists on the planet, most notably an array of brilliant émigrés. Noted social scientists and humanists had also arrived and gained academic posts at UC. This gave rise to tensions as these émigré internationalists displaced the old provincial elites that had long controlled the university. The anti-Communist crusade of the late 1940s exacerbated these tensions, as evident in the Loyalty Oath controversy of 1950 in which a number of distinguished faculty, including émigrés, were dismissed (temporarily, as it turned out) because they refused to sign a required loyalty oath. So, too, were these Cold War tensions reflected in state government, with the formation in Sacramento of the Joint Fact-Finding Committee on Un-American Activities in California, chaired by state senator John Tenney, whose only previous claim to fame had been his composition of the song "Mexicali Rose." For nearly a decade, the Tenney Committee busied itself finding Communist agents in just about every sector of the state and each year publishing its conclusions. An offended Thomas Mann, named in one such report, left California for Switzerland. Republican congressman Richard Milhous Nixon, a lawyer from Whittier who had served as a naval officer in the Pacific during the war, rode the anti-Communist crusade into the U.S. Senate in 1950, defeating the Democratic candidate, former actress Helen Gahagan Douglas, on the basis of her alleged softness on communism. In 1945, Nixon had been a somewhat rumpled lieutenant reviewing contracts for the military. By 1954, he was vice president of the United States.

In the post–World War II era, taxpaying Californians, acting through their elected representatives, bought into a program that was most fully articulated by UC president Clark Kerr in his Godkin Lectures at Harvard, later published as *The Uses of the University* (1963). The modern research university, Kerr argued—not just the University of California, but any great research university—was actually a diversified institution, a multiversity, serving the various needs of society, including its economic and cultural development, through research and (to a lesser extent) through teaching. The multiversity was society's think tank, essential to progress. Even as he lectured, Kerr was sustained in his argument by the success of the UC experiment. In the decade following the war, the University of California transformed itself from a first-rate regional university into a first-rate world university, and it did this, in significant measure, because the taxpayers of California saw in the UC system a vehicle for their own betterment. The fact that the California taxpayer was buying Kerr's vision became even more apparent with the adoption of the Master Plan for Higher Education in 1960. Taxpayers were now willing to support the University of California even though nearly ninety percent of them would never see their children enrolled at a UC campus. The Master Plan concurrently consolidated state college campuses into a multicampus California State University with its own board of trustees. The CSU system would serve the top thirty percent of high school graduates. A two-year community college system, meanwhile, would offer vocational and paraprofessional training and the first two years of arts and sciences, transferable to either the CSU or the UC system. Thus postwar California conceptualized itself as a higher-education utopia in which all Californians would be offered the opportunity to maximize their potential, whatever their individual capacities and talents might be. It was a vast and grand democratic plan; and like the schools, freeways, and housing tracts everywhere under construction in these years, it expressed the optimism of a state that had gone to war and prevailed and would never be the same. In later years, the drama and energy of this period and its aftermath, centered on the gubernatorial administration (1959–67) of Edmund G. "Pat" Brown—a skilled and astute Democrat from San Francisco, centrist in his politics, loving California and devoted to the building of its infrastructure—seemed a golden age of consensus and achievement, a founding era in which California fashioned and celebrated itself as an emergent nation-state.

10

O BRAVE NEW WORLD!

Seeking Utopia Through Science and Technology

Mount Palomar Observatory, San Diego County

CALIFORNIA STATE LIBRARY

Through engineering and technology, California invented itself as an American place. The completion of the trans-Sierra portion of the transcontinental railroad can be seen as an engineering feat of the highest order. The development of mining technology led to the Pelton turbine, a California invention, which in turn brought hydroelectricity to California, which in turn made possible an industrial infrastructure. Aviation had been a preoccupation since the 1880s, and when the airplane arrived in California, it was adopted and perfected there. By the 1920s, California had taken the lead in vacuum tube technology, making possible radio and television. By the 1930s, Californians were taking the lead in smashing the atom. In the 1950s, Californians were bringing into being, through the semiconductor, the digital revolution. Then came biotechnology, in which California has always led the nation. In each instance, the specific scientific, engineering, or technological advance emerging from California was linked to the effort to discover a truth, solve a problem, make a profit, make productive use of one's time, and, in the process, make the world a better and more interesting place. Open, flexible, entrepreneurial, unembarrassed by the profit motive, California emerged as a society friendly to the search for utopia through science and technology.

Nor were the natural sciences absent, even in the early years. A number of scientific expeditions had visited California in the Spanish and Mexican eras; John Charles Frémont was in his own way an explorer-scientist; and California produced a remarkable feat of ornithology in its first American decade. Andrew Jackson Grayson, an artist from Louisiana, had arrived in California with his wife and son in October 1846, having crossed the continent by covered wagon and narrowly escaped being marooned with the Donner party. (Grayson would later paint a portrait of himself, his wife, and his infant son arriving in California that remains one of the iconic images of transcontinental migration.) Serving as an officer with Frémont's volunteer battalion during the conquest, Grayson went into business in San Francisco following his release from service. Sometime in 1853, at the Mercantile Library in San Francisco, he had a life-changing experience: he saw an exhibit of Audubon's *Birds of America* (1827–38), and it inspired him to create a pictorial record of the birds of the Pacific Coast. For the next thirteen years, before his untimely death, Grayson devoted himself to the documentation and description (which the Smithsonian Institution published) and the painting of an ornithological portfolio, which he intended to issue as *Birds of the Pacific Slope.* Not until 1986 was this book published, by the Arion Press of San Francisco, and it then became immediately clear that John James Audubon had had a notable counterpart on the Pacific Coast.

The decade of Grayson's creativity, the 1850s, was an increasingly science-oriented period, topped off by the publication of Charles Darwin's *The Origin of Species* (1859). In 1847 Yale founded its Sheffield Scientific School, which would send a number of talented geologists out to California. Since 1848, the Swiss-born zoologist and geologist Louis Agassiz had been on the faculty at Harvard, working on his four-volume *Contributions to the Natural History of the United States,* which began to appear in 1857 and which would eventually address a number of California topics. On the evening of April 4, 1853, seven San Francisco gentlemen of scientific inclinations—their number included five doctors, one lawyer, and one real estate broker—set in motion the establishment of the California Academy of

Sciences, whose goal would be the "systematic survey of every portion of the state and the collection of a cabinet of rare and rich productions." Within a few years, scientists supported by the academy were conducting tidal and coastal, floral and faunal, riparian and montane, surveys of long-term importance.

Active in California since 1850 (and later president of the academy) was the English-born geographer and astronomer George Davidson, sent by the U.S. Coast and Geodetic Survey to chart the Pacific coast for navigational purposes. Davidson reported his findings in *Directory of the Pacific Coast* (1858), subsequently updated as the *Pacific Coast Pilot* series. The initial surveys sponsored by the academy and by the federal government concentrated upon the coast. Yet inland California—its mighty mountain ranges especially—beckoned as well, and in 1860 the state legislature established the Geological Survey under the direction of state geologist Josiah Dwight Whitney, a graduate of the Sheffield Scientific School and the author of *Metallic Wealth of the United States* (1854). Whitney gathered around him a team of similarly trained Yale men—William Henry Brewer and Clarence King, most notably, along with non-Yalie Lorenzo Yates—and set about the task of geologically surveying California. Recently returned from two years of climbing and study in Europe, and trying to recover from the shattering loss of his wife and child, Brewer, field director of the survey, spent four years in the wilds of California, measuring its heights and land formations. His younger colleague, Clarence King, was at once a first-rate geologist and a talented writer. King's *Atlantic Monthly* essays, collected as *Mountaineering in the Sierra Nevada* (1872), remain, according to Wallace Stegner, the best writing to come out of California during the frontier period other than Mark Twain's *Roughing It,* published that same year.

Even before the establishment of the survey, Californians had been aware of a great valley in the central Sierra Nevada, which in 1852 they began to call Yosemite. Years before academically trained geologists arrived there, however, yet another English émigré, James Mason Hutchings, began to promote the beauty of the Yosemite Valley through *Hutchings' Illustrated California Magazine,* which he founded in 1856, edited, and single-handedly wrote during the following years. Thanks in great measure to this magazine and Hutchings's *Scenes of Wonder and Curiosity in California* (1860), the Yosemite Valley began to emerge in the consciousness of Californians as a symbol of the physical grandeur—even the moral possibilities—of the new state. Visiting Yosemite in 1860, Unitarian minister Thomas Starr King urged Californians to build within themselves "Yosemites of the soul." A group of Californians led by Frederick Law Olmsted, the noted traveler and landscape architect, lobbied through Congress a bill (which Lincoln signed in 1864) setting aside under the protection of the state a huge tract of Sierra land that included the Yosemite Valley and the Mariposa Big Trees. For the rest of the century—indeed, for the twentieth century as well—camping trips to Yosemite became a rite of passage and celebration for Californians eager to define to themselves just exactly what California was all about.

For the Scottish-born naturalist John Muir, encountering the Yosemite Valley and the mountains of California gave rise to a lifetime vocation. Muir was not a purely scientific writer, but a descriptive naturalist with a solid scientific background. As a conservationist, he played an important role in having the Yosemite Valley transferred to federal jurisdiction in 1890. He also served as first president of the Sierra Club, founded in 1892. In May 1903, Muir camped out in Yosemite for two days with President Theodore Roosevelt. Then and thereafter, he ceaselessly advocated the creation of a national park system.

Muir's contemporary at the Sierra Club, Professor Joseph Le Conte of Berkeley, a Georgia native who had studied at Harvard with Agassiz and had joined the faculty of the University of California shortly after its founding, pursued an important academic career in geology and natural history. As a scientist, Le Conte was interested in the origins of mountain systems. As a philosopher with a theological orientation, he was interested in reconciling Darwinism and Christianity, as was evident in his *Religion and Science* (1874) and the popular course he taught at Berkeley on this topic. Among his students was Frank Norris (and possibly Jack London, if only as an auditor during London's brief stay there), who absorbed from Le Conte a sense of human nature as grounded in natural (read animal) life yet struggling for a higher consciousness: the theme of many a Norris (and London) short story and novel, and a topic to be taken up as well by John Steinbeck.

From its opening in 1869, the University of California was interested in mining, geology, agriculture, and mechanical engineering because these enterprises were crucial to the developing economy of the state. The greatest mechanical invention to come out of California during this period, however, the Pelton turbine, was not a product of academic research but—like the reaper, the telephone, and the airplane—the product of intuition and practical experimentation. The Pelton turbine would come from the world of mining, the seedbed for technological development in California through the 1870s.

For thousands of years, the technology of the waterwheel had remained essentially unchanged: running water flowed into a series of receptacles around the rim of a wheel, rotating the wheel and in turn operating the mechanism to which it was connected. The problem was, as every high school student of physics knows, that for every action there is an equal and opposite reaction, hence approximately half the power of the running water was lost when it hit the receptacle. Lester Pelton, an Ohio-born mechanic, carpenter, and millwright, arrived in California for the Gold Rush in 1850 and worked in the mining industry as it made the transition to an industrial enterprise using waterwheels to drive stampers to crush ore. Sometime in the early 1870s, Pelton observed a spinning water turbine whose misaligned cups allowed incoming water to be deflected promptly out of the cups; yet instead of rotating more slowly, that turbine spun even faster. Pelton experimented further with a double cup with a wedge-shaped divider in the middle; the new configuration drove the turbine faster yet. In 1880 Pelton obtained his first patent for a water turbine that multiplied the power of running water, hence the speed of the turbine, as much as sixfold. From this increased speed came not only more power for stamping ore, but the premise for hydroelectrical generation as spinning turbines, driven by water dropped from dams through penstocks, generated energy in hitherto undreamed-of amounts.

A SELF-TRAINED CALIFORNIA MECHANIC had thus advanced a technology that had remained static for thousands of years. But what about flight? Was this not a challenge of equally long standing? And who was to solve it? On the morning of August 28, 1883, on the edge of the Otay Mesa south of San Diego on land once belonging to the Rancho Tía Juana, the brothers John and James Montgomery assembled a 38-pound wood-and-fabric heavier-than-air glider that John, after much experimentation, had designed. Born in Yuba City in 1858, John Montgomery had grown up in a very Californian way—fascinated by flight. As early as the Gold Rush, Californians were speculating about the possibility of dirigible balloon flights to California from the East Coast. By the 1860s, Californians were experimenting with various forms of lighter-than-air flight. At the age of eleven, John Montgomery watched aeronaut Frank Merriott fly a steam-propelled hydrogen balloon above a Fourth of July crowd in Shell Mound Park on San Francisco Bay. Fascinated from that moment on by aviation, Montgomery pursued pioneering experiments in the design of a heavier-than-air glider through his education at Santa Clara College south of San Francisco and St. Ignatius College in San Francisco, where he took his master of science degree.

The Italian Jesuits who staffed St. Ignatius College were thoroughly at home with the scientific Enlightenment, and Montgomery received a first-rate education there; indeed, in 1880 the U.S. Bureau of Education ranked St. Ignatius College—despite its remoteness and small size—in the superior category as far as its scientific program and laboratory facilities were concerned. Much of the credit for this high ranking was due to Jesuit scientist Joseph Neri, chairman of the natural sciences department, who throughout the 1870s had been conducting pioneering experiments in electrical arc lighting. For the Centennial celebration of July 4, 1876, Neri illuminated Market Street with electrical arc lights and reflectors, the earliest such demonstration—by a decade!—of public illumination by electricity anywhere throughout the world. From Neri and from the two other Jesuits teaching at St. Ignatius—especially mathematician Aloysius Varsi and mechanical engineer Joseph Bayma—Montgomery absorbed a taste for experimentation, together with the conviction that fundamental scientific problems could be addressed, directly and effectively, in California as well as anywhere else.

By that August 1883 morning, all was in readiness. Inserting himself into a gull-winged glider that seemed to float out of the notebooks of Leonardo da Vinci, Montgomery was pulled aloft by his brother, tugging a long rope as one would fly a kite. Gaining an altitude of fifteen feet, the 130-pound Montgomery glided for six hundred feet, then safely landed. It was the first recorded heavier-than-air flight in human history, and it took place in California. It also confirmed something essential about the Golden State: that air travel—as engineering, as science, as metaphor, and as dream—was totally commensurate with the California identity. Over the next century, aviation would shape California, and California would shape aviation.

The Wright brothers flew their powered heavier-than-air craft on December 17, 1903, near Kitty Hawk, North Carolina. But neither North Carolina nor the Wrights' home state of Ohio was destined to capitalize upon the new invention. That role belonged to California. In January 1910, the Los Angeles County Chamber of Commerce organized an air show, held from the tenth through the twentieth at Dominguez Hills, that asserted once and for all that California—its climate, its engineering and technology, its entrepreneurial spirit and capital—intended to insert aviation into the very DNA code of the state. Over the next ten years, the names associated with aviation in California—Glenn Curtiss, Allan and Malcolm Loughead (later changed to Lockheed), John Northrop, Glenn Martin, Donald Douglas, T. Claude Ryan—would become brand names synonymous with flight itself.

Even as the Los Angeles Air Meet was being held in January 1910, the Lockheed brothers were busy with the design and production of a passenger-carrying seaplane, first flown in 1911. Glenn Curtiss and Glenn Martin were also designing and building pioneering aircraft. Graduating from MIT in 1914 with the first degree in aeronautical engineering granted by that institution, Donald Douglas joined Glenn Martin the next year at an assembly building near the present-day Los Angeles International Airport. In 1920, after a brief sojourn in Cleveland, Douglas opened his own aviation company in the back room of a barbershop on Pico Boulevard. By the fall of 1922, Douglas was manufacturing an airplane a week out of a former movie studio on Wilshire Boulevard in Santa Monica. T. Claude Ryan, meanwhile, had established Ryan Airlines of San Diego, a mail and passenger carrier. This got Ryan interested in the problem of long-distance flight. The result was the M-1, soon refined into the M-2 monoplane. Further modified as the N-X-22 Ryan NYP, Ryan's monoplane, christened the *Spirit of St. Louis*, was flown across the Atlantic in May 1927 by one of Ryan's young pilots, Charles Lindbergh.

So, too, did California—Southern California especially—pioneer passenger flight. By the mid-1920s, fully a third of the aviation traffic in the United States was operating from fifty private landing fields in Greater Los Angeles, where there were some three thousand licensed pilots (a group that included a notable number of women and minorities, especially African Americans). Four passenger lines—Western Air Express, Maddux Air Lines, Pacific Air Transport, and Standard Airlines—were offering regularly scheduled service to Salt Lake City, San Francisco, Seattle, and the Southwest. In 1929, Western announced plans for service to Kansas City, connecting to New York, in Fokker DP-32 passenger planes. Maddux Airlines, in which film director Cecil B. DeMille was an early investor, flew Ford Tri-Motors. On August 26, 1929, the gigantic (776 feet in length) German passenger dirigible *Graf Zeppelin* arrived in Los Angeles at Mines Field, site of the present-day LAX, on a round-the-world cruise. An estimated 150,000 visitors flocked to the airport by automobile and streetcar to catch a glimpse of the tethered behemoth whose very arrival signaled an impending era of international flight.

The following decade, thanks in part to pioneering aeronautical research at Caltech, Donald Douglas took a two-engine passenger/freight carrier through the evolutions of DC-1 and DC-2 to the DC-3, arguably the most serviceable aircraft in the history of aviation. Announcing the DC-3 in 1935, Douglas sold 803 of these aircraft in the next two years. By 1937, DC-3s were carrying 95 percent of the civilian traffic in the United States. During World War II, more than ten thousand DC-3s (redesignated the C-47 Skytrain or the C-54 by the Americans, the Dakota by the British) ferried hundreds of thousands of troops and an uncountable amount of freight. Even at this writing, DC-3s are still taxiing to and from terminals in remote regions of the planet.

Like Icarus in the Greek myth, John Montgomery fell to his death from a flying machine on October 31, 1911, having taken to the skies some fifty-five times on fabricated wings. The industry he had helped bring into being, however, would continue. In time, it would develop, through rocketry, to even more daring flights. In the postwar era, the breaking of the sound barrier by Chuck Yeager on October 14, 1947, over Muroc Air Base in the high California desert ushered in a new era of flight that would eventually extend itself into space, thanks to an upgraded version of the Atlas missile being manufactured in San Diego. In 1958 the National Aeronautics and Space Administration established its research-and-development-oriented Jet Propulsion Laboratory near the campus of Caltech, which oversaw its operation. Here the technology of space flight was fine-tuned, although Texas and Florida provided the actual flight centers, and early in the new millennium, the robotic exploration of Mars and the rings of Saturn was being directed and controlled from Pasadena.

ALREADY FOR NEARLY A CENTURY, Californians had been showing a special proclivity for the penetration of space through astronomy. As in the case of mining during the first frontier, astronomy stimulated pure science and the intricate technology required for its service. Three San Franciscans—George Davidson, James Lick, and Richard Samuel Floyd—played key roles in establishing this astronomical tradition. In 1879, Davidson, after nearly three decades of scientific activity in California, built the first astronomical observatory on the West Coast atop a hill in San Francisco. Although the instrumentation of the Davidson observatory was not particularly impressive, he used his 6.4-inch refracting device and auxiliary instruments to make a valuable series of astronomical observations keyed to geodetic research. He also evangelized constantly regarding the preeminence of astronomy as a pure and practical science in which California, given its superb atmospherics, might assume national leadership.

San Francisco millionaire James Lick was impressed by Davidson's call for astronomy to make California its home. When Lick died in October 1876, he left funds for an observatory supporting the most powerful telescope on the planet. Already, two years before his death, Lick had established a trust to supervise the construction of such an observatory, which would be turned over to the University of California when completed. To direct this enterprise, Lick chose Richard Samuel Floyd, a dashing former Confederate naval captain who had come to San Francisco following the war and married into wealth and social prominence. Floyd spent twelve years finding the site for the observatory—Mount Hamilton in Santa Clara County, 4,250 feet above sea level—building the necessary roads to the summit, constructing the observatory and auxiliary buildings, and, most important, casting and grinding (in Paris) a 36-inch lens, the largest in the world at that time, and designing and building not only the telescope to hold the lens but an apparatus to support its mechanical structures. The Lick Observatory—with the departed James Lick reinterred beneath the telescope—was ready for business by 1887. On his very first night on the telescope, on September 9, 1892, astronomer Edward Emerson Bernard discovered the faint fifth satellite of Jupiter, one of the great astronomical discoveries of the nineteenth century. The Lick Observatory also stimulated the founding of the Astronomical Society of the Pacific to support the observatory and other astronomical projects.

George Ellery Hale, a wealthy young Chicagoan and recent graduate of MIT who had been involved in astronomy since age fourteen, visited the Lick Observatory in July 1890 while on his honeymoon. Hale had already decided upon astronomy as his career, assisted in this desire by an observatory with a 12-inch lens, designed by the famed Chicago architect Daniel Hudson Burnham and presented to Hale by his father. By the time he was twenty-five, Hale was on the faculty of the University of Chicago. In the spring of 1903, he was back in California, this time exploring Mount Wilson above Pasadena as the site for a 60-inch mirror telescope to be financed by the newly established Carnegie Institution in Washington. Hale had a reflector telescope, which did not require an observatory, in operation by early 1904. He then led the effort to construct an observatory with a 60-inch mirror lens. This time the distinguished Pasadena architect Myron Hunt designed the structure, which was ready for use on December 20, 1908. That night, Hale took photographs of the Orion Nebula through what was then the most powerful telescope on the planet. Almost immediately, he began planning for a 100-inch lens, for which he found a patron in Los Angeles businessman John Hooker. The lens was cast in St. Gobain, France. There had never before been a disk of such magnitude, 13 inches thick and weighing five tons. It arrived in Pasadena in December 1908, and it took nine more years to polish it and to design and build for it an unprecedented reflection telescope housing. The Hooker telescope was ready for business in November 1917. It received nearly three times as much light from the stars as its 60-inch predecessor, which is to say, it increased the observable universe by 300 percent.

George Ellery Hale then turned his attention to two further scientific projects: a 200-inch disk and the upgrading of the Throop Polytechnic Institute into a first-rate center of scientific research. Founded in 1891 by Chicago businessman Amos Throop, the institute had been plodding along for nearly three decades as an amiable but mediocre school committed to technical training. This would not be good enough, Hale determined. In January 1907, Hale announced his dream of transforming Throop Polytechnic into a cutting-edge scientific institution. In the spring of 1910, the entire student body of Throop, five hundred strong, were asked (with twenty or so exceptions) to continue their educations at other places. That fall, Throop reopened its doors to a select thirty-one students. In 1920, the trustees voted to rename their institution the California Institute of Technology. On the faculty by that time were future Nobel Prize winner Robert Millikan and the renowned chemist Arthur Noyes, with whom Hale formed a triumvirate that led Caltech, as it was commonly called, to a new level of excellence. Soon, a Mount Wilson–based astronomer and Caltech faculty member, Edwin Powell Hubble, would be building upon the work of Harvard astronomer Henrietta Levitt and the Harvard-trained Belgian mathematician Abbé G. H. Lemaître, a Roman Catholic priest, to document the expanding universe—researches that would bring Albert Einstein to Pasadena on New Year's Day 1931 with some pressing questions on his mind as to how his calculations fit in with Hubble's observations. Caltech chemistry professor Linus Pauling, meanwhile, was applying quantum theory to calculations of molecular structure in order to better understand the nature of chemical bonding—work for which Pauling would receive the Nobel Prize for chemistry in 1954.

GEOLOGY, MINING, ASTRONOMY, AVIATION: here were some basic stimulants to scientific creativity in California. Now emerged yet another cause and matrix of scientific and technological virtuosity: electronics. At Palo Alto, new inventions would soon be making an entirely new world of transcontinental phone calls, radio, television, and high-speed electronics possible. Lee de Forest had earned his Ph.D. in 1899 from the Sheffield Scientific School at Yale University and entered the business world as a variously employed but mainly freelance inventor, who would eventually have 180 patents to his credit. In

1910 de Forest moved to Palo Alto, where he was associated with the Federal Telegraph Company. While there, in 1912, de Forest invented a vacuum tube called the Audion that converted alternating current to direct current and functioned as an amplifier. On the day it was invented, de Forest and his colleagues amplified by 120 times the sound of a housefly walking across a sheet of paper. That very summer, Edwin Howard Armstrong, a junior at Columbia, working in his home in Yonkers, New York, completed what was essentially the same invention, thereby setting in motion a lifelong patent battle with de Forest that would ultimately drive Armstrong to suicide. A much more attractive figure than de Forest, who was something of a P. T. Barnum, Armstrong was championed by Westinghouse, while de Forest's cause was taken up by the American Telephone and Telegraph Company, to which de Forest had sold his Audion tube for $50,000 as an amplifier for transcontinental phone calls. De Forest then went on to develop the Audion as an oscillator for radiotelephone transmission, thereby making possible the broadcast and reception of voice and music over the airways. Armstrong, meanwhile, was achieving similar—and, many would claim, superior—results. From Armstrong's and de Forest's inventions, however the credit must finally be apportioned, would come radio, motion picture sound, and television. De Forest himself moved to Hollywood, where he married the silent film star Marie Mosquini and continued to invent, to take out patents, and, to the legitimate distress of Edwin Armstrong, to promote himself as the Father of Radio.

But what about the transmission of images? Enter Philo T. Farnsworth, a native of Utah who moved to San Francisco at the age of twenty-one in 1925 and there conducted experiments with the electronic projection of images: *further* experiments, it should be noted, because at the age of fourteen, this precocious genius had grasped the fundamental technique of such projection—the scanning of images line by line—while plowing a field in repetitive furrows. Setting up a laboratory in a loft in the Cow Hollow section of San Francisco, Farnsworth attracted some local investors and with the help of his wife, his brother, and a small number of assistants created a technology based on a dissector tube he called the "orthicon" that allowed him on September 7, 1927, to transmit a simple image—a black glass with a line drawn down the center—through purely electronic means and thus demonstrate the basic technology of television. Farnsworth patented his invention shortly thereafter, but it came into competition with an earlier (1923) patent by the Russian émigré Vladimir Zworykin, whose experiments had been unsuccessful. Not until 1934 did the U.S. Patent Office award Farnsworth priority, but he was never able to capitalize on this recognition owing to the preexisting relationship between Zworykin and the all-powerful Radio Corporation of America. As in the case of the Pelton turbine, the pattern embodied by Farnsworth—that of a self-instructed Westerner bringing an important scientific experiment to conclusion in California—fit an established paradigm.

Lee de Forest and Philo T. Farnsworth had backing from members of the Stanford community. In the first three decades of the twentieth century, Stanford University developed a special expertise in electrical engineering, thanks in significant measure to Professor Frederick Emmons Terman. Born with the century, the son of a noted Stanford professor (the co-inventor of the Stanford-Binet IQ test), Terman took a bachelor's degree in chemistry at Stanford and a master's degree in electrical engineering there in 1922 before going on to MIT for a doctorate (1924) in electrical engineering under the renowned theoretician Vannevar Bush. Returning to Palo Alto to recover from an attack of tuberculosis, Terman soon began teaching at his alma mater. Fascinated with the commercial possibilities of the vacuum tube, he devoted his research energies to this device, which had already stimulated a whole new range of industries.

Terman was especially interested in Philo T. Farnsworth's experiments with television, and he took his students on field trips to San Francisco to observe Farnsworth's research. As the 1920s became the 1930s, Terman became ever more strongly convinced that Stanford University should participate not only in theoretical research relating to electrical engineering, but in its commercial implementation as well.

In 1937, Terman made available faculty advice, laboratory facilities, and one hundred dollars' worth of supplies to Stanford graduate Russell Varian, who had worked for Farnsworth, and his brother Sigurd, a former pilot with Pan American Airways, as they worked on a new kind of vacuum tube designed to amplify microwave signals into an ultra-high-frequency current. On the evening of August 19, 1937, the first klystron tube, as the Varian brothers called it, was put into operation, as subsequently described in the *Journal of Applied Physics.* Work continued on the klystron tube at Stanford through the rest of the decade. When war came, it was a key component in the success of radar.

Two other Stanford graduates, meanwhile—David Packard and William Hewlett, each of them a student of Terman's—were, with his guidance, designing and building an audio oscillator that would generate electrical signals within the frequency range of human hearing and would, when connected to a loudspeaker, produce a high-quality tone. Terman instantly saw the commercial possibilities of the audio oscillator. He had personally recruited Packard from Schenectady, New York, where Packard had gone to work for General Electric, inducing him to return to Palo Alto and work with Hewlett on the project. Hewlett and Packard formed a company, headquartered in Palo Alto in the one-car garage of the house Packard and his wife were renting, with Hewlett moving into the backyard cottage. By the late 1930s, they had perfected the audio oscillator and the Hewlett-Packard Company had made its first big sale: four oscillators to Walt Disney Productions for the enhancement of the music for *Fantasia* (1940).

Across the Bay in Berkeley, meanwhile, a contribution was being made to the most important scientific and technological feat of the twentieth century: releasing the power of the atom. There, UC Berkeley physics professor Ernest Orlando Lawrence, yet another Yale graduate, had invented and developed by 1931 a cyclotron that generated high-energy beams of nuclear particles that made possible the exploration of the atomic nucleus, which is to say, the ability to peer into the very building blocks of matter. In 1939 Lawrence was awarded the Nobel Prize in physics for both the development of the cyclotron and his researches into atomic structure and transmutation. It would be ridiculous to claim for California any exclusivity in the task of releasing the power of the atom; on the other hand, Lawrence and his colleague J. Robert Oppenheimer, who also held an appointment at Caltech, were in the 1930s making Berkeley a center of nuclear research, with Oppenheimer doing important work on the quantum theory of molecules and the nature of antiparticles. From 1942 to 1945, Oppenheimer directed the atomic energy research project at Los Alamos, New Mexico, to which he recruited a number of his Berkeley students and colleagues. After the war, he chaired the general advisory committee of the Atomic Energy Commission. The Lawrence Laboratory at Berkeley emerged as an epicenter of further nuclear research, with seven of its scientists winning Nobel prizes.

The Second World War, during which Terman worked on the top-secret radar project at Harvard, further expanded his horizons as he witnessed the electronics field burgeoning geometrically. So, too, did the Varian brothers and Hewlett and Packard, also involved in defense manufacturing, have their horizons broadened during the war years as they came into contact with mass markets beyond their prewar dreams. Through the tragedy of war, a brave new world of electronics was being brought into existence; and Stanford University, Terman determined, would play a key role in its development. That university, after all, already held a leadership position in electrical engineering and electronics. It also owned more than eight thousand acres of prime land available for development. Returning to Stanford as dean of engineering in 1946 (becoming provost in 1955, senior vice president in 1958), Terman pursued his plan to make Stanford and Palo Alto the world headquarters of electronics research and development. Terman's program was threefold: bring talented inventors into interface with Stanford faculty, establish a research institute that was distinct from the university, and open an industrial park. He succeeded in all three ventures. In 1949 the Varian brothers formed Varian Associates to provide klystrons and other electronic devices for military and commercial use. In 1953 Varian and Associates became the first company to establish its operation at the newly formed (1951) Stanford Industrial Park. All told, Stanford University would recover $2.56 million in licensing fees before patents expired in the early 1970s for the $100 in seed money it had provided to the Varians in 1937. When profit margins such as this became known, investors took notice, most notably Arthur Rock of San Francisco, who pioneered a new form of business financing in which investors took risks alongside company officials and had a say in the development and management of the enterprise. By the late twentieth century, Palo Alto had become the epicenter of high-tech venture capitalism, serving Silicon Valley start-ups.

ENTER THE SEMICONDUCTOR. For four decades, vacuum tubes of various kinds had been making possible the electronic era through the transmission of electricity in various formats. But vacuum tubes, elegant and diverse as they might be, were fragile, bulky, energy-consuming, and given to overheating. The more complex the electronics, moreover, the more vacuum tubes were needed. When the high-speed computer age dawned in 1945, the ENIAC computer (the Bank of America was a pioneer in its commercial use) required more than seventeen thousand tubes and consumed a prodigious amount of electricity. During the war, scientists began to ask the question: was there another way to conduct and amplify electricity into a variety of formats and uses? Could the vacuum tube be replaced with some kind of solid material: not a conductor such as copper, but a semiconductor such as silicon—a nonmetallic chemical element, number fourteen on the periodic table, found in rocks and minerals—that would do the work of vacuum tubes? In 1945, Bell Laboratories in Murray Hill, New Jersey, formed a team to look into the problem. Just before Christmas 1947, two members of that team, John Bardeen and Walter Brattain, observed that power increased when electrical signals were passed through a crystal of germanium, a rare grayish-white metal chemically similar to tin. Bardeen and Brattain called this amplifying circuit a "point-contact transistor." Their colleague William Shockley, while not present at this first observation, began to explain it theoretically through quantum physics and to develop the theory of an even more sophisticated amplifying device: a crystal in a sandwich shape, with various impurities added, which Shockley called the "junction transistor." In 1951 the first of these sandwich-shaped junction transistors based on Shockley's semiconductor theory was produced, and in 1956 Shockley, Bardeen, and Brattain shared a Nobel Prize in physics.

By this time, Shockley had reestablished himself in Palo Alto, where he had grown up. There, in February 1956, with financing from Beckman Instruments, he founded the Shockley Semiconductor Laboratory. His goal: to develop and produce a silicon transistor. Germanium was rare, but silicon was a common chemical element and could also tolerate high temperatures. Headstrong and paranoid, Shockley alienated his younger staff, eight of whom broke away in 1957 under the leadership of MIT Ph.D. Robert Noyce to found Fairchild Semiconductor. Noyce and, working independently, Jack Kilby of Texas Instruments separately invented the integrated circuit chip, and Fairchild was very soon raking in $130 million a year. Shockley joined the Stanford faculty as professor of engineering in 1963, and his company folded in 1968. (At Stanford, Shockley, straying from his field, became involved in race-related IQ studies, which made him a pariah among his colleagues.) In 1968 Noyce and his colleague Gordon E. Moore left Fairchild to found the Intel Corporation. At Intel, electrical engineer Ted Hoff, a Rensselaer graduate with a Stanford Ph.D., invented a microprocessor chip into which intelligence could be programmed via software. Brought on the market in 1971 as the 4004, Hoff's microprocessor was one sixteenth of an inch long and consisted of 2,300 transistors. The 4004 had as much calculating power as the ENIAC computer of 1945, which had occupied three thousand cubic feet and required more than seventeen thousand vacuum tubes.

Making such computer power personally available to millions of Americans was the mission of two talented young Californians in their twenties, Steven Paul Jobs, who had been raised in Mountain View and Los Altos and had dropped out of Reed College, and San José native Stephen Wozniak, who had recently dropped out of UC Berkeley. Working together in the Jobs family garage in Los Altos, Jobs and Wozniak designed and built the prototype for a personal computer they called "Apple I." Shown the prototype, a local electronics retailer ordered twenty-five. Jobs sold his Volkswagen microbus and Wozniak his Hewlett-Packard calculator to raise the $1,300 necessary to go into production. Apple I went on sale in 1976 for the biblical price of $666.66 and earned $774,000 in sales. Apple II, with built-in circuitry that allowed it to interface directly with a color monitor, made its appearance the next year. Some sixteen thousand software programs were written for its use. Apple II earned $139 million within three years.

Silicon Valley, as the region triangulated by Palo Alto, Sunnyvale, and San José soon came to be called, was a place, a culture, a center of invention and manufacture that revolutionized society itself by taking to new levels the way people communicated, stored and retrieved information, analyzed problems, and, increasingly, thought. It was as if a new neural network had been created for the human race: a digital and silicon-based circuitry that extended the capacity of the individual human being by linking him or her to a vast ocean of data and to software applications capable of driving a myriad of programs for navigating that ocean. The introduction to the public in 1983 of the Internet—in the invention of which California-based scientists played key roles—compounded this collective noosphere (to use the terminology of the Jesuit mystic Teilhard de Chardin), this shared and integrated community of information. No wonder Silicon Valley companies were so different in their organizational structure, so nonhierarchical, so quick to cluster talent for specific purposes, then reassemble it for other tasks! Their very product represented an evolutionary step forward for the human race.

AND THE BIOLOGICAL BASIS of life itself was also being probed and manipulated—sometimes controversially—through the new DNA-based science of genetics and the biotechnology that could manipulate the digital code of life to useful effect. In contrast to computer technology, no exclusive California claim could be made for biotechnology, although by the millennium forty percent of all biotechnological research and manufacturing in the United States was located in California. In Amgen, Inc., of Thousand Oaks and Ventura County could be found the largest biotech company in the world, with sales reaching more than $3 billion annually by the year 2000. Most biotechnology companies tended to cluster in dedicated suburban office parks, with the Bay Area and San Diego in the lead. The posh San Diego suburb of La Jolla near the UC San Diego campus exfoliated in a coterie of companies bearing such Dr. Seuss–like names (Theodor Geisel, otherwise known as Dr. Seuss, lived in La Jolla) as Amylin, Biosite, Cytel, Gensia, Lidak, Ligand, Mycogen, Stratagene, Telios, and Viagene, each of them promising to unlock the secret of life. Most biotech companies were working on medically related initiatives: a cure for cancer, AIDS, strokes, heart attacks, blood clots, or hepatitis; gene therapy; better skin graft techniques for burns; treatments for hypertension and other chronic ailments. As in the case of computer technology, biotechnology spread from the university into such for-profit companies as Cetus, BioGrowth, CalBio, Gilead, and Genentech, where the very building blocks of life were being engineered not for the sake of pure science (although the spirit of science pervaded the enterprise) but for the sake of putting useful and marketable products before the public. Gilead Sciences of Foster City, for example, devoted itself to pioneering a new class of potential human therapeutics based on nucleotides, the primary molecules of life.

In contrast to the Silicon Valley software boom launched by the microprocessor, with its sudden and breathtaking breakthroughs and overnight riches, the development of biotechnology was a more gradual process. It was seeking to imitate, after all, processes that had taken hundreds of millions of years in the evolution of animal and human biology. Universities, moreover, were playing catch-up in the field, creating biotechnology parks near their campuses, forming research and profit-sharing programs with for-profit companies. UC San Diego had been the Stanford of biotechnology, in that the very establishment of this UC campus in the mid-1960s was based on the developing biotechnology culture of that city, which it intensified. Attracted to the Torrey Pines section of La Jolla as well was the Salk Institute for Biological Studies, brought there in 1963 by its founder, Dr. Jonas Salk, known for his work in developing a vaccine against poliomyelitis. Ensconced in a breathtaking campus designed by Louis Kahn atop a mesa overlooking the sea, the Salk Institute supported such Fellows as Sir Francis Crick, co-discoverer of DNA, and in turn attracted other nonprofit research institutes such as the nearby Neurosciences Institute, dedicated to the study of the mind-body relationship. Thanks to the continuing efforts of Scripps Institute of Oceanography professor Roger Revelle, the regents of the University of California authorized the creation of a science-oriented campus in San Diego. By 1964 two Nobel laureates and thirteen Academy of Sciences members were establishing the foundations of UC San Diego as an important center of scientific research. According to longtime newspaper columnist Neil Morgan, UC San Diego completed the de-provincialization of California's southernmost metropolis—transforming it, that is, from a Lisbon-like enclave, a garrison resort, into the sixth largest city in the United States and a national center of scientific research, with more Ph.D.s in its population than in that of any other city in the nation.

Across 150 years, aspiring Californians had adopted nature as the primary symbol of what they hoped to achieve as a society. Nature as wilderness, true, as in the case of John Muir; but also nature working in tandem with technology: moving land and water in mining and irrigation; generating electricity by multiplying the power of water-driven turbines sixfold; taking to the air on wings of fabric and bamboo; peering into the multi-billion-year past of the cosmos through lenses ground to exquisite purity. Californians had harnessed electromagnetic waves to transmit sound and images; had helped release the power of the atom; had devised chips and circuits storing information in quantities that only the mathematics of exponents and the refashioned language of ancient Greece could express. And then, at the end of one millennium and the beginning of the next, they had begun to appropriate into science, medicine, and industry the genetic building blocks and structure of nature herself.

One side effect of this orientation to science was to make California an epicenter of science fiction, as exemplified by, among others, Ray Bradbury, Robert Heinlein, and Ursula LeGuin. California even supported the rise of a homegrown religion, the Church of Scientology, founded in Los Angeles in 1954 by science and science-fiction writer L. Ron Hubbard. Sometimes this proclivity could run into bizarre channels, as in the case of the thirty-nine members of the Heaven's Gate cult who committed suicide in Rancho Santa Fe in San Diego County in late March 1997, believing that they were scheduled to rendezvous with a spaceship trailing the Hale-Bopp comet. Yet so fervent had become this faith in science that 59 percent of the Californians voting in the November 2004 election passed Proposition 71 authorizing the sale of $3 billion in bonds over a ten-year period to finance state-monitored programs of stem cell research. Bypassing the National Institutes of Health, which had been sponsoring biological research at the federal level for 117 years, Proposition 71 asserted California as a nation-state enamored—beyond considerations of theology and/or fiscal prudence in the midst of a continuing budget crisis—of seeking utopia through science and technology, which had become a way of life.

11

AN IMAGINED PLACE

Art and Life on the Coast of Dreams

Poet Robinson Jeffers and art patron Albert Bender, Tor House, Carmel, 1930s

CALIFORNIA STATE LIBRARY

The twentieth century witnessed the debut of three entertainment media—film, radio, and television—dependent upon electronic technologies developed in California. Each of these media, film especially, took root in Southern California as it matured. To the traditional concerns of literature in California—nature, naturalism, and bohemia—were added the *noir* worldview and the apocalypse. A prior concern, meanwhile—the frontier—migrated into motion pictures in the form of the Western. Continuing its commitment to landscape, painting remained en plein air and Postimpressionistic into the 1920s before exploding into Fauvist color with the group of artists known as the Society of Six. Painting embraced Expressionism and abstraction at midcentury, then diversified into a number of styles at the end of the century. Photography made a similar transition from the dreamy painterly values of Pictorialism in the early 1900s to the austere purities of the work of Edward Weston and Ansel Adams. Likewise did architecture sustain its commitment to Arts and Crafts and Mediterranean Revival into the 1920s, until modernism emerged to dominate the midcentury. Serious music, at first an almost exclusively performance art, ran to pattern. It was traditional, even retardaire, into the 1930s. Then arrived the émigré composers. Following the war, the modernism of the émigrés attracted a second generation of California composers and seeped into West Coast jazz. Through all these transformations—in film, radio, television, writing, painting, architecture, and music—California continued to energize the arts as matrix, occasion, and subject. Cumulatively, across the century, the arts defined and redefined California as an imagined place.

Motion pictures did not initially establish themselves in California, which is ironic given that the experiments in 1872 of photographer Eadweard Muybridge, proving that a horse raised all four feet from the ground simultaneously when trotting, together with the Zoopraxiscope that Muybridge invented to project images of the running horse on a screen, prophesied the near-simultaneous invention of the motion picture camera in France, England, and the United States in March, April, June, and October 1895. The early studios were in New York (Vitagraph, Biograph), Philadelphia (Lubin), New Jersey (Edison), and Chicago (Essanay, Selig). But with the exception of Chicago, these locations were perilously close to the New Jersey–based Motion Picture Patents Company, known more familiarly as the Trust, which sought nothing less than an all-encompassing regulation of the new industry through the payment of taxes for each piece of equipment in use and per-foot royalties on film either produced or exhibited. Then there was the mercurial nature of East Coast weather, which rendered filming in the outdoors a persistent uncertainty. In the winter of 1907–08, Selig director Francis Boggs and cameraman Thomas Persons, needing good weather, entrained for Los Angeles, where they filmed the outdoor scenes for *The Count of Monte Cristo* (1908). Liking Los Angeles as a location, they established a Selig operation there, filming *In the Sultan's Power* (1908), the first complete film to be made in Los Angeles, and used a Classical Revival villa and gardens as background for *The Roman* (1908). Then came a production of *Carmen* (1908), which involved the building of an entire set. Not only did the Selig staff appreciate the reliably good weather of Los Angeles, they also relished the distance from the subpoena servers constantly being dispatched by the lawyers hired by Edison Laboratories to initiate suits against producers who were not always willing to pay what Edison considered their fair share of licensing and reel footage fees.

Between 1908 and 1909 a number of other filmmakers, equally reluctant to pay tribute to the Trust, arrived in Los Angeles. In the winter of 1910, director David Wark Griffith arrived, returning to Southern California in the winters of 1911, 1912, and 1913 to film outdoor scenes. For his first all-California film, *The Thread of Destiny* (1910), a story of Old California starring Mary Pickford, Griffith moved his troupe out to Mission San Gabriel. Another all-California film, *In Old California* (1910), soon followed. Most of the movies Griffith made in these early years—including *The Converts* (1910), *The Way of the World* (1910), and *Over Silent Paths* (1910)—were set in Spanish or Mexican California and filmed in the missions of San Gabriel, San Fernando, or San Juan Capistrano. A Southerner with Confederate sympathies, Griffith loved the missions as icons of lost grandeur and a vanished way of life.

In the summer of 1912, comedy director Mack Sennett, a disciple of Griffith's, arrived in Los Angeles, and within thirty minutes of his troupe's arrival at the train station, Sennett was busy filming the first of many Keystone comedies. A brash Irish Canadian given to liquor, cigars, and women (tradition assigns to him the invention of the casting couch), Sennett loved Los Angeles and featured it as the environment and background of countless Keystone comedies. Taking to the streets for innumerable chase scenes, Sennett caught Los Angeles in the process of becoming a major American city. Viewing these comedies across the country, Americans caught glimpses of inviting bungalows on broad avenues lined with palm, pepper, or eucalyptus trees. It was always sunny, and there was never any snow on the ground.

The New York director Cecil Blount DeMille arrived in Los Angeles in December 1913 to film a Western entitled *The Squaw Man* (1914), which he was making in partnership with the San José–born New York vaudeville producer Jesse Lasky and Lasky's brother-in-law, Samuel Goldfish (later Goldwyn), who was in the wholesale glove business. "I'm in," said Goldfish with typical laconicism the night the Jesse L. Lasky Feature Play Company was organized by Lasky, DeMille, and Goldfish over dinner at the Claridge Grill in New York. (As Samuel Goldwyn, Goldfish became famous for saying "Include me out" when he didn't like a deal.) In Los Angeles, DeMille located an L-shaped barn abutting an orange grove on the corner of the dirt roads Selma and Vine, which he rented and transformed into a makeshift studio. Released in February 1914, *The Squaw Man* earned $244,700, which represented an enormous return on investment. Not only did DeMille decide to stay in Hollywood, he became, along with Griffith, the iconic Hollywood director, dressed in quasi-military style (jodhpurs and riding boots, epaulets on his shirt), directing large-scale films in the studio or outdoors like a general on campaign. Griffith's *The Birth of a Nation* (1914) and *Intolerance* (1916) set new standards for ambitious production, and in such films as *Carmen* (1915) and *The Ten Commandments* (1923), DeMille was not far behind. Each of them owed a debt (especially DeMille) to David Belasco, a San Francisco–born New York producer specializing in opulent presentations that Belasco helped transmute into the Hollywood approach, with its obsession with lavish production values, its taste for pageantry, and, above all, its belief that *story, story, story* must ever energize the film and move it forward. DeMille himself acknowledged Griffith as the preeminent master. "He was the teacher of us all," DeMille later said of his fellow founder. "Not a picture has been made since his time that does not bear some trace of his influence."

By the 1920s it was apparent that the production of films in Hollywood—a district of Los Angeles in the foothills of the Santa Monica Mountains eight miles northwest of downtown—would be on an industrialized basis, which is to say, in corporately owned studios in which screenwriters, directors, actors and actresses, technicians, and support staff were on salary. Even Griffith, who was very much an independent director in the European manner, made his peace with the studio system in 1919 when he joined Mary Pickford, her husband Douglas Fairbanks, and comedian Charlie Chaplin to found United Artists. Griffith's three partners were already giants in their field and destined to remain so. Chaplin's best films—among them *The Kid* (1921), *The Gold Rush* (1925), and *City Lights* (1931)—established the Little Tramp as the best-known comedic figure of the twentieth century. Pickford and Fairbanks, meanwhile, not only defined stardom in the new medium, but made "Pickfair," their hilltop estate in Beverly Hills, the White House of Hollywood: the very essence of glamor and respectability (as envisioned in the movie kingdom).

Through the 1920s and early 1930s, the film studios—with such founding entities as Fine Arts, Fox, Famous Players, and Metro consolidating into such larger presences as Metro-Goldwyn-Mayer (1924), RKO (1928), Warner Bros. (1929), Twentieth Century–Fox (1935), and Paramount in its final form (1935), and such earlier presences as Universal (1915), United Artists (1919), and Columbia (1922) managing to hold their own—continued to develop as sophisticated corporations, with integrated links to theater chains and distribution companies. Thanks to Adolph Zukor, a Hungarian émigré of long rabbinical lineage, Paramount was especially successful in this regard, as attested by its studios in Hollywood, its corporate headquarters on Times Square in New York City, and its connection to the German film industry—a connection that helped give Paramount films from this period a kind of slinky finish. Studios did have personalities and preferences, which developed even further after the introduction of sound in the late 1920s.

What was amazing about Hollywood was that, decade after decade, it never fell into a slump. In the early 1900s film was conceptualized as narrative and made a vital connection with the masses. In the 1910s, just about every genre—comedies, tragedies, biblical and historical epics, domestic dramas, the Westerns favored by Carl Laemmle at Universal—was introduced in fully realized formats. In the domestic dramas of Cecil B. DeMille from this period—*The Cheat* (1915), *Old Wives for New* (1918), *Male and Female* (1919), *Don't Change Your Husband* (1919), *For Better or Worse* (1919), *Why Change Your Wife?* (1920)—a generation of recently derusticated Americans was exposed to the amenities, niceties, and dangers of urban life, including adultery and divorce. During the 1930s, Hollywood can be said to have helped stabilize the nation by offering intensities of psychological release for the stress everyone was experiencing: gangster films (*Little Caesar* [1930], *Public Enemy* [1931], *Scarface* [1932]) with which to question capitalism itself; horror films (*Dracula* [1931], *Frankenstein* [1931], *Freaks* [1932], *Doctor X* [1932]) to express the dread of sudden and catastrophic collapse; sexually charged films (*Dishonored* [1931], *Red Dust* [1932]) that expressed a sense of rebellion against the established order; and, toward the end of the decade, great costume dramas (*Anthony Adverse* [1936], *The Prisoner of Zenda* [1937]) that showed the triumph of individual courage over hostile historical forces; Westerns (*Stage Coach* [1939], *Union Pacific* [1939]) renewing hope in the American experiment; and *Gone with the Wind* (1939), in a class by itself, recasting the American experience as an epic of defiance in the face of defeat. Never, as historian Arthur Schlesinger, Jr., has pointed out, have so many great films been produced in such rapid succession, and never did Hollywood play such a powerful and direct role in the subliminal and public life of the nation.

Starting in the mid-1930s, the takeover of Germany by National Socialism set in motion a mass emigration of talented Europeans—academics, scientists, doctors, psychiatrists and psychoanalysts, writers, artists, actors, film directors—to the United

States. With its opportunities for employment in the film industry, its salubrious climate, and perhaps even its greater distance from the conflict, Southern California got more than its fair share of these creative émigrés. Already, a cadre of cinematic Mitteleuropeans—directors Ernst Lubitsch, Max Reinhardt, and William Wyler, screenwriter and director Billy Wilder, actor and director Erich von Stroheim, actor Peter Lorre, actress Marlene Dietrich—had found homes and happiness in the Southland, based in part upon the long-standing connections between the American and German film industries. With the rise of Nazism, this vanguard became a phalanx as such creative personalities as writers Thomas Mann, Heinrich Mann, Alfred Doblin, Lion Feuchtwanger, Christopher Isherwood, and Franz Werfel; playwright Bertolt Brecht; directors Otto Preminger and Jean Renoir; actress Hedy Lamarr; composers Igor Stravinsky, Dmitri Tiomkin, Franz Waxman, Max Steiner, Erich Wolfgang Korngold, Miklos Rozsa, Darius Milhaud, and Arnold Schoenberg; conductors Otto Klemperer and Bruno Walter; artist Man Ray; and so many others flocked to Southern California, where the majority of them found employment in the film industry. Settling in Pacific Palisades, novelist Thomas Mann—known to the émigré community as "the Kaiser"—functioned as something like the head of a government in exile, a Charles de Gaulle without portfolio. The émigrés dramatically internationalized the film industry, the academy, music, medicine, and other aspects of life in California. In doing so, they anticipated and foreshadowed the even greater internationalization that would occur after the reformation of federal immigration laws in the mid-1960s.

The direct and powerful connection among event, audience, and the movies intensified during the years leading up to the Second World War as the United States weighed its alternatives. A pro-British lobby, operating under the direction of Alexander Korda with a discretion approaching secrecy, stimulated the productions of such pro-British films as *Gunga Din* (1939), *Goodbye, Mr. Chips* (1939), *Nurse Edith Cavell* (1939), *The Sea Hawk* (1940), *That Hamilton Woman* (1941), and others. Such films made it seem inevitable that the United States would eventually join Great Britain in its fight for survival, and were followed by the Academy Award–winning *Mrs. Miniver* (1942) to tell Americans why they had done the right thing by signing up. Hollywood solidly enlisted in the war effort, and numerous film stars and some directors—Jimmy Stewart, Robert Montgomery, Tyrone Power, Sabu, Gene Autry, Clark Gable, John Ford, and William Wyler, among others—compiled distinguished records in active military service. The 1st Motion Picture Unit at the Hal Roach Studio in Culver City, more commonly known as Fort Roach (Captain Ronald Reagan was serving there), supervised the production of training films, and the Bureau of Motion Pictures of the Office of War Information encouraged the production of patriotic scripts.

In the Cold War that followed, the pro-Soviet sentiments in some of these scripts—even such a slight suggestion as that in *Action on the North Atlantic* (1943), with a screenplay by John Howard Lawson, in which Humphrey Bogart, playing a merchant marine officer, identifies a Soviet plane as "one of our own"—brought Hollywood on the carpet before the House Un-American Activities Committee. Dalton Trumbo, one of the "Hollywood Ten" who refused to testify before HUAC in the fall of 1947, called this period the Time of the Toad; and it was a fearful time, to be sure—the testimonies, the naming of names, the recantations, all this followed by a blacklist that would remain in force for the better part of a decade—but it must also be pointed out that some Hollywood writers, including most of the Ten (Lawson was especially active) were in fact at one time or another members of the Communist Party, which was reputed to throw the best parties in Hollywood. The Cold War reactivated the tensions of the prewar era. The Department of Justice broke the connections between studios, theaters, and distributorships, and television constituted its own form of threat.

But even as these troubles were occurring, Hollywood was reaching yet another high point of art and social commentary in the film noirs of the period: dark, brooding dramas expressing the political tensions, the buried animosities based on race and class that were now beginning to surface, the mistrust between men and women separated too long by war, the distrust of the governments that had sent millions to their deaths. Then, in the 1950s, fully recovered from both television and the breakup of its monopolies, Hollywood began to issue a new string of biblical and costume dramas—*Quo Vadis?* (1951), *The Robe* (1953) (this in the new CinemaScope process), *The Ten Commandments* (1956), *Ben-Hur* (1959)—that recapitulated the way that Hollywood had won the hearts and minds of the American people earlier in the century.

THE FILM NOIR of the late 1940s was inspired by a new genre of writing, namely, the hard-boiled detective story. Such writers as Robinson Jeffers, John Steinbeck, and William Saroyan, however, still maintained their preoccupation with the California themes of nature, naturalism, and bohemia, now transmuted to a more politicized community of resistance. Among the most noted poets in California during the twentieth century, Robinson Jeffers took the fundamental aesthetic premise of California since the mid-nineteenth century, nature, and made of it a lifestyle, a philosophy, and a poetic practice. Jeffers described his approach as "In-Humanism," by which he meant the effort to transcend the limits of the weak and faltering biological self in favor of what was permanent in nature. In one of his best poems, a hawk alights upon a stone, and Jeffers sees in this image a perfect text from nature itself: the fierce consciousness of the hawk, the final indifference of the stone. In 1919 Jeffers had himself escaped into what he termed "the massive mysticism of stone" by building for himself a stone tower on the Carmel coast where he lived until his death in 1962, producing an array of long narrative poems based on classical or biblical themes and set in the backcountry of Big Sur, together with intense lyrics and such hyper-isolationist jeremiads as "Shine, Perishing Republic" (1924).

For John Steinbeck, nature was not so much a symbol of transcendence as the very matrix of the here and now. Nature was the all and the everything, the tide pool on the Monterey coast (Steinbeck's favorite metaphor) in which all living creatures were contained within the same boundaries and led a common life, devoid of ends and goals ("non-teleological" was the way Steinbeck put it) beyond surviving in their immediate environment. For all his reputation as a social commentator, Steinbeck, who had studied biology at Stanford in the late 1920s, saw human life in more elemental terms: biologically, that is, as living organisms in a landscape, and collectively as "group-man" (again, Steinbeck's term) held together by biological linkages. Animal imagery abounds in Steinbeck's fiction. His characters are fascinated by animals and frequently compared with them. They also live communally—whether they are strikers, or the Joad family, or loafers on Cannery Row—and in such collectivity they achieve their finest moments and fullest definitions.

The sheer insistence of nature in California, what he experienced as its overwhelming yet uninterpreted presence, got very much on the nerves of critic Edmund Wilson, the quintessential Easterner, when he was living in Santa Barbara in the 1920s. Later, in the 1930s, Wilson would return to California as a reporter and would see no reason to change his mind. The Pacific Ocean, Wilson noted in *The Boys in the Back Room* (1940), was the prime case in point. The Atlantic bespoke culture, history, Europe. The Pacific, by contrast, was vast and uninterpreted. There was no metaphor for it; indeed, there were few metaphors for California, which to Wilson seemed a big, beautiful, but empty place. Hence, California writers tended to adhere to a simplistic relationship to nature, or, if dealing with urban matters—as writers of detective stories commonly do—to sustain a near-solipsistic drama of the self against society. A minimalist culture, Wilson argued, encouraged the minimalist style so pervasive in the hard-boiled fiction of the 1930s then being pioneered by James M. Cain, Horace McCoy, Richard Hallis (Eric Knight), and John Steinbeck. The San Francisco-based Pinkerton-detective-turned-novelist Dashiell Hammett—the Ernest Hemingway of the detective story—introduced the hard-boiled style in such classics as *Red Harvest* (1929) and *The Maltese Falcon* (1930), in which detective Sam Spade asked nothing of anyone and expected even less. As in the case of Steinbeck's *The Grapes of Wrath* (1939) becoming John Ford's brilliant movie of 1940, *The Maltese Falcon* became equally well known through the 1941 film directed by John Huston and starring Humphrey Bogart in one of the most riveting performances of his career.

Hammett moved to Southern California in the early 1930s to work in Hollywood, as did F. Scott Fitzgerald, James M. Cain, Horace McCoy, and William Faulkner. In such figures, fiction and film coalesced. Edmund Wilson, in fact, described *The Grapes of Wrath* as the first major American novel to be written as a movie script. While most writers had their difficulties with the assembly-line techniques of the studios, their cinematic experiences strengthened their novels and vice versa. Fiction in California became tense, telegraphic, story-driven. It also began to explore more completely the life and times of the Golden State. The protagonist of Knight's *You Play the Black and the Red Comes Up* (1938) ends his story with an evocation of California as an emotionally empty place: "I could remember everything about California," he notes, "but I couldn't feel it. I tried to get my mind to remember something that it could feel, too, but it was no use. It was all gone. All of it. The pink stucco houses and the palm trees and the stores built like cats and dogs and frogs and ice-cream freezers and the neon lights around everything."

Such an evocation of bleakness and emotional disconnect characterized the life and art of Raymond Chandler both before and after a measure of fame came to him: his voyage into a heart of darkness, an existential void—the edge of nothingness, as Chandler described it—which Edmund Wilson saw as the matrix of the best writing in California during this period. Even Chandler's exacting biographer, Frank MacShane, seems to despair of chronicling the innumerable moves, up to two or three a year, and the numerous places in which Chandler and his wife lived through the 1930s. They lived alone, almost claustrophobically, because they wanted it that way. Although Chandler published his first full-length novel, *The Big Sleep,* in 1939, he was essentially a writer of the 1940s and 1950s. In these novels Chandler created a world as coherent as William Faulkner's Yoknapatawpha County. Since he had not enjoyed much of a life (or so he felt), Chandler re-created himself as Philip Marlowe—not autobiographically, but metaphorically—and through Marlowe, Chandler was able to reappropriate the City of Angels and its attendant suburbia. Los Angeles had eaten up his life, kept him on the edge of nothing, as he put it. Yet without Los Angeles, he, and Marlowe, were less than nothing, disembodied ghosts.

Likewise did William Saroyan seek to fill the void—in his case, the suspected emptiness of the universe itself—with his version of that perennial concern of California writers, bohemianism, which is to say, the shoring up of threatened identities through art and "hanging out." Writers in frontier San Francisco had done this and would soon be doing it again in the Beat era; but in the meantime, William Saroyan of Fresno and San Francisco made his debut with *The Daring Young Man on the Flying Trapeze and Other Stories* (1934), with its Depression-defying message of anarcho-individualism, supreme and triumphant, contemptuous of politics and economics as the measuring rods of worth. Born in Fresno and raised in an Oakland orphanage before being brought back to Fresno, where he absorbed the detail and color of the Armenian community, Saroyan moved to San Francisco in 1927 at the age of nineteen (his mother and brother eventually joined him), got a job as a counter clerk for the telegraph company, rented a flat on Carl Street in the Haight-Ashbury district, and began to divide his time among his telegraph job, playing the ponies at the Tanforan Race Track, drinking in North Beach dives, losing money in card games, and writing, writing, writing, on his upright Royal in his Carl Street flat. He turned out short stories about himself, written in a headlong, free-associational manner and concerned (in the midst of every kind of aside, anecdote, and shaggy-dog story) with the perennial theme of the human condition: the existential drama of a prismatic Saroyan-Self through whom, in a manner that mingled Montaigne and the Marx Brothers, he explored questions of love, life, creativity, death, the universe, "the full catastrophe," as Zorba the Greek would later put it. In 1939 Saroyan won the Pulitzer Prize for his Broadway play, *The Time of Your Life,* set in a bar on the Embarcadero in San Francisco. He also directed the play, which was easy in that it consisted of characters delivering Saroyanesque declarations to one another. Since Saroyan was Saroyan, he turned down the Pulitzer in order to make a statement (as to exactly *what* remains unclear) but also, one suspects, strictly for the hell of it, for the sake of the gesture, the projection of an autonomous self against the universe.

Another Bohemian of the period was John Fante, who projected himself into the void as the Italian American Bandini, living in cheap lodgings on Bunker Hill and, like the Saroyan-Self, countering the void with words in such novels as *Wait Until Spring, Bandini* (1938), and *Ask the Dust* (1939), in which Bandini/Fante wanders the streets of the city, a fierce hunger raging in his heart for all that Los Angeles was promising, wanting so desperately a slice of the Big Orange. "Los Angeles, give me some of you!" Bandini cries. "Los Angeles, come to me the way I came to you, my feet over your streets, you pretty town I loved you so much, you sad flower in the sand, you pretty town." And yet Bandini/Fante is more than half aware that Los Angeles (and by extension California) has a way of promising things—the gorgeous girls on the street, the golf clubs in the window at Spalding's on Sixth, the cool lawns and green swimming pools of Bel Air—that it will never deliver. "You'll eat hamburgers year after year," he tells himself, "and live in dusty, vermin-infested apartments and hotels, but every morning you'll see the mighty sun, the eternal blue of the sky, and the streets will be full of sleek women you will never possess, and the hot tropical nights will reek of romance you'll never have, but you'll still be in Paradise, boys, in the land of sunshine."

Nathanael West and Aldous Huxley had similar responses. An Easterner in exile (yet fitting in rather well, given his own capacity for self-fabrication and deception), West found Los Angeles (and again, by implication, California) a great big lie, destined to implode upon itself, which is exactly what it does at the conclusion of West's *The Day of the Locust* (1939): explode into a riot of disappointed Los Angelenos who take revenge upon the city by burning it down. Huxley's *After Many a Summer Dies the Swan* (1939)—which some consider the best Los Angeles novel ever—satirizes California's fake promise of youth through the figure of an aging tycoon based on William Randolph Hearst. It too ends apocalyptically.

This sense of California as promise betrayed and doom impending provides a leitmotif of writing in the postwar period, most notably in the fiction and essays of Sacramento-born Joan Didion. The daughter of a staunchly Republican pioneer family, Didion graduated from UC Berkeley in 1955, then went to New York to write for *Vogue* and in her off hours to complete her first novel, *Run River* (1963), decrying what postwar suburban development—in which both her father and her brother were engaged—had brought to the Sacramento Valley. Returning to Los Angeles, Didion produced a series of books—the nonfiction *Slouching Towards Bethlehem* (1968) and the novels *Play It As It Lays* (1970) and *A Book of Common Prayer* (1977)—bristling with a brilliant ambivalence about California. Eventually, in the memoir *Where I Was From* (2003), Didion more than implied that both her personal California, in terms of the myths she had absorbed as a child, and the larger California experiment contained what she believed to be a crippling level of deceit and self-deception.

The Beats of the 1950s (the era in which Didion came of age intellectually at UC Berkeley) agreed. Although the Beat movement alighted in San Francisco, its origins were in New York, at Columbia University and in the bohemian Greenwich Village neighborhood. After New York–born poet Lawrence Ferlinghetti arrived in San Francisco (where he settled after Columbia, naval service in World War II, and a doctorate at the Sorbonne on the G.I. Bill), his City Lights bookstore and publishing house became the epicenter of the Beat movement. The best-known Beats, among them Jack Kerouac and Allen Ginsberg, came and went with some frequency between the West Coast (especially North Beach, the rest of the Bay Area, Big Sur, and the Venice district of Los Angeles), Mexico City, the East Coast, and Morocco. In 1956 City Lights published Ginsberg's *Howl*, the poetic manifesto of the Beat movement. *Howl* evoked the anguish of a postwar generation oppressed by the soulless materialism of corporate America and taking refuge in sex, rebellion, and drugs, often to their own destruction. An obscenity trial followed, in which publisher Ferlinghetti was acquitted. The Beats revived bohemia in San Francisco and exported it to Venice Beach in Los Angeles. As in the case of most bohemianism, theirs was a style, a posture, an attitude—as much political as literary—toward postwar America, which they believed had become corporate, right-wing, cold, and conformist. As such, the Beat movement, however amorphous and semicoherent, fed into the much more focused protest movement of the 1960s.

The two most important post-Jeffers poets of California, however, William Everson and Gary Snyder, while each associated with the Beats, ultimately eschewed politics in favor of a nature-oriented mysticism that had been a persistent theme of imaginative writing in California since the frontier. Everson began his career with *San Joaquin* (1939), poems written while the Central Valley–born Everson was doing farm labor. He spent the war as a conscientious objector clearing trails and crushing rocks in Oregon. Converting to Catholicism in 1948, Everson spent the 1950s as a Dominican lay brother, writing (under the name "Brother Antoninus") some of the most impressive religious poems of the twentieth century. Leaving the Dominicans to marry, Everson spent the rest of his life in Santa Cruz, associated with the UC campus there as a poet, a fine art printer, and the author of verse and critical studies promoting a Jeffers-influenced view of California as transcendental nature. Gary Snyder followed a similar path, except in the direction of Zen Buddhism rather than Roman Catholicism. Depicted as Japhy Ryder in Jack Kerouac's Big Sur Zen novel *The Dharma Bums* (1958), Snyder had from the beginning the ambience of a seeker. He spent twelve years studying Zen Buddhism in Japan and also visited India in search of enlightenment. Snyder's poetry—appearing in collections titled *Riprap* (1959), *Myths and Texts* (1960), *Riprap and Cold Mountain Poems* (1965), *The Back Country* (1968), and the Pulitzer Prize–winning *Turtle Island* (1974)—burned with a hard, gemlike flame, its emotion under control, its vision precise. As artist, Gary Snyder was the greatest of the Beats, a notable American poet of any school, and, in his nature orientation and environmentalism, the example *par excellence* of the California tradition he represented and fulfilled.

Wallace Stegner of Los Altos and Stanford University, meanwhile, was combining an equally focused environmentalism, expressed in brilliant nonfiction, with keen social observation in a series of fictions set in the suburbs in and around Stanford that kept the novel of manners alive in California during the late 1960s and 1970s. Prior to his arrival at Stanford as a professor of creative writing at the end of the war, Stegner's primary fictional theme had been the Great Big West, as might be expected of a writer born in Saskatchewan and raised there and in Utah on hardscrabble ranches. Once at Stanford, Stegner directed his interest in the Great Big West into his nonfiction, including environmental writing and biographies of John Wesley Powell and Bernard De Voto, and turned his fictional lens onto the elegantly developed upper-middle-class suburbs of the mid–San Francisco peninsula. In 1972 Stegner won the Pulitzer Prize for *Angle of Repose* (1971), a novel based (perhaps a shade too closely, as the literary world would debate three decades later) upon the letters and journals of the nineteenth-century California writer Mary Hallock Foote. In 1976 the San Diego–born novelist Oakley Hall wrote the libretto for the opera of the same name, with music by UC Berkeley professor of music Andre Imbrie, and it was produced in San Francisco. Like Stegner, Hall combined teaching (at UC Irvine) and writing (in San Francisco). Hall's existential Western, *Warlock* (1958), coming after Walter Van Tilburg Clark's *The Ox-Bow Incident* (1940) and *The Track of the Cat* (1949), sustained a connection between California, the Great Big West, and the Western as film and literary genre.

SUCH A REAFFIRMATION was a healthy thing, in that California was already becoming by midcentury what it formally became by Census 1990—the most urbanized and suburbanized state in the nation—and needed to be reminded of its continuing, if embattled, wilderness. The painters of California remained preoccupied with landscape through the 1920s, most of them working in plein air Postimpressionist style: retardaire as far as modernism was concerned, and more than a little provincial, it can be argued, but continuing to produce a well-received painterly gazetteer of the Golden State. The "Society of Six," however—a loose fraternity of East Bay painters socializing and painting together beginning in the 1920s—changed all that, bringing to art in California new realms of chromatic vigor and figurative verve. Masculine, bohemian, resembling Jack London in their direct, even tough-guy approach to art, the Six defied the prevailing genteel ethos of Postimpressionism to create a series of canvases exploding in vivid color and depicting, not from an aesthetic distance but in close-up, California's hillside cabins and seaside docks, its farms and towns, its yellow hills and golden sunlight, its coastal enclaves and fishing villages, its people. Above all else, the Six perceived a whole new range of hues in the landscape and the built environment of the Bay Area: the hills of Tiburon on San Francisco Bay, for example, in Selden Gile's *Boat and Yellow Hills* from the late 1920s, exploding in yellow, with trees presented in blue-green with a rose-red underpainting; or Gile's *The Soil* (1927), with its sunburst-orange mountain, its ocher paths, its aquamarine sky. Here were colors that Californians knew instinctively to be their own: colors that had been seen in the mind long before they were experienced in the landscape.

Through the 1920s, Frank Van Sloun, a student of Robert Henri in the early 1900s in New York, stood as a lonely exponent of Social Realism on the West Coast, a one-man outpost of the so-called Ashcan School, as evident in Sloun's *Flossie* (1920), a life-size oil portrait of a young lady of the night, utterly defiant of the genteel tradition that then held sway in California. The Depression at last brought Social Realism to California, especially among watercolorists, who were almost like photographers in their ability rapidly and directly to capture the passing scene. Thanks to the watercolorists of the California School, as their movement is now called, daily life—a backyard barbecue in suburbia, a Sunday afternoon in Elysian Park in Los Angeles, trucks unloading on the Embarcadero in San Francisco—made its way into painting. One member of the California School, Millard Sheets, turned to oil on canvas for *Angel's Flight* (1931), a depiction of apartment life on Bunker Hill. What George Bellows's *Cliff Dwellers* (1913) was to New York, Sheets's *Angel's Flight* was to Los Angeles: an unabashed, unapologetic evocation of urbanism in all its density and human drama. In May 1934, Maynard Dixon, a practitioner of stylized Native American themes, created a series of Socialist Realist works in subdued documentarian tones, while continuing under WPA sponsorship his career as a muralist dealing with Native American and Old California themes.

North and south, the mural—with its capacity for political statement—was experiencing a golden age in California during the 1930s, as it was throughout the rest of the United States. The Mexican muralists José Clemente Orozco, David Alfaro Siqueiros, and Alfredo Ramos Martínez were active in Southern California. The great Diego Rivera, accompanied by his wife Frida Kahlo, came to San Francisco from Mexico on three separate visits in the 1930s to create three ambitious works: *Allegory of California* (1931) at the Pacific Stock Exchange Club, *The Making of a Fresco, Showing the Building of a City* (1931) at the San Francisco Art Institute, and *Pan-American Unity* (1940) for the Golden Gate International Exposition. More than half a dozen local artists, meanwhile, created a series of murals for Coit Tower atop Telegraph Hill (1933) that for sweep, detail, and sociological complexity remains among the most successful mural projects of its kind in the nation.

Art historian Bram Dijkstra has chronicled the struggle among modernism, Expressionism, and Social Realism in the

1930s and 1940s for the artistic soul of America. While expressive and figurative paintings of everyday life continued to flourish through the 1940s, Dijkstra argues that modernism was more congenial to an increasingly corporate society that preferred the abstract and the general over the local and the specific. Whatever the causes, abstract modernism came to California in a vivid way following the Second World War—through the works of such painters as Clyfford Still, Ronald Bladen, Edward Corbett, and Richard Diebenkorn—but sustained within itself as well throughout these years a figurative impulse: a desire, that is, to depict California people and places, evident in such artists of the Bay Area figurative school as David Park, Elmer Bischoff, James Weeks, and Joan Brown. Richard Diebenkorn, who became the most noted of them all, made the progress from Abstract Expressionism to figurativism to the sui generis style of his semiabstract *Ocean Park* series depicting the neighborhood in Santa Monica, fronting the Pacific, where Diebenkorn lived and maintained his studio. The *Ocean Park* paintings constituted an epic of line, plane, and color that critics such as Robert Hughes were soon calling the most impressive abstract landscapes done by an American artist in the twentieth century. Metropolitan Sacramento, meanwhile—centered on the art department at UC Davis—was emerging in the 1960s and beyond as an epicenter of pop art (Wayne Thiebaud), neoluminism (Greg Kondos), and figurative funk (sculptor Robert Arneson). By the 1970s and beyond, art in California was running through many channels. In Oakland, Mel Ramos was creating a series of neorealistic pop art female nudes, depicted in association with fruits, animals, or commercial products, that by the turn of the century had won him a European reputation. In Los Angeles, Alexis Smith was doing collages in which actual images from the mass-produced, the quotidian—a *Life* magazine cover, an advertisement for Foster Freeze ice cream cones—were played off one another as pulp fiction text. John Register and Robert Bechtle, by contrast, were creating photo-realistic depictions of urban and suburban California landscapes that brought with them a sense of subliminal dread, isolation, and loneliness suggestive of the work of Edward Hopper. Even the outwardly genial and optimistic English-born David Hockney concealed, behind the joyous colors and deliberately childlike figurativism of his Southern California swimming pools, a world that could also seem tenuous, barely held together.

PHOTOGRAPHY IN CALIFORNIA entered the twentieth century seeming to wish to escape the purely photographic values of Watkins and Muybridge in favor of the self-consciously literary dreaminess of the Pictorial style, the equivalent of Postimpressionism in painting. Two Californians, however—Edward Weston and Ansel Adams—by word and deed led a campaign to restore photography to its own terms. They were joined in this effort by a coterie of Bay Area photographers calling themselves "Group f/64" in tribute to the lens aperture that provides the greatest depth of field for maximum precision of line and detail. In the mid-1920s a three-year sojourn in rural Mexico returned Weston, a Glendale portrait photographer, to the practice of photography as a direct and elemental art. After a period of Abstract Expressionism in the late 1920s—seashells, rocks, bell peppers that looked like nudes and nudes that looked like bell peppers—Weston, by now based in Carmel, returned to the outdoors, where he became the equivalent of Robinson Jeffers (whom he photographed brilliantly) in emphasizing nature as an end in itself, complete on its own terms. The San Francisco–born photographer Ansel Adams, spokesman for Group f/64, sustained such an affinity with nature from the beginning of his career. By the time Adams was fifteen, he had become an accomplished photographer, as his early studies of the sand dunes at Baker Beach in San Francisco clearly demonstrate. What Mexico was to Weston, the

Sierra Nevada—the Yosemite Valley especially—was to Ansel Adams: the galvanizer and consolidator of a mature talent. In the summer of 1923, on a pack trip into the mountains south of Mount Lyell, Adams took his first famous photograph, *Banner Peak and Thousand Island Lake.* He would later describe his technique as "visualization": the full and complete integration of the photographer, the object photographed, environmental conditions, and the photographer's conception of the print he wished to see. Guided by this visualization, this judgment of light and shadow, the photographer, Ansel believed, would instinctively choose the appropriate technology of lens and filter, and then wait—seconds, minutes, hours, as long as it took—for the right moment to come before pressing the shutter.

Thus when the Depression came to California, a tradition of true photographic realism was in place when the San Francisco–based society photographer Dorothea Lange, shocked at the breakup by police of a demonstration outside her studio, turned her attention to the social turmoil that was all around her in San Francisco and in the agricultural fields of the state. Taking to the road as a photographer with the Resettlement Administration (renamed the Farm Security Administration in 1937) in the company of UC Berkeley labor economist Paul Taylor—whom she had met at a Group f/64 meeting in Oakland and would later marry—Lange began a series of photographs intended to document for Washington the plight of migrant labor in California. One of these photographs, taken in March 1936—of Florence Thompson and her three children stranded in a roadside canvas lean-to outside Nipomo on the Central Coast—would, under the title *Migrant Mother,* become one of the best-known photographs of the twentieth century.

ARCHITECTURALLY, CALIFORNIA MAINTAINED its preference for the Arts-and-Crafts-inspired shingle style—as represented by, among others, Bernard Maybeck in the Bay Area and by Charles Sumner Greene and his brother Henry Mather Greene in the Southland—through the first two decades of the twentieth century. Along with other Americans, Californians also experimented with varieties of Tudor, Jacobean, Georgian, even Hansel and Gretel Storybook in their domestic design. Mediterranean Revival—whether Spanish, Spanish Colonial, Italian, or French—dominated the 1920s. This did not prevent modernism, however, from making a dramatic appearance in the pre–World War I era in the *sui generis* work of the San Diego–based architect Irving Gill, whose clean lines and surfaces and minimalist presentation paralleled Viennese Secessionism. In the 1920s, modernism was further articulated in Southern California through the work of the Austrian émigrés Richard Neutra and Rudolf Schindler and was continued through the 1930s by a brilliant array of younger modernists—J. R. Davidson, Gregory Ain, Raphael Soriano, Craig Ellwood, Pierre Koenig, A. Quincy Jones—whom historian Esther McCoy has dubbed the Second Generation. In Northern California, William Wurster led a movement for a softer modernism, less machine-oriented and hard-edged, which maintained many continuities with the earlier wood-oriented Bay Region style.

With the exception of the homes built by Joseph Eichler in the Bay Area during the 1950s, however, high modernism did not dominate the postwar building boom. Even as modernism flourished among artist-architects and their discriminating clients, another domestic tradition—California Ranch, as practiced by designer Cliff May—proved more attractive to a general audience, including the upscale market. The editors of the Menlo Park–based *Sunset* magazine, for one thing, favored the Ranch style; indeed, in the late 1940s they commissioned May to design the *Sunset* headquarters (completed in 1952) in Menlo Park, and this imprimatur had great effect, for *Sunset* was playing an important role in defining the design and lifestyle of postwar suburban California. Nevertheless, modernism—as represented by the works of Gardner Dailey and Joe Esherick—continued to characterize high-end architecture in California through the rest of the century.

MUSIC, TOO, fits into this paradigm of a shift from the conservative to the avant-garde with little in the way of transition. San Francisco had a musical tradition that went back to the Gold Rush, when a performance of Rossini's *Stabat Mater* was performed in the frontier city as early as 1849. By the late 1870s, San Francisco was supporting a flourishing theatrical and musical culture. It also had Wade's Opera House (1876), one of the most ambitious venues of its kind in the country. (Enrico Caruso was singing there the night before the great earthquake.) In 1923 an opera company was established in San Francisco under the direction of émigré Gaetano Merola. Moved in 1932 to a magnificent new Beaux Arts opera house on Van Ness Avenue, the San Francisco Opera—along with its symphony orchestra established in 1911 and flourishing under the direction of Pierre Monteux—sustained for fifty years San Francisco's claim to be the performing arts capital of the Far West. Los Angeles, meanwhile, nurtured a burgeoning choral music community from the early 1900s, the legacy of its strong Anglo-Protestant population. In 1919 a philharmonic orchestra was established under the direction of Alfred Hertz with the financial support of mining heir William Andrews Clark, who sometimes sat in as second violin. In Daisy Dell, meanwhile—a canyon amphitheater in Hollywood—a tradition of religious services and choral music led to the establishment of the Hollywood Bowl in 1922, for which architect Lloyd Wright, son of Frank Lloyd Wright, designed a performance shell that soon emerged as one of the primary icons of Southern California.

When sound came to motion pictures, a whole new career field—writing music for films—was opened to composers. In the 1930s, émigrés such as Erich Korngold, Dmitri Tiomkin, Max Steiner, Miklós Rózsa, and others achieved eminence in this field. Steiner's score for *King Kong* (1932) and Korngold's scores for *Captain Blood* (1935), *Anthony Adverse* (1936), *The Adventures of Robin Hood* (1938), *The Constant Nymph* (1943), and *Of Human Bondage* (1945) represented a new venue and mode for serious music. The rise of Nazism in Germany, followed by the outbreak of war in September 1939, brought to Los Angeles two major modernists, Igor Stravinsky and Arnold Schoenberg. An instinctive showman, Stravinsky adapted easily to the movie studios, beginning with the featuring of his music in Walt Disney's *Fantasia* (1940). While in Los Angeles, Stravinsky would complete *Symphony in C* (1940), *A Symphony in Three Movements* (1941/45), his *Mass* (1944/47), *Concerto in D* (1946), and the music for *Rake's Progress* (1948/51), for which W. H. Auden wrote the libretto. He would also compose the *Ebony Concerto* (1945) for bandleader Woody Herman and *Circus Polka* (1942), a dance for the elephants of the Ringling Bros. and Barnum & Bailey circus. An advocate of atonalism, Schoenberg did not connect with a popular audience; nevertheless, the work of his Los Angeles years—especially the oratorio *Moses and Aaron* (1951)—took musical modernism to new heights.

Another notable modernist, the French composer Darius Milhaud, had long since been using jazz in such scores as *La Création du monde* (1923); so it was not surprising that after the war, when Milhaud was teaching at Mills College in Oakland, an aspiring jazz musician by the name of Dave Brubeck should come under his influence. Through Brubeck in the late 1940s and early 1950s, jazz on the West Coast moved into increasingly progressive realms. Bandleaders Stan Kenton and Artie Shaw were equally eager to take their medium, the jazz orchestra, into comparably progressive modes, although the effort cost each of them his popularity as a purveyor of danceable music. Torn by the conflict, Artie Shaw, one of the greatest musicians of his generation, left music entirely. Composers such as John Cage, Philip Glass, and John Adams, however, kept modernism alive and well in California, as did maestro Kent Nagano, who frequently scheduled modernist composers on the program of the Berkeley Symphony that he continued to lead while holding podiums at various times in Lyon, Los Angeles, Berlin, and London. Meanwhile, working alone or in partnership with arranger-lyricists Tony Asher and Van Dyke Parks, composer Brian Wilson of the Beach Boys was fusing the worlds of pop and modernism in such song cycles as *Pet Sounds* (1966), *Smiley Smile* (1967), and the long-delayed *Smile* (2004), which, taken together, help justify Leonard Bernstein's assertion that Wilson was one of the most important American composers of the twentieth century.

A dividend of the migration from the Dust Bowl states during the Depression was an intensification of country music. Nurtured in the honky-tonks and dance halls of Bakersfield in Kern County and dozens of other Central Valley places, California country music—as exemplified in such performers as Gene Autry, Bob Wills, Spade Cooley, Rose and the Maddox Brothers, Buck Owens, Merle Haggard, and Dwight Yoakam—reminded the nation that California was not exclusively a chardonnay-and-cheese enclave of coastal sophisticates, but was also the hardscrabble home of flag-waving working men and women whose musical loyalties lay with the Grand Ole Opry: truck drivers, waitresses, small farmers, linemen, and mechanics, sometimes down on their luck, who spoke with a twang, wore boots and jeans, and were living and loving, smoking and drinking, cheating and repenting, and singing about it all in a cavalcade of songs that had a way of getting to the heart of America itself.

THE OUTDOOR LIFE, mountaineering especially, and sport—boxing, swimming, tennis, baseball, football, and track and field most notably—had characterized the California lifestyle since the late nineteenth century; and so the number of athletic champions emerging from the state is no surprise. If California has made any contribution to sport on a national level, it is in the democratization of pursuits that were previously the prerogatives of elites. Most of the champions of the twentieth century who come from California first developed their skills in publicly subsidized circumstances: municipally supported swimming pools, golf courses, and tennis courts in particular, where middle-class Californians, thanks to the recreational policies of Progressivism, were introduced to these previously social-register sports.

As in the case of early childhood education, this orientation in its earliest phases owed much to German culture, especially strong in the San Francisco Bay Area, where in 1860 a group of German immigrants, highly influenced by the physical fitness movement in their homeland, founded an Olympic Club devoted to gymnastic pursuits, one of the oldest clubs of its kind in the nation. Boxing was especially prized at the Olympic Club, and one of its members, James "Gentleman Jim" Corbett, defeated John L. Sullivan in 1892 for the heavyweight boxing championship of the United States. The Olympic Club and the Los Angeles Athletic Club, established in 1880, played important roles as well in introducing organized track and field competition, which developed dramatically in the twentieth century as an affordable, low-maintenance high school and college sport. Bob Mathias of Tulare County in the Central Valley, for example, won the decathlon at the 1948 Olympic Games as a seventeen-year-old public high school student.

The tennis courts of California, many of them municipally funded, tended to favor hard surfaces, which were more economical and could be used year-round, and encouraged a quicker and more competitive mode of play than the game played on the grass or clay surfaces of the East. Hence the early champions in this field—May Sutton (Wimbledon 1907), Maurice McLoughlin (Wimbledon 1913), Helen Wills (an eight-time Wimbledon winner in the 1920s and 1930s)—tended to come up through public courts rather than country clubs and to play a fast and edgy kind of game. Likewise did swimming champion Florence Chadwick—a policeman's daughter who set new English Channel records in August 1950—hone her skills as a youngster in the free public surf off San Diego. From the beginning, rough-water swimming had been a popular pursuit in the Golden State, as attested by the many swimming and boating clubs fronting San Francisco Bay by the 1880s. One aspect of this rough-water-oriented culture—yachting, centered in the clubs and associations of San Francisco, Catalina, and San Diego—remained elite; yet in time another rough-water sport—surfing, brought to California in 1907 by Anglo-Hawaiian George Freeth—would become yet another affordable, widespread pursuit. By the late twentieth century, in fact, the California surfer, male and female alike, had become an icon of the California lifestyle, celebrated in song, film, advertising, and other media. So, too, did another inexpensive shoreline pursuit, beach volleyball, gain comparable popularity during these years and become similarly representative of an endless summer on the shores of the sundown sea in a place called California, where everyone was forever young and looked great in swimming trunks or bikini.

As far as baseball was concerned, California—where the sport was introduced in 1859 and flourished through the rest of the nineteenth century as a club pursuit—remained a minor league state until the arrival of the Giants and the Dodgers in 1958. And yet the Pacific Coast League—organized in 1903 from the club-oriented California League that had emerged in the 1880s—was for more than half a century an extraordinarily popular and successful venture in terms of the number of cities represented, of successful stadiums, and of notable players, including two of baseball's greatest stars, Joe DiMaggio (San Francisco Seals) and Ted Williams (San Diego Padres). Another great California player, Jackie Robinson of Pasadena, became the first African American to integrate major league baseball via a team (the Dodgers) that subsequently came to Los Angeles.

Mountaineering, meanwhile, remained a largely elite endeavor, pursued by such upper-middle-class Sierra Club members as Walter A. Starr, Jr., whose posthumously published *Starr's Guide to the John Muir Trail and the High Sierra Region* (1934) literally cost Starr his life to research. Skiing, an allied pursuit, was equally upper-middle-class in the pre–World War II era but, unlike mountaineering, expanded in the postwar era to a widespread resort-based culture. Rock climbing, however, an edge-sport affiliate of mountaineering, remained a sport of the few, given its great dangers. On November 12, 1958, Warren Harding became the first rock climber to scale the face of El Capitan in the Yosemite Valley. In the decades that followed, new materials and technologies made rock climbing an even more ambitious sport and introduced two new pursuits—windsurfing and hang gliding—whose skilled interfacing of nature and science further reinforced the "DNA code" of California.

Thus through sport and the arts California participated in, and frequently initiated, the recreational and aesthetic developments of the twentieth century. In literature, architecture, painting, photography, and music, moreover, strong arguments can be made for a truly Californian tradition, or at the least for distinct California variations on larger movements. The internationally renowned Los Angeles–based architect Frank Gehry, for example, can be fully understood only within the context of the city that nurtured his talents and built one of his greatest buildings, Disney Hall (2004), atop Bunker Hill. Whether adopted, adapted, or indigenous in inspiration, the arts have long functioned as an imaginative matrix for living and interpreting life, California style.

12

ECUMENOPOLIS

Forging a World Society

César Chávez addresses rally of United Farm Workers, late 1970s

CALIFORNIA STATE LIBRARY

If there is such a thing as DNA codes for states—and there may very well be!—then crucial to the sociogenetic heritage of California would be ethnic diversity. It began in the Native American era with its seventy to eighty language groups and its multitude of tribelets and kinship groups, and it continued through the Spanish and Mexican eras. Were one to see the first settlers of Los Angeles assembling in the plaza-to-be in September 1781 and examine them from the perspective of their genetic heritage, one would encounter European, Native American, and African bloodlines mixed in every possible combination. Ask these settlers what they were, and they would reply "Spaniards," possibly even "Mexicans"; for (technically at least) to be a subject of the Spanish crown was not a matter of bloodline but of Hispanic culture, Roman Catholicism, and loyalty to viceroy and king. The brief Mexican era only intensified this diversity with the arrival of English, American, French, and Russian settlers. During the Gold Rush, diversity exfoliated into brilliant hues as nearly every portion of the planet sent its people to California—as, in the words of historian J. S. Holliday, "the world rushed in."

No one claims that everyone was treated fairly in any of these periods. Far from it. The Spanish settlement represented an intrusion—even an aggression—against Native Americans, whatever the motivations of the Franciscan padres might have been. As far as their own populations were concerned, Spain and Mexico each had its own caste system based on Spanish descent, although the remoteness of California (and the consequent preciousness of the human stock that had been transported there) tended to soften distinctions based on bloodlines; and a number of the leading Californio families were of partial Indian and/or African ancestry.

So, too, was American California founded on racial distinctions and repressions: the disenfranchisement of blacks and Asians, the aggression against Mexican land titles, the lynch law in the mines that seemed to have such a special preference for Hispanic victims. The lynching of Chinese in Los Angeles in October 1871 and the "Chinese Must Go!" crusade that followed, most strongly in San Francisco, continued to give evidence of this proclivity, as did the anti-Japanese "White California" movement of the early twentieth century, culminating in the segregation of Japanese schoolchildren in San Francisco, the barring of Japanese immigrants from land ownership, and the incarceration of Japanese Americans during World War II. The great agricultural strikes of the 1930s can be seen in terms of color as well as economics, given the preponderance of minorities in the agricultural workforce. Jim Crow was a well-known figure to Mexican, African, and Japanese Americans in the first half of the twentieth century. Even the so-called Okies were targets of ethnic prejudice. They were white people, true, but they were also racialized, which is to say, they were despised in their very physical selves as denizens of Tobacco Road, slack-jawed and incestuous.

San Francisco's considerable German Jewish and Sephardic Jewish colonies, meanwhile, which migrated to Los Angeles in the 1850s as well, were augmented at the turn of the century by a large influx of Eastern European Jews; and this population was increased even further in the 1930s by refugees from Fascist Europe, until Los Angeles emerged as one of the two or three most important centers of Jewish civilization on the planet. Anti-Semitism was rare in the nineteenth and early twentieth century, when Jewish names were listed among the founders of dozens of major enterprises as well as private clubs, but that viral infection of the soul did seep into the California bloodstream between the First and Second World Wars, especially in metropolitan Los Angeles.

By the early 1900s, San Francisco had a higher proportion of foreign-born residents relative to its total population than any other city in the United States, including New York. That population included the first Korean immigrants to California, harbingers of a migration that would more than half a century later make Los Angeles the second or third largest Korean city on the planet. The 1920s also witnessed a second influx of Mexicans into the fields of California, where they joined the Filipinos, the Japanese, the Sikhs, and the other peoples already working there. Armenians, meanwhile, fleeing Ottoman Turkish persecution, were settling in the Great Central Valley. In the 1930s as well, nearly half a million Anglo-Americans from the Dust Bowl states flocked to California. John Steinbeck's *The Grapes of Wrath* is their story. There had always been a sizable African American population in California, from the Gold Rush onward, but the Second World War brought thousands of African Americans to California to work in the shipyards and other aspects of the defense industry. Beginning in 1965 with the Immigration and Nationality Acts amendments, the United States embarked upon a program of reforming its immigration laws, with the result that previously excluded groups, Asians especially, could not only immigrate into the United States on an equal basis, but were granted expanded quotas to compensate for past restrictions. Further amendments favored the reuniting of families. Over the next three decades, California experienced a dramatic rise in its Asian population. Upheavals in Iran, in Vietnam and other countries of Southeast Asia, in Bangladesh, in the Soviet Union and its successor nations, and in other troubled parts of the world where there was American involvement eventually brought to

California hundreds of thousands of refugees from these various populations. By the end of the twentieth century, eighty-plus languages in addition to English were spoken by children in the Los Angeles Unified School District.

Yet there were—and remain—tensions. Racial, ethnic, and religious covenants of exclusion had been characteristic of real estate in California throughout most of the twentieth century. In 1963 Assemblyman W. Byron Rumford of Berkeley, an African American, successfully authored a law banning such discrimination. The California Real Estate Association retaliated with Proposition 14 repealing the act, which passed by more than two to one in the November 1964 election. Although the U.S. Supreme Court nullified this revocation in 1967, the popular rejection of the Rumford Act nevertheless testified to continuing tensions based on race and religion in California.

Such an ingathering of the human race into American society and institutions has not come easily, especially in light of existing prejudices. A number of immigrant groups brought to California long-seated enmities against each other. Then there is the continuing divide between black and white, complicated by the fact that California has been becoming increasingly brown, with both blacks and whites (blacks especially) foreseeing the time when they would be on the margins of society. Two catastrophic events—the Watts riots of 1965 and the Los Angeles riots of 1992—and one public spectacle—the O. J. Simpson trial of 1995—underscored the fact that California is far from exempt from what the Swedish sociologist Gunnar Myrdal correctly described in 1940 as the American dilemma: race.

Breaking out in the predominantly black Watts district of Los Angeles, southwest of downtown, on August 11, 1965, the Watts riots were unambiguously racial in motivation. A black man was arrested by white police for drunk driving. An angry crowd gathered. The mostly white police officers responded by roughing up the crowd and making more arrests. Five days of rioting including the torching of stores and automobiles by roving bands, sniping, looting, and angry mobs roaming the streets exceeded the ability of the LAPD to handle the situation, and Governor Edmund G. "Pat" Brown sent in the National Guard. When it was over, thirty-four bodies lay in the morgue, and more than a thousand people had been injured. The subsequent investigation, chaired by former CIA director John A. McCone, revealed an abyss of monumental dimensions between black and white: not only economic—the lack of jobs, the dearth of local stores and public transportation, indeed, the dearth of local institutions of any sort other than churches—but psychological as well. For all their propinquity, the people of Watts and the other peoples of the City of Angels might not even be said to be living in the same city.

When a group of Los Angeles policemen stopped another black motorist, Rodney King, twenty-six years later, and beat him so severely (fifty-six baton blows in all) that he had to be hospitalized, that was evidence aplenty that race remained an issue in the City of Angels. The incident might have gone unremarked, save for the fact that a resident of a nearby apartment complex captured the beating on video camera, and local, state, national, and international television endlessly reprised this tape in all its horror. When the four officers, indicted on felony charges, were acquitted by an all-white jury in Ventura County on April 29, 1992, a repeat of the Watts uprising seemed inevitable, and indeed it happened: one of the worst urban riots in American history, in fact, leaving Los Angeles five days later with forty-five bodies in the morgue, a smoking haze hanging over the city from multiple fires, national guardsmen and marines in full battle gear patrolling the city in jeeps and Humvees or standing guard on street corners behind gunnysack emplacements.

While the Watts riots of August 1965 were black versus white, the Los Angeles riots of April–May 1992 pitted blacks and browns against whites and Koreans, whose stores were the special targets for looting and arson. Latino rioters, moreover, seemed mainly interested in looting as opposed to violent personal attacks on people of other races. As in the case of 1965, follow-up investigations revealed deep fissures based on race throughout the metropolitan region.

While arising from a domestic tragedy—the murder on June 12, 1994, of a white wife and a white bystander who happened to be in the wrong place at the wrong time—the internationally monitored O. J. Simpson trial, which occupied two thirds of 1995, increasingly became a referendum on race, or at least on whether a black defendant could get fair treatment from the LAPD and court system. On October 3, 1995, a predominantly African American jury acquitted Simpson, and a predominantly African American and Latino crowd outside the courthouse broke into joyful cries and applause when they heard the verdict.

As difficult as the black/white issue might be, it ultimately took second, even third, place in the minds of the public to another race- and/or ethnicity-related issue: illegal immigration. In the 1990s, this anxiety surfaced around three issues—public aid to illegal immigrants, affirmative action, and bilingual education—and would be especially focused on the flood of illegal immigrants into California, from Mexico especially. A September 1993 poll in the *Los Angeles Times* revealed that 86 percent of those polled ranked illegal immigration as one of the three major problems facing California, with the other two—crime and the economy—related to that issue. At the time, there were more than thirty bills under consideration in Sacramento restricting state services to illegal immigrants. Residents of San Diego were parking their cars on bluffs overlooking the border and turning on their headlights to illuminate illegals as they slipped across. In the June 1992 presidential primary, Republican Pat Buchanan advocated the digging of an impassible trench along the border.

All this involved a number of challenges and contradictions. In the 1960s, thanks to the reform of immigration laws begun by the Kennedy administration, white California became increasingly yellow and brown. By the 1990s, there were more than one million Californians of Chinese descent in the state and another million Filipinos—two groups who had been excluded from California in earlier eras. Through birth, legal immigration, and federal amnesties in 1986, the legal Latino-American and legally resident Latino population of California stood at 7.7 million by 1990, which is to say, a quarter of the total population. California, in short, had become a significantly—and legally—Mexican American society, with Los Angeles as the third largest Mexican city in the world and Mexican Americans active in every phase and level of California life. Mexican American Californians were proud of their identities—their bilingualism, their culture and religion, their strong family ties, their capacity for hard work, their ambition to make a better life for themselves in the United States—and they also understood that they would soon (as by 2000 they in fact did) constitute the dominant demographic group of color in the state: a fact that was already evident in the growing number of Mexican Americans in local government and the state legislature. They saw themselves, in short, as being as American as any other immigrant group: multigenerational Americans in many instances, with distinguished war records in World War II, Korea, Vietnam, and the Persian Gulf.

Now came the problem. As the anti-illegal campaign gained momentum, it focused upon illegals from Mexico; and in doing so, it seemed to call into question the validity, hence the value, of the Mexican American presence in California, despite the distinctions that were repeatedly being made between legal and illegal immigrants. Such a sensitivity on the part of Mexican Americans, moreover, had its justification; for—despite the legitimate arguments being made, especially regarding the corruption of the American legal system by illegal immigration—there were many who saw in the anti-illegal crusade an opportunity to give vent to a more pervasive dislike of the direction California was taking in terms of its demographic makeup.

The grievous fissure, the affronted pride, the fear and resentment, gave rise to the placing of the "Save Our State" initiative, Proposition 187, on the November 1994 ballot. Proposition 187 called for the withdrawal of all public support, with the exception of emergency medical services, for undocumented Californians. It was endorsed by Republican incumbent governor Pete Wilson, running for a second term, and opposed by state treasurer Kathleen Brown, the Democratic challenger. Very soon Proposition 187 became a de facto referendum on race and culture in California, to such an extent that the president and incoming president of Mexico each denounced it; and when it passed, 59 to 41 percent, there were deeply hurt feelings among Mexican Americans. Proposition 187 was never implemented; it went immediately into the courts—especially on the issue that states cannot regulate immigration—and it stayed there. It did, however, help create a climate of opinion in Washington, among Republicans and Democrats alike, that illegals were costing the country a great deal of money. In August 1996, Congress passed and President Clinton signed into law the Personal Responsibility and Work Opportunity Reconciliation Act making illegal immigrants ineligible for state and federal benefits, with the exception of emergency medical care, immunization, and emergency disaster relief. Cutting off food stamps and other benefits, giving states the right to cut off Medicaid to legal immigrants as well as illegals, the act was even more draconian than Proposition 187.

The debate regarding race and ethnicity now shifted to a new but related matter, affirmative action, which is at once a theory of history and a set of programs. Certain groups, ran the theory, had been excluded from certain sectors of American life and were now eligible for appointments and/or promotions that would redress this historical imbalance. Equity was involved, as well as diversity; for a diverse society, it was argued, was not only more fair but more functional. Affirmative action was based, moreover, on the theory that men and women were primarily who and what they were because of race, ethnicity, gender, class, or some combination thereof. Sacramento businessman Ward Connerly, however, an African American and a regent of the University of California, did not believe this. Connerly believed, rather, that personhood transcended race, ethnicity, gender, class, or any combination thereof. Each individual was equal before the law, Connerly argued. It was the duty of society not to redress history but to maintain itself blind to color or gender. As a regent of the University of California, Connerly was especially disturbed by affirmative action programs that were keeping Asian students with perfect 4.0 grade point averages from top UC campuses while admitting African American or Latino students with 3.0 averages or lower. Affirmative action may have been necessary at one time, Connerly admitted; but to make it a permanent part of society was to claim, by implication, that certain minorities were less talented than nonminorities and would forever require special treatment.

Almost single-handedly, Ward Connerly, joined by his close personal friend and fellow UC regent Governor Pete Wilson, at a meeting of the regents in San Francisco on July 20, 1995, ended race- and gender-based preferences at UC, effective in 1998, by a vote of 14 to 10. Shock waves reverberated throughout the state. Far from being intimidated, an unfazed Connerly went on to take a leadership position in placing the California Civil Rights Initiative, Proposition 209, on the November 1996 ballot, outlawing affirmative action in state and local governments. On election day, Proposition 209 passed by 54 percent, losing only in Los Angeles County and the Bay Area. As usual, it was immediately taken into the courts and was halted by an injunction. This time, however, a three-judge panel of the U.S. Court of Appeals for the Ninth Circuit overturned the injunction, and on November 3, 1997, the U.S. Supreme Court let this decision stand without comment.

Next on the agenda was bilingual (Spanish-English) education. By 1997, some 1.4 million students in the California school system had limited proficiency in English. The question became: was it best to immerse them in English until their skills improved, or to run a Spanish-language track through the fifth grade or beyond if necessary? Educators made arguments on both sides of the question. Pro-bilingual arguments and politics prevailed, and by middecade some 1.4 million K–5 students were being instructed in Spanish. Previously, however, in 1986, California voters had approved Proposition 63, declaring English the official language of the state. Given this declaration—and continuing reality, it was assumed—opponents of bilingual education argued that students being taught in Spanish-only classrooms were being relegated to second-class citizenship, especially given the fact that their transition from an all-Spanish environment remained uncertain. A strong proponent of this point of view was Silicon Valley multimillionaire Ron Unz, who joined with longtime Orange County teacher Gloria Matta Tuchman, a Mexican American, to qualify for the June 1998 ballot Proposition 227 calling for the disestablishment of California's $400-million-plus bilingual education program in favor of a one-year immersion in English language proficiency.

While Proposition 227 did not strike the same chords of disaffection as Proposition 187—indeed, Latinos lined up on both sides of the question—it did represent a strong cultural statement: to wit, that California was in its public and commercial life an English-speaking society and that all immigrant groups who wished to function as fully equal members of that society must have a command of English. Receiving up to

$5,000 a year in bonuses, teachers in bilingual programs were especially adamant in their opposition. The distinguished Bolivian-born mathematics teacher Jaime Escalante, however—whose ability to teach calculus to Latino students was celebrated in the film *Stand and Deliver* (1998)—favored the measure. His own family, Escalante pointed out, spoke both Spanish and English at home, but only English in the workplace. The purpose of school, he argued, was to prepare students to function in society, which demanded proficiency in English. In June 1998, Proposition 227 passed with 61 percent of the vote. This time, while there was some resistance—and a waiver option was made available—English-language immersion went into effect. By March 2003, state superintendent Jack O'Connell was reporting that the students of California, whatever their ethnicities, were showing comparable advances in their English-language skills. Conversely, more non-Latinos were learning Spanish.

The 1990s had been wrenching, even heartbreaking, in the hostile undertones and reverberations of Proposition 187. Indeed, the issue of just exactly how the state should respond to undocumented Californians, the majority of them Latino, remains a continuing question. The economy of California, for one thing, is dependent upon the estimated two-million-plus undocumented workers in the state. They, after all, hold down the hard and disagreeable—but essential—jobs, which other groups either cannot or will not perform. What kind of society, the question remains, would have in its very economic structure a need for undocumented workers, while at the same time continuing to keep them in a semi-pariah status? This argument surfaced in the state legislature in the fall of 2003, when the legislature passed, and Governor Gray Davis, fighting a recall campaign, signed a bill authorizing the issuance of driver's licenses to undocumented workers. If the work is necessary, sponsors of the bill argued, why are we hobbling the ability of the workers to get to their jobs? This new law, however, struck a strong chord of opposition and was immediately repealed when Arnold Schwarzenegger succeeded Gray Davis as governor.

Still, for all these difficulties, a common culture seems to be holding, although cultural critics such as Victor Davis Hanson of the Hoover Institution, writing in *Mexifornia: A State of Becoming* (2003), and Samuel Huntington of Harvard, writing in *Who Are We: The Challenges to America's Identity* (2004), have expressed pessimistic views. A distinction has to be made, Hanson argues, between Mexican Americans committed to this country, and Mexicans coming to California exclusively to get work, their loyalties remaining with Mexico—the one group being an essential building block of California, the other an unassimilated mass threatening to take over the state. Huntington's argument postulates an irreducible and non-negotiable Anglo-Protestantism at the core of American identity. Groups who assimilate to this core become good Americans; those who do not, do not. In one sense, Hanson's and Huntington's arguments were déjà vu all over again in terms of the early 1990s; but this time around, the Mexican American population of California had long since become a determining voting bloc, wooed by Republicans and Democrats alike, and there were no hostile propositions on the ballot. The election in May 2005 of city councilman Antonio Villaraigosa, a former Speaker of the Assembly, as the first Hispanic mayor of Los Angeles since Cristóbal Aguilar left office in 1872 underscored the growing political clout of the Hispanic population of California. Even more subtly, the election of Villaraigosa suggested the re-Hispanicization of California as a society, especially in its southern counties.

As the writer Richard Rodríguez has argued, the center is holding. There is a common society called "California," diverse but emergently ecumenical. Californians, Rodríguez argued in his many newspaper and television appearances and his book

Brown (2002), are becoming more like each other. At an earlier time, Rodríguez had been severely castigated by many Mexican American academics because he refused to take up the then-fashionable adversarial position against the predominant Anglo culture. Growing up in Sacramento in the 1950s, Rodríguez had been educated by Irish nuns who seemed oblivious to his race, or at least did not consider his being Mexican American a barrier to learning how to solve equations or diagram sentences. Educated at Stanford, the Warburg Institute in London, Oxford University, and UC Berkeley, where he took a Ph.D. in Renaissance literature, Rodríguez turned down a tenure-track appointment to Yale because, in his opinion, it smacked of affirmative action. The more he experienced California as a cultural critic and working journalist, the more Rodríguez believed that Californians were becoming more like each other—that a common culture was beginning to emerge.

Then there is the question of multiple identities: the ability of California, that is, to allow its people to sustain within themselves, simultaneously, multiple allegiances. Thus, defenders of this position (including *Los Angeles Times* correspondent Gregory Rodríguez) argued, when a predominantly Mexican American crowd cheered for Mexico against the United States team in February 1998 at a World Cup soccer championship game in Los Angeles, the fans were not disrespecting the United States or renouncing their political allegiance, but merely acting like Irish Americans on St. Patrick's Day, French Americans on Bastille Day, Italian Americans on Columbus Day, or Chinese Americans at the Chinese New Year. California does not demand of its immigrants that they sacrifice cultural loyalties to their country of origin, only that they be loyal and observant Americans. Since the population of California is one-third immigrant, almost any given Californian has a number of cultural tracks playing in his or her mind. Well and good, critics of this position replied. But some people at the soccer game had thrown beer bottles on the field and booed the American flag. California might allow for multiple tracks, but a citizen's ultimate American identity and allegiance must still prevail.

A look at the demographic data makes a refreshing break from the arguments. Census 2000 revealed that, far from destabilizing California, immigration has actually shored up the social structures of the state. At a time when the traditional family has been coming under increasing stress—there were more than 834,000 single-mother families and 292,000 single-father families in California as of 2000—immigrants have shown a remarkable stability in their family ties. American-born groups might be talking the talk about family values, but at the same time they are getting divorced in record numbers, having children out of wedlock, or not having children at all, while immigrants have been marrying and having children and staying married and taking care of their old people. They have also been accommodating themselves to other immigrant and nonimmigrant groups in the twenty-four California cities in which the ethnic equivalent of "white flight" has not been happening. Census 2000 showed a recurring mosaic in California of three to four ethnic or racial communities coexisting under a single political umbrella. Neighborhoods tend to be ethnic, true, but no one group is driving any other group out. A pattern of accommodation has been asserting itself.

According to Census 2000, moreover, younger Californians, specifically the under-eighteen Millennial Generation, seem to be weaving a tapestry combining disparate elements and common values. Eighteen-and-under Californians made up 27.3 percent of the total population in 2000, but only 34.8 percent of those 9.2 million Californians were Caucasian. The rest were Hispanic (43.8 percent), Asian (9.6 percent), African American (6.7 percent), American Indian and Alaska Native (0.5 percent), and finally, Native Hawaiian and Pacific Islanders (0.1 percent). Millennial California, then—which is to say, the California of the first two decades of the twenty-first century—will have a strong Hispanic majority, a secondary sector of whites, a noticeable Asian American community, a declining African American population, and a very small percentage of people in other ethnic categories. These identities, moreover, are commingling, and 7.3 percent of Californians under the age of eighteen were claiming two or more racial and/or ethnic identities in 2000. The 2000 census also revealed that California has become a society in which minorities constitute the majority. Culturally, the question has now become: will these groups be sealed off from one another, or will Richard Rodríguez be proved correct? Will there be an ecumenical interchange among the various groups, a forging of a common California amid the diversity? In 1982, Ridley Scott's film *Blade Runner* forecast Los Angeles/California as being, on the street at least, culturally eclectic to the point of pandemonium: a sum total of mutually repellent parts. But is this inevitable? Could not the Millennial Generation sustain its multiple identities within a context of interchange and common ground? That remains the question—and the hope.

13

ARNOLD!

Stewardship or Squandered Legacy?

Arnold Schwarzenegger and his wife Maria Shriver, inauguration day, November 17, 2003. Sharon and Gray Davis look on.

SAN FRANCISCO CHRONICLE

PHOTO CHRIS STEWART

The question remains: is California governable? And if it is, what kind of government do Californians want? For all its impressive growth, there remains a volatility in the politics and governance of California, which became perfectly clear to the rest of the nation in the fall of 2003 when the voters of California recalled one governor and elected another.

Behind that recall election could be found proximate causes—an energy crisis, a crushing shortfall of revenues following the collapse of the dot-com industry, an imprudently expanded state budget, the particular personalities of the incumbent governor Gray Davis and his chief challenger, screen actor Arnold Schwarzenegger—but there were also more long-standing problems, structural as well as psychological, regarding what exactly Californians valued in the public sector and were willing to pay for.

To Joan Didion's way of thinking, California—especially the public works system by means of which it had invented itself through water—had been the result of federal largesse. From the beginning, Didion argued, the federal government, representing the entire people of the United States, had brought American California into being and had been paying most of its bills through spending on defense and public works. Californians, meanwhile, so Didion maintained in *Where I Was From* (2003), had from the beginning been envisioning themselves as an independent-minded pioneer people, prizing self-reliance and basing their culture upon it. While not as comprehensive in his arguments as Didion, state treasurer Phil Angelides made a similar point before, during, and after the fiscal crisis and recall. Californians, Angelides argued, had the wherewithal to afford a flourishing public sector; the Republican leadership was just too cheap to pay for it. Nonsense, Republican leaders retorted: state government had ballooned into a $100-billion-plus monster. It was time to kill the beast.

Despite its reputation for radicalism and eccentricity, California was for its first 110 years a predominantly Republican state. Most of its governors, state legislators, county supervisors, mayors, and council members—even in the San Francisco Bay Area—had been Republicans. The more suburbanized California became in the twentieth century, the more Republican it became, up until the 1960s. In the nineteenth century, California Republicanism was conservative and oligarchic. After 1910, however, it fused with a reform-oriented Progressivism through the two gubernatorial administrations (1911–17) of Hiram Johnson, a San Francisco attorney elected in 1910 as a reform candidate promising to kick the Southern Pacific out of California politics. There were also Progressives in the Democratic Party, such as Senator James Duval Phelan and former San Francisco city attorney Franklin Lane, secretary of the interior in the Wilson administration.

The question was: were the Progressives reforming liberals or reforming conservatives? The answer is that they were a little of each and something in between. The California Progressives distrusted big government, big corporations, and big labor. They preferred to see a reforming elite, namely, themselves—professional men of the upper middle class, a kind of nobility of the robe—in authority. They were ardent conservationists, yet they also believed in public works: the dams and reservoirs that made modern California possible, even at the loss of the Hetch Hetchy Valley. They were distrustful of partisan politics and put in place a system of appointive commissions to oversee water and power, harbors, and other ongoing functions of government. They also mandated nonpartisanship in local elections and an open primary system that allowed candidates to enter party primaries regardless of their own political affiliations. (In 1946 Earl Warren would win both the Republican and Democratic nominations for governor.) Yet they also sponsored the initiative, the referendum, and the recall, which placed in the hands of the voters an extraordinary ability to make an end run around representative government. Thanks to the Progressive reforms of the pre–World War I era, the voters of California could place proposed laws directly on the ballot through petition, express their opinion on laws passed by the legislature, or recall public officials without cause or judicial procedure.

Thus, California Progressivism contained within itself both liberal and conservative impulses, as judged by the standards of today. In their continuing animosity toward the Japanese, in fact, Progressives could show themselves as a hard-edged Right. During the 1920s, the generally conservative drift of the country detached California Republicanism from its Progressive alliance. The social conflict of the 1930s precipitated a turn to the right. In such a figure as Earl Warren, however, governor from 1942 until 1953 when he accepted an appointment as chief justice of the U.S. Supreme Court, Progressivism resurfaced in Republican circles. Earl Warren was a law-and-order man, a crime-fighting anti-Communist district attorney and attorney general; but he also had liberal leanings regarding the social responsibilities of government: traits that surfaced dramatically when he became chief justice. Between 1942 and 1966—which is to say, during the gubernatorial administrations of Warren, Goodwin Knight, and Edmund G. "Pat" Brown, two Republicans and a Democrat—Progressivism characterized state government during a period of extraordinary growth. Despite their differences, Democrats and Republicans saw sufficiently eye to eye to build the infrastructure—schools, colleges, and universities; freeways, roads, and bridges; public buildings; and public programs of every sort—serving the rise of postwar California. For a later generation, caught in partisan turmoil and gridlock, the Warren-Knight-Brown years of confident creation seemed a golden age of vision and consensus in which Democrats and Republicans alike had held a shared membership in the Party of California.

The 1960s witnessed a challenge to this consensus. Throughout the Sun Belt, which included Southern California, Republicanism became populist and antigovernment: a tide that lifted the political boat of actor and television commentator Ronald Reagan. The Democratic Party, meanwhile, was moving in the other direction, with left-liberal Democrats playing the determining role in primary elections. Unlike the governors of the 1950s and the first half of the 1960s, who agreed on a significant percentage of all issues, the governors of the subsequent era staked out for themselves more differentiated points of view. In 1966, Ronald Reagan ran as an antigovernment Republican reformer, although he eventually compromised with his Democratic legislature and signed into law the single largest tax hike in California history. Governor Edmund G. "Jerry" Brown, Jr., sustained an idiosyncratic blend of left, right, and New Age perspectives. His successor, former attorney general George Deukmejian, was a moderate Republican, who sought to resteady state government after the frequently brilliant and sometimes not-so-brilliant experimentations of the Jerry Brown era. Former San Diego mayor and U.S. senator Pete Wilson, who succeeded George Deukmejian, was a moderate Republican doing his best to remain moderate when the collapse of the Cold War economy cut state revenues by more than 40 percent.

The Party of California, meanwhile, was being challenged by the Party of Dissent. Ever since the nineteenth century, dissent had been a way of life on what many considered to be the "Left Coast" of the nation. Such dissent was focused primarily on industrial and labor-related issues, although in the case of the IWW, revolutionary socialists such as Jack London, and the in-your-face Communists of the 1930s, more fundamental changes were in mind. The second half of the 1900s witnessed an explosion of dissent—into politics, feminism, sexuality and other aspects of personal fulfillment, education, literary and artistic value and practice, drug usage, military service, and corporate culture and control—that either originated in California or consolidated itself here and gave the state a reputation for kookiness, even as critics of California were themselves being transformed by what was going on in the Golden State. Thanks to upheavals in California, the rest of the nation had by the twenty-first century become significantly California-ized.

This process began during the Second World War with the arrival in California of numerous pacifists, anarchists, and general resisters, many of them in federal custody. In 1944, bohemian writer Henry Miller planted the flag of anarchy in Big Sur, and this event, as well as any other, represented a watershed in the consolidation of dissent on the Left Coast. For the rest of the war and after, Miller and his friends in Big Sur formed a kind of free-floating resistance community that soon established satellite communities in San Francisco, Berkeley, Santa Monica, and Venice Beach. Berkeley itself emerged in these postwar years as a leftist enclave, as evidenced by the founding there in 1949 of the radically oriented Pacifica Foundation and its radio station KPFA-FM by pacifist Lewis Hill, an outspoken opponent of the recent war. Throughout the 1950s, a number of cultures ran parallel in Berkeley: a university culture on the UC campus, by and large conservative in nature; its polar opposite at Pacifica/KPFA; a blue-collar culture on the flatlands spilling over from Oakland, with half a dozen or so old-time Communists from the 1930s still in residence; and in the hills an upper-middle-class/professional elite, many of them academics, of generally liberal orientation. Liberalism, however, took on a more militant edge in 1960 in the course of two controversies: hearings by the House Un-American Activities Committee in San Francisco's City Hall, which provoked riots, and the execution of convict Caryl Chessman, author of the international bestseller *Cell 2455, Death Row* (1954), who many believed had been railroaded into a death sentence by a hostile Los Angeles County court.

The Beat movement, meanwhile, while primarily literary in its expression, also had political overtones. Although they rarely talked directly about politics, the Beats wanted out of what they considered a culture increasingly dominated by corporate values and a corporation-driven politics and foreign policy. Whether the Beats should be considered to have been radicals or radical conservatives, however, remains an open question. San Francisco poet Lawrence Ferlinghetti (who may or may not have been a Beat in the first place) was a classic radical; but many conservatives, it must be remembered, were also decrying the effects of the new corporate culture. Jack Kerouac ended his career as an avid supporter of William F. Buckley, Jr., and his *National Review.*

By 1964 the radical component of the Bay Area identity, aroused by resistance to the Vietnam War, had taken root on the UC Berkeley campus, as the eruption there of the Free Speech Movement in September 1964 dramatically attested. The proximate cause of the outbreak, led by philosophy student Mario Savio, was an administrative decision to prohibit political activity on Sproul Plaza. This provocative restriction tapped into a magma of dissent among many Berkeley students, arising in mixed degrees from their opposition to the Vietnam War, their fear of being drafted, their espousal of various critiques of capitalist society, their desire for more sex, drugs, and rock 'n' roll, and their general antipathy for what a great big uncaring place UC Berkeley seemed to have become. Before it was over, the Free Speech Movement resulted, on the night of December 2–3, in the greatest mass arrest in California history as 750 students were hustled out of Sproul Hall, where they had been staging a sit-in. Long-term effects were even more significant: the election of Ronald Reagan to the governorship in 1966 on an outspokenly anti-student-protest platform, followed by the firing the following year of university president Clark Kerr by a Reagan-dominated Board of Regents. But even more important, the Free Speech Movement helped launch a sensibility, an attitude, in the Baby Boomer generation that would affect its values and behavior for the next forty years.

Across the Bay in San Francisco, meanwhile, a movement of young Americans calling themselves "hippies" was raising even more havoc with traditional values. Berkeley students, after all, were attending college (most of them, at least), and most of them were headed—whether they wished to admit it or not—toward traditional careers. The hippies, by contrast, were, as LSD guru Timothy Leary was urging them to do, tuning in and dropping out, often short-circuiting their lives (in many cases killing themselves) in street life and drug usage. In 1964 the hippie movement had been attached to symbols of peace and friendship, as expressed in the poetry and public readings of onetime Beat poet Allen Ginsberg, now deeply into Asian mysticism and aesthetics. Hippies dressed in motley arrangements of tie-dyed fabrics, beads, headbands, and flowers, as if they were themselves mystics or dervishes from some enchanted land. As late as 1967, singer Scott McKenzie was urging young America to come to San Francisco, wearing flowers in its hair, for the Summer of Love. Nineteen sixty-seven opened with a mass rally in the Great Meadow of Golden Gate Park adjacent to the Haight-Ashbury district of the city, where the hippie movement was based. Some twenty thousand hippies, weekend hippies, wannabe hippies, fellow travelers, and the merely curious attended the event. Amplified psychedelic music blared over the crowd, and marijuana smoke hovered above the gathering like a low-lying San Francisco fog. Tablets of various pharmaceuticals were freely distributed. There were overdoses aplenty, of course, and that was the Catch-22 of the hippie movement. It became drug-driven, and burned itself to a cinder.

Whether or not he was ever a hippie (or whether, in fact, the term "hippie" had any meaning at all after the Summer of Love), the murders perpetrated by cult leader Charles Manson and his followers in August 1969 in a canyon above Beverly Hills (the victims included actress Sharon Tate, coffee heiress Abigail Folger, and international hairstylist Jay Sebring) put an end once and for all to the movement by offering up an image of terminal horror. By the early 1970s, the Haight-Ashbury district, before 1964 a quiet neighborhood of picturesque Victorians fronting Golden Gate Park, seemed a war-torn no-man's-land, which it remained for the next two decades.

In another part of the city, by contrast, the Castro district was looking spiffier and more stylish each year; its citizens, the gay community, had come to San Francisco out of dissent, true, but also to find a place where they could be more openly themselves. As a port city with a live-and-let-live attitude, San Francisco had from the nineteenth century onward tolerated gays and lesbians, provided that certain rules of discretion were adhered to. The lavender-friendly nature of the city was intensified during the Second World War as thousands of gay and lesbian service personnel passed through San Francisco, where they had positive experiences despite intermittent clampdowns by the military police, shore patrol, and local cops. The gay character of the city steadily increased through the 1950s, and by the mid-1960s word was out across gay America that San Francisco was a good place to be. This period and the following half-decade witnessed the transformation of the Castro district; the increasing presence of gay people in the cultural and civic life of the city; the creation of gay-oriented newspapers, churches, and other institutions; and the rise of the gay community as a political force. By the mid-1970s, Harvey Milk, a camera store owner from the Castro, was sitting on the Board of Supervisors, the first openly gay elected official in the nation. Tragically, however, Milk and San Francisco mayor George Moscone were assassinated in November 1978 by recently resigned supervisor Dan White, a former policeman and fireman. Deftly defended, White was convicted on reduced charges and given a lenient sentence, which scandalized many and provoked demonstrations of outrage in the gay community.

San Francisco was already reeling from a catastrophe the previous month in the jungles of Guyana, on the north coast of South America, that has to be considered part of the California history of this era. The church community involved, the People's Temple, originating in Indianapolis, had begun its California existence in Mendocino County and grew to strength in San Francisco, where, under the leadership of the Reverend Jim Jones, it became a force in local politics. Press scrutiny of human rights violations at the temple, however, led Jones to move his congregation—a racially mixed amalgam of blacks, poor whites, and a small cadre of middle-class adherents—to an agricultural commune in Guyana which he called Jonestown. As California congressman Leo J. Ryan and two aides, visiting the settlement in Guyana to investigate continuing allegations against the temple, were boarding an aircraft to leave, they were ambushed by temple members; Ryan was left dead on the tarmac beneath his plane, and the others were seriously wounded. That night and the next morning, urged on by the Reverend Jones, members of the People's Temple settlement, following a prearranged suicide plan, gave cyanide-laced punch to 276 children before drinking it themselves. By morning, a total of 914 Jonestown residents, including Jones, who shot himself, lay dead. It was the largest mass suicide in American history.

GIVEN THE POLARIZATION and turmoil that began in the 1960s and lasted through the 1970s—compounded by the assassination of presidential candidate Robert Kennedy in June 1968 in the Ambassador Hotel in Los Angeles on the night of his victory in the California primary election—it is not surprising that California seemed to the rest of the nation to be such an unstable political place. From the 1960s forward, California was in fact showing a dichotomous diversity verging on the eccentric in its politicians and public officials. On the right, there were such figures as U.S. senator George Murphy, superintendent of public instruction Max Rafferty, Los Angeles mayor Sam Yorty, and Congressman Robert "B-1 Bob" Dornan of Orange County. On the left were such figures as San Francisco congressman Philip Burton and state chief justice Rose Bird, whom Jerry Brown had appointed despite her total lack of judicial experience. U.S. senator S. I. Hayakawa, a Democrat turned Republican, occupied a political space of his own. The majority of elected officials in California, it must be said, were mainstream Democrats and Republicans; yet the state nurtured a vivid spectrum of ideologues who expressed the seismic volatility of a politically immature state—immature in that, with the exception of local government, Californians were not all that interested in politics, nor did they have to be. Thanks to the reforms of the Progressives, a significant proportion of the business of government was done by boards and districts that were nearly anonymous in their composition. By the 1990s, state government itself seemed to be in eclipse, if one were to judge by the amount of coverage given state government in local media. Many influential newspapers, in fact, did not even maintain a bureau in Sacramento.

What were the issues facing government in California, regardless of the particular level of public attention being paid to them at any given time? As in the case of every state and every community in the nation, the primary task of government is to do the day-to-day work necessary to keep society functioning. From this perspective, the work of government in California—

local, county, regional, and state—was prosaic and yet vitally necessary. "All politics are local" is the way that House Speaker Thomas Phillip "Tip" O'Neill expressed this truism. Yet the drama of politics is not always evident in the day-to-day operations of government, particularly when things are going reasonably well. Politics is a theater of opinion, and it requires a drama with a plot, a story to tell. Certain issues surface in politics as shorthand terms for a larger cultural debate. What were they in California? Immigration, most vividly, as has already been discussed; but also the environment, especially as it relates to matters of growth and/or no-growth, together with education, social programs, and taxation.

Since so much of nature had been destroyed by the Gold Rush, it is not surprising that there eventually came corrective action in the form of a judicial decision in 1884 by U.S. circuit court judge Lorenzo Sawyer, who had himself been a gold miner in 1850, that the Malakoff Hydraulic Mine must cease operation because its debris, flowing downriver, was polluting other properties. This decision can be seen as the beginning of the environmental movement. Eight years later, in San Francisco, the Sierra Club was founded to promote awareness and preservation of the Sierra Nevada. The first Sierra Club president, John Muir, played an important role in helping establish a national park system.

In modern times, the most significant environmental wake-up call was the Santa Barbara oil spill of January 28, 1969, when an oil drilling platform five miles offshore malfunctioned, creating a sea of ooze that extended thirty-five miles in diameter and polluted twenty miles of the Santa Barbara coast. This catastrophe spurred environmental groups to militant action, as symbolized by the growing activism of Sierra Club president David Brower, who eventually became too militant for even the Sierra Club and formed his own group, Friends of the Earth. Pesticide contamination of the Kesterson National Wildlife Refuge in the

San Joaquin Valley, starting in 1980, killed and deformed wildlife on a massive scale. The level of Mono Lake, meanwhile, had sunk by more than forty feet owing to drain-offs by the Department of Water and Power of Los Angeles, and its population of nesting gulls had begun to disappear.

A considerable literature arose chronicling and predicting the destruction of California by runaway growth, and voters began to pay attention. When Southern California sought more water from the north via a Peripheral Canal running past the wetlands of the Sacramento River delta northeast of San Francisco, voters rejected the measure by 62 percent when it came on the ballot in June 1982. Gradually, though, over the next two decades, California went increasingly Green. Founded in the early 1990s, the Green Party of California looked to David Brower as its prophet and avatar, along with actors Peter Coyote and Ed Begley, Jr., singer Bonnie Raitt, and former Democratic congressman Dan Hamburg of Ukiah, who mounted a million-dollar campaign for governor in 1998, winning thirteen local seats and putting a Green in the state Assembly. When the Pacific Lumber Company threatened to harvest old-growth redwoods in the Headwaters Forest of Humboldt County, Earth First! activist Julia Butterfly Hill in December 1997 ascended a thousand-year-old redwood tree she named Luna, and remained there until December 1999, when her demands were met. As dramatic as such a gesture might be, however, California had as of the millennium no statewide program for dealing with the further growth that will inevitably come. The population of the state, the department of finance has estimated, will be approaching sixty million people by 2040. How is such growth to be accommodated without the complete destruction of precious farmland, open space, and forests?

And how are the children and young people of the state to be educated so that they can survive in an increasingly competitive technological and economic environment? In the so-called Golden Age following World War II, the schools of California were considered among the best in the nation, and test scores proved it. But by the early 1990s, California had dropped to the lowest rankings in terms of scores and dollars spent on K–12 education. In 1993, for example, fourth-graders in California were vying with fourth-graders in Mississippi for the dubious distinction of being the worst readers in the nation. In 1996 the state legislature authorized nearly a billion dollars to be spent on reducing class sizes, and by the time Pete Wilson left office, California was spending 43 percent of its budget on K–12 education. Was this high percentage of expenditure a sign of failure, some were asking, or the inevitable result of the work that the public schools of California were performing on behalf of the rest of the nation in assimilating millions of non–native English speakers into American life? Were test scores being used to stigmatize immigrant students? Such a query remained a touchy question as the new millennium began.

The growing number of social programs were also a subject of debate. The New Deal came late to California, but social democratic New Deal thinking remained characteristic of the state for the next sixty years. Few, if any, states in the nation were sustaining by the 1990s such a full range of state-supported health and social welfare programs as was California. The 1960 Master Plan for Higher Education was still in effect, and, as in the case of its social programs, few states could point to such a comprehensive state-supported education program. A three-strikes-and-you're-out law passed in 1994, mandating long prison terms for third felony convictions, was filling state prisons to capacity and beyond. Then there was the question of bond indebtedness on billions of dollars that had been borrowed over the preceding thirty years for construction projects. When mandated programs, including paying interest on bonds and debt retirement, were factored in, the state had less than 17 percent of its revenues to operate on. It had to do this, moreover, within the context of Proposition 13.

Passed by two thirds of the voters in June 1978, Proposition 13 reduced residential property taxes by 57 percent and permanently capped the rate of future taxation. Its primary supporter, the Howard Jarvis Taxpayers Association, described it as the Boston Tea Party of California. It certainly reduced state and local finances dramatically. Deprived of funds, state government began confiscating local revenues to maintain itself. As new residential properties not covered by Proposition 13 came on the market, revenues increased; but the state maintained its control of these funds, thereby creating a permanent conflict between state and local government.

Local government was embattled, and never more so than when faced with a series of natural and (as in the case of the Los Angeles riots) man-made catastrophes that put a terrific strain on local resources. On October 17, 1989, an earthquake measuring 7.1 on the Richter scale, centered in the Loma Prieta section of the Santa Cruz peninsula, struck the San Francisco Bay Area. It was the most serious earthquake to hit the region since April 1906. A portion of the I-880 elevated freeway running through West Oakland collapsed just as commuter traffic was beginning, and forty-two motorists met horrible deaths beneath tons of concrete. Altogether, sixty-six people died, and there was $7 billion in damage.

Then, on a hot, windy Sunday, October 20, 1991, a 2,000-degree inferno broke out in the Oakland hills, fueled by oil-rich eucalyptus trees that exploded like bombs in the heat. Twenty-five people lost their lives, one hundred fifty suffered serious injuries, and twenty-seven hundred structures were destroyed. Over the years California had had many such fires, but in terms of death and destruction the Oakland fire is in a class by itself.

Two years later, fires raged along the entire south coast of

Southern California, from Malibu to northern San Diego County. Three hundred homes were lost. Pepperdine University came within a few hundred yards and a few shifts of wind to losing its new multimillion-dollar campus. On the morning of January 17, 1994, a magnitude 6.7 earthquake, centered in the Northridge district of Los Angeles in the eastern San Fernando Valley, shook the city for ten terrible seconds. Fifty-seven people died, most of them as a result of collapsing structures, and $20 billion in property was lost. Rainstorms swept the Southland in January and February 1992, causing five deaths. In the winter of 1995, El Niño storms struck north and south, flooding Sacramento, the Russian River area, San José, and Los Angeles County. In January, February, and March of 1998, El Niño returned with a vengeance. For three straight months, California, north and south, was pelted with lashing rains, the worst in a century. Along the coast, mudslides destroyed valuable homes and property, forcing evacuations. When it was over, El Niño had caused $500 million in damage and deaths numbering into the dozens (exact figures were never compiled). State and federal disaster areas had been declared in forty-one out of fifty-eight counties.

Each of these natural catastrophes, while its results were alleviated by federal relief programs, cost local and state government hundreds of millions of dollars in emergency expenditures.

Two further catastrophes, these of human making—an energy crisis and the collapse of the dot-com industry—brought California to the brink. On September 23, 1996, Governor Pete Wilson signed into law the Electric Utility Industry Restructuring Act calling for the deregulation of electricity in California by March 1998. The act was intended to keep manufacturing and other large-scale enterprises in California by allowing them to buy their electricity at competitive rates from private nonregulated sources within and outside the state. The law also allowed the regulated public utilities in California to sell their electrical generation plants to private companies. Starting in March 1998, Californians would be buying their electricity on a spot market administered by the Power Exchange, with the transmission of this electricity under the supervision of a nonprofit entity called the California Independent System Operator (ISO). This new system was intended to flood the state with electricity providers eager to do business at competitive prices.

Within a year of beginning operation, the system was coming under stress. The regulated public utilities, first of all, almost immediately sold off $3 billion worth of generators and related equipment, to the delight of their stockholders, flush with unexpected dividends. Within a year or so, California, having disestablished a system of regulated public utilities in effect since the Progressive era, had transferred its electrical generating capacity to private, unregulated—and mostly out-of-state—companies such as Duke Energy of North Carolina and Enron and Reliant Energy of Texas. Then the rains dwindled, and the hydroelectric capacity of California and its suppliers in the Northwest fell off drastically. Between December 1999 and December 2000, the price of the natural gas driving most electrical generators increased sixteenfold. A concern for polluting emissions took other generators off-line in a state in which no new generators had been built within the last ten years. Nuclear energy had long since been demonized into marginality. Phoenix, Las Vegas, Portland, and Seattle were meanwhile developing voracious appetites for the electricity that had previously been diverted to California, while in-state consumer demand had increased by 24 percent since 1995.

As electricity became increasingly scarce, the private companies—"the boys from Texas"—began to "eat California's lunch," as one energy official put it, driving the cost of electricity on the spot market to astronomical heights. Summer 2000 saw the state's electrical bill increase by $10.9 billion over the previous summer, with most of the money going to the boys from Texas. Houston-based Reliant Energy alone experienced a 600 percent increase in profits, $100 million of it coming from California. By January 2001 the ISO controlling the distribution of electricity was declaring alerts and enforcing blackouts. Suddenly California found itself facing the unthinkable: the catastrophic collapse of its energy grid. Californians turned off their air conditioners, dimmed their lights, unplugged their appliances, turned their downtowns into sepia tones, in an effort to reduce their consumption of electricity. Governor Gray Davis castigated the energy companies as price gougers and sought relief, unsuccessfully, from the federal government. In April 2001 the Pacific Gas & Electric Company, bulwark of the Northern California economy, filed for bankruptcy protection under Chapter 11. The State of California, meanwhile, was being forced to buy electricity at exorbitant prices in order to forestall the total collapse of the state's economy. By early 2002, California was seeking a market for $12.5 billion in bonds to pay for electricity that had already been consumed.

The dot-com industry, meanwhile, was in a comparable state of collapse. In April 2000 the NASDAQ had peaked at 5,048. Then, over the next eighteen months, a steady, then precipitous decline ensued. By mid-August 2001, the NASDAQ index had dropped to 1,930, and by autumn some 129,310 workers had lost their jobs at Internet-based companies. This resulted in a dramatic—nearly 40 percent over the next two years—reduction in state revenues, owing especially to the fact that a significant amount of those revenues came from taxes on Californians earning $100,000 or more annually, a sector significantly wiped out by the dot-com collapse. During the flush times, starting in 1998, the state government had increased its budget by 40 percent, from $67 billion to $97 billion, in the belief that the money machine would never stop. Everyone, Democrats and Republicans alike, seemed to be happy at the pork barrel.

All this—the increased expectations of government, the dependency of local government on state support, the usurpation of the state budget by debt service, compounded by the energy crisis and other mandated programs—came to a head in 2003 as the State of California faced a $38 billion shortfall in revenues, if current programs were to be maintained. The problem was that the supernova of state government had swept up into its force field old and new, effective and ineffective programs alike. Throughout 2002 and 2003 the department of finance slashed social and other programs indiscriminately, or so it seemed, with the exception of prison guards' salaries, which were increased dramatically, thanks to the political clout of their union. By the summer of 2003, the very viability of state government was coming into question. Cut services, Republicans urged—and no new taxes. Cut services, if possible, Democrats countered—but do not disestablish the New Deal; raise taxes selectively, rather, and borrow from Wall Street to get through the crisis. Official legislative analyst Elizabeth Hill disagreed. The state, she pointed out, was already paying $2.6 billion annually in debt service. Further debt could drive California into insolvency. Already, Standard & Poor's had dropped California's bond rating to its lowest category, and in February 2003 Moody's Investors Service followed suit, which meant that it would now cost the state a lot more to borrow money.

A growing number of taxpayers, meanwhile, had become disillusioned with Governor Gray Davis, then at the beginning of his second term. Someone, after all, had to be responsible for this mess, and it might as well be the governor. Using a recall provision approved by the voters in January 1911 during the Progressive era, the anti-Davisites began in January 2003 to circulate a petition to put a recall measure before the voters in the fall. Not only did California allow for such a recall, but the January 1911 measure called for the election of a new governor simultaneously. Any Californian could file his or her candidacy for a small fee plus the endorsement of fewer than one hundred voters of the same political party. On July 23, 2003, Secretary of State Kevin Shelley certified that the recall petition had qualified for the ballot. The next day, Lieutenant Governor Cruz Bustamante set the recall election for October 7, 2003. A cornucopia of candidates filed: a former television star, an actress in adult films, a lady bartender in the Mother Lode, earnest activists of every persuasion, and a list of politicians and celebrities that included a sitting congressman, the lieutenant governor, a state senator, a former secretary of state, a syndicated newspaper columnist, a former congressman who had served as White House chief of staff, the chairman of the 1984 Olympics—and, declaring his candidacy on August 6 on Jay Leno's *Tonight Show,* action-film star Arnold Schwarzenegger, a naturalized Austrian immigrant. The following October, Davis was recalled, and Schwarzenegger was overwhelmingly elected governor with 48.6 percent of the total votes cast.

Historians of the future will have a field day drawing comparisons between California and its new governor. Both, in a sense, are figments of their respective imaginations. In 1849, American California had invented itself as a state through a sheer assertion of will, and so had Arnold Schwarzenegger invented himself through sheer force of will as a bodybuilder, a businessman, an actor, and a viable political candidate, strengthened in this process by his astute and equally determined wife, author and television journalist Maria Shriver, and through her the entire Shriver-Kennedy legacy, now translated to California. All things considered, California and Schwarzenegger were equally improbable, and so was the new relationship between them. How could a young and impoverished immigrant have accomplished so much since his arrival in the United States in the early 1970s: the Mr. Universe titles, the successful real estate investments, the college degree, the movie career, the brilliant marriage, the growing reputation in the 1990s as an effective political activist, the end run around the primary system to the governorship, and the success and general respect on both sides of the political aisle that unfolded in his first year in office?

State government, of course, remained a continuing problem. Largely through Schwarzenegger's leadership, voters approved a cap on spending, the creation of a reserve fund, and a bond issue to deal with the shortfall without collapsing social programs to a draconian degree. The governor also launched a comprehensive review of state operations with an eye to harmonizing programs and revenues. Deploying his personal popularity, Schwarzenegger negotiated with group after group, asking them to take cuts so as to stabilize the state in exchange for renewed participation when things got better. He even got teachers and prison guards to take a cut in pay and Indian tribes to cough up another $1 billion in casino revenues. Whatever his political future—whether or not he would run for a second term as governor, whether or not he would ever hold higher office—Schwarzenegger had already edged himself into the front ranks of notable governors of California since 1850.

The fact that Arnold Schwarzenegger was an immigrant spoke for itself. He was leading an immigrant state. In his inaugural speech, Schwarzenegger noted that he had long thought of California as a golden dream by the sea. It had been a long time since any politician had talked that way about California. The golden dream had become sadly tarnished in the last decade of the old millennium. In times past, boosters of California might easily cite statistics supporting the notion that California was offering Americans one of the best societies in which to live. No one surveying the costs and problems of California in the new millennium, however—soaring housing prices, gridlocked freeways, embattled public schools, rising crime and the costs of long-term incarceration, a state government that had weakened itself through runaway growth, a tax revolt that made the financing of legitimate state services problematic, natural catastrophes of earthquake, fire, flood, and mudslide—would cite California as an unambiguous triumph. But did that mean (as in the title of a novel from this period) that California was over—that it had lost its promise entirely? There has always been something slightly bipolar about California. It was either utopia or dystopia, a dream or a nightmare, a hope or a broken promise—and too infrequently anything in between. Now it was something in between: a society of great promise with a $1.5 trillion economy, making it the fifth largest GNP on the planet. The world was still rushing in—legally and illegally, as it turned out—not to escape reality in California, to bask in the unearned increment, but to struggle competitively in a society that had only recently begun to internalize in its myth of itself what the Spanish philosopher Miguel de Unamuno called the tragic sense of life.

Even before Unamuno coined this apt phrase, however, the California-born philosopher Josiah Royce had said something similar. California, Royce noted, was a promise, but it was also a struggle for redemption in the face of failure. California was not perfect; nor was the United States of America, in which California played such a significant role, perfect; nor was the world in which California functioned as a nation-state and global commonwealth perfect. Other regions of the country—the American South especially, but also the flinty shores of New England and the snow- and tornado-swept Midwest—had long since become used to the idea that nothing was perfect, even the American dream. Californians were now getting used to that same idea, although, as native daughter Joan Didion was pointing out, they had a long way to go before they fully internalized such a limiting recognition. But they also had many advantages to work with: a blessed portion of the Pacific Coast; the freedoms and political institutions of the American republic; a polyglot, diversely talented, and ambitious population; and a cumulative heritage of aspiration to a better life—a chance of breaking through, of finding a golden dream by the sea—that was continuing to bring people to these Pacific shores. Across the long years of California's existence in modern times—under the jurisdictions of Spain, of Mexico, and of the United States—there have been cruelties, injustices, and mistakes aplenty. The record shows this to be the case. But there has also been an equally sustained persistence of what Josiah Royce called "the Hope of the Great Community": a place, a society, in which the best possibilities of the American experiment can be struggled for and sometimes achieved.

Acknowledgments

Fifteen years ago, historian Richard Allison suggested that I attempt a one-volume history of California. Years later, Scott Moyers of Random House provided me with the opportunity to do so. David Ebershoff, Moyers's successor as editor of the Modern Library Chronicles series and a noted novelist in his own right, was most encouraging regarding the first draft of this book and made many fine editorial decisions on its behalf.

For assistance with Spanish and Mexican references, I am grateful to Professor Iris Engstrand of the University of San Diego, Professors Rose Marie Beebe and Robert M. Senkewicz of Santa Clara University, and the La Jolla–based independent historian Harry W. Crosby. I am indebted to these experts, but I take responsibility for any errors in these sections of the text.

For assistance in selecting and obtaining photographs, I am grateful to John Cahoon and Jonathan Spaulding of the Seaver Center for Western History Research at the Natural History Museum of Los Angeles, Dace Taube of the Doheny Library at the University of Southern California, and Gary Kurutz, curator of special collections at the California State Library. Literary agent Sandra Dijkstra played her usual astute and encouraging role in the evolution of this book. Sheila Starr served as editorial adviser and helped me prepare the final manuscript.

I dedicate this brief history—so challenging to write, given my narrative proclivities—to Kathryn and Steven Sample in gratitude for their leadership and for the supportive environment they have helped to create at the University of Southern California, where since 1989 I have been privileged to be a member of the faculty.

Recommended Readings

GENERAL REFERENCE

Beck, Warren, and Inez Haase, *Historical Atlas of California* (1974)

Dunlap, Carol, *California People* (1982)

Hart, James D., *A Companion to California* (new edition, 1987)

Hoover, Mildred Brooke, Hero Eugene Rensch, and Ethel Grace Rensch, *Historic Spots in California* (third edition, revised by William Abeloe, 1966)

Hynding, Alan, and Mark Still, *California Historymakers* (second edition, 1999)

Pitt, Leonard, and Dale Pitt, *Los Angeles A to Z: An Encyclopedia of the City and County* (1997)

Works Progress Administration, Federal Writers' Project, *California: A Guide to the Golden State* (1949)

GENERAL HISTORIES

Cleland, Robert Glass, *From Wilderness to Empire: A History of California, 1542–1900* (1944)

Engstrand, Iris, *San Diego: California's Cornerstone* (2005)

Lavender, David, *California: A Bicentennial History* (1976)

Rawls, James, and Walton Bean, *California: An Interpretive History* (eighth edition, 2003)

Rice, Richard, William Bullough, and Richard Orsi, *The Elusive Eden: A New History of California* (third edition, 2002)

Rolle, Andrew, *California: A History* (fifth edition, 1998)

Rolle, Andrew, and James Gaines, *The Gold State: California History and Government* (fourth edition, 2000)

1. QUEEN CALAFIA'S ISLAND

Bakker, Elna, *An Island Called California* (1984)

Fagan, Brian, *Before California: An Archaeologist Looks at Our Earliest Inhabitants* (2003)

Fradkin, Philip, *The Seven States of California* (1995)

Heckrotte, Warren, and Julie Sweetkind, editors, *California 49: Forty-Nine Maps of California from the Sixteenth Century to the Present* (1999)

Margolin, Malcolm, *The Ohlone Way: Indian Life in the San Francisco–Monterey Bay Area* (1978)

McLaughlin, Glen, with Nancy H. Mayo, *The Mapping of California as an Island: An Illustrated Checklist* (1995)

McPhee, John, *Assembling California* (1993)

"The Queen of California," *The Atlantic Monthly* (March 1864)

Quinn, Arthur, *Broken Shore: The Marin Peninsula, A Perspective on History* (1981)

Rawls, James, *Indians of California: The Changing Image* (1984)

Schoenherr, Allan, *A Natural History of California* (1992)

2. LAWS OF THE INDIES

Bobb, Bernard, *The Viceregency of Antonio María Bucareli in New Spain, 1771–1779* (1962)

Bolton, Herbert Eugene, *Anza's California Expeditions* (five volumes, 1930)

Chapman, Charles Edward, *The Founding of Spanish California* (1916)

Costo, Rupert, and Jeannette Henry Costo, editors, *The Missions of California: A Legacy of Genocide* (1987)

Couve de Murville, M.N.L., *The Man Who Founded California* (2000)

Crosby, Harry, *Antigua California: Mission and Colony on the Peninsular Frontier, 1697–1768* (1994)

Crosby, Harry, *Gateway to Alta California: The Expedition to San Diego, 1769* (2003)

Geiger, Maynard, *The Life and Times of Fray Junipero Serra* (two volumes, 1959)

McLaughlin, Glen, with Nancy Mayo, *The Mapping of California as an Island* (1995)

Meyers, Paul A., *North to California: The Spanish Voyages of Discovery: 1533–1603* (2004)

Nunis, Doyce B., Jr., editor, *The Founding Documents of Los Angeles: A Bilingual Edition* (2004)

Phillips, George, *The Enduring Struggle: Indians in California History* (1981)

Phillips, George, *Indians and Intruders in Central California, 1769–1849* (1993)

Priestley, Herbert Ingram, *José de Galvez, Visitor-General of New Spain* (1918)

Quinn, Arthur, *Broken Shore: The Marin Peninsula, A Perspective on History* (1981)

Richman, Irving Berdine, *California Under Spain and Mexico, 1535–1847* (1911)

Sandos, James A., *Converting California: Indians and Franciscans in the Missions* (2004)

Schultz, John, *Spain's Colonial Outpost* (1985)

Sunset Editors, *The California Missions: A Pictorial History* (1981)

Time-Life Editors, *The Spanish West* (1976)

Wagner, Henry Raup, *Spanish Voyages to the Northwest Coast of America in the Sixteenth Century* (1929)

Weber, David, *The Spanish Frontier in North America* (1992)

3. A Troubled Territory

Beebe, Rose Marie, and Robert M. Senkewicz, editors, *Lands of Promise and Despair: Chronicles of Early California, 1535–1846* (2001)

Chaffin, Tom, *Pathfinder: John Charles Frémont and the Course of American Empire* (2002)

Dakin, Susanna Bryant, *The Lives of William Hartnell* (1949)

Dakin, Susanna Bryant, *A Scotch Paisano: Hugo Reid's Life in California, 1832–1852, Derived from His Correspondence* (1939)

Grivas, Theodore, *Military Governments in California, 1846–1850* (1963)

Gutiérrez, Ramón, and Richard Orsi, editors, *Contested Eden: California Before the Gold Rush* (1997)

Hague, Harlan, and David Langum, *Thomas O. Larkin: A Life of Patriotism and Profit in Old California* (1990)

Harlow, Neal, *California Conquered: War and Peace on the Pacific, 1846–1850* (1982)

Miller, Robert Ryal, *Juan Alvarado: Governor of California, 1836–1842* (1998)

Monroy, Douglas, *Thrown Among Strangers: The Making of Mexican Culture in Frontier California* (1990)

Perez, Crisotomo, *Land Grants in Alta California* (1996)

Robinson, W. W., *Land in California* (1948)

Rosenus, Allan, *General M. G. Vallejo and the Advent of the American* (1995)

Stewart, George, *The California Trail: An Epic with Many Heroes* (1962)

4. Striking It Rich

Blodgett, Peter, *Land of Golden Dreams: California in the Gold Rush Decade, 1848–1858* (1999)

Boessenecker, John, *Badge and Buckshot: Lawlessness in Old California* (1988)

Boessenecker, John, *Gold Dust and Gunsmoke: Tails of Gold Rush Outlaws, Gunfighters, Lawmen, and Vigilantes* (1999)

Brands, H. W., *The Age of Gold: The California Gold Rush and the New American Dream* (2002)

Caughey, John, *The California Gold Rush* (1975)

Delmatier, Royce, Clarence McIntosh, and Earl Waters, *The Rumble of California Politics: 1848–1970* (1970)

Dillon, Richard, *Burnt-Out Fires: California's Modoc Indian War* (1973)

Ellison, Joseph, *California and the Nation, 1850–1869* (1927)

Ellison, William Henry, *A Self-Governing Dominion: California, 1849–1860* (1950)

Garnett, Porter, *Papers of the San Francisco Committee of Vigilance of 1851* (1910)

Gay, Theressa, *James W. Marshall: The Discoverer of California Gold, A Biography* (1967)

Holliday, J. S., *Rush for Riches: Gold Fever and the Making of California* (1999)

Holliday, J. S., *The World Rushed In: The California Gold Rush Experience* (1981)

Johnson, Susan Lee, *Roaring Camp: The Social World of the California Gold Rush* (2000)

Kurutz, Gary F., *The California Gold Rush: A Descriptive Bibliography of Books and Pamphlets Covering the Years 1848–1853* (1997)

Lapp, Rudolph, *Afro-Americans in California* (1979)

Levy, JoAnn, *Unsettling the West: Eliza Farnham and Georgianna Bruce Kirby in Frontier California* (2004)

Melendy, H. Brett, and Benjamin Gilbert, *The Governors of California: Peter H. Burnett to Edmund G. Brown* (1965)

Mullen, Kevin, *Let Justice Be Done: Crime and Politics in Early San Francisco* (1989)

Olin, Spencer, Jr., *California Politics, 1846–1920: The Emerging Corporate State* (1981)

Paul, Rodman, *California Gold: The Beginning of Mining in the Far West* (1947)

Paul, Rodman, *The California Gold Discovery: Sources, Documents, Accounts and Memoirs Relating to the Discovery of Gold at Sutter's Mill* (1966)

Quinn, Arthur, *The Rivals: William Gwin, David Broderick, and the Birth of California* (1997)

Rawls, James, and Richard Orsi, editors, *A Golden State: Mining and Economic Development in Gold Rush California* (1999)

Rohrbough, Malcolm, *Days of Gold: The California Gold Rush and the American Nation* (1997)

Royce, Josiah, *California: A Study of American Character* (1886)

Shinn, Charles, *Mining Camps* (1885)

Starr, Kevin, and Richard Orsi, editors, *Rooted in Barbarous Soil: People, Culture, and Community in Gold Rush California* (2000)

Wheat, Carl, editor, *The Shirley Letters from the California Mines, 1851–1852* (1949)

Williams, Mary Floyd, *History of the San Francisco Committee of Vigilance of 1851* (1921)

5. REGULATION, RAILROAD, AND REVOLUTION

Atherton, Gertrude, *California: An Intimate History* (second edition, revised and enlarged, 1927)

Bain, David Howard, *Empire Express: Building the First Transcontinental Railroad* (1999)

Barth, Gunther, *Bitter Strength: A History of the Chinese in the United States, 1850–1870* (1964)

Bookspan, Shelley, *A Germ of Goodness: The California State Prison System, 1851–1944* (1991)

Burchell, R. A., *The San Francisco Irish: 1848–1880* (1980)

Cleland, Robert Glass, *The Cattle on a Thousand Hills: Southern California, 1850–1880* (1951)

Deverell, William, *Railroad Crossing: Californians and the Railroad, 1850–1910* (1994)

Hinckley, Helen, *Rails from the West: A Biography of Theodore D. Judah* (1969)

Lavender, David, *Nothing Seemed Impossible: William C. Ralston and Early San Francisco* (1975)

Lewis, Oscar, *The Big Four* (1938)

Lewis, Oscar, *Silver Kings* (1967)

Lewis, Oscar, *The War in the Far West: 1861–1865* (1961)

Orsi, Richard, *Sunset Limited: The Southern Pacific Railroad and the Development of the American West, 1850–1930* (2005)

Pitt, Leonard, *The Decline of the Californios: A Social History of the Spanish-Speaking Californians, 1846–1890* (second edition, 1998)

Shumsky, Neil Larry, *The Evolution of Political Protest and the Workingmen's Party of California* (1991)

Tutorow, Norman E., with Evelyn Tutorow, *The Governor: The Life and Legacy of Leland Stanford, A California Colossus* (two volumes, 2004)

6. The Higher Provincialism

Baur, John E., *Health Seekers of Southern California* (1959)

Bean, Walton, *Boss Ruef's San Francisco* (1952)

Brown, J. L., *The Mussel Slough Tragedy* (1958)

Bullough, William A., *The Blind Boss & His City: Christopher Augustine Buckley and Nineteenth-Century San Francisco* (1979)

Deverell, William, *Whitewashed Adobe: The Rise of Los Angeles and the Remaking of Its Mexican Past* (2004)

Dumke, Glenn, *The Boom of the Eighties in Southern California* (1944)

Fradkin, Philip L., *Magnitude 8: Earthquakes and Life Along the San Andreas Fault* (1998)

Fradkin, Philip L., *The Great Earthquake and Firestorms of 1906: How San Francisco Nearly Destroyed Itself* (2005)

Hansen, Gladys, and Emmet Condon, *Denial of Disaster* (1989)

Hughes, Edan Milton, *Artists in California, 1786–1940* (1986)

McGinty, Brian, *Strong Wine: The Life and Legend of Agoston Haraszthy* (1998)

Meyerson, Harvey, *Nature's Army: When Soldiers Fought for Yosemite* (2001)

Mowry, George E., *The California Progressives* (1951)

Palmquist, Peter E., *Carleton E. Watkins: Photographer of the American West* (1983)

Royce, Josiah, *Race Questions, Provincialism, and Other American Problems* (1908)

Starr, Kevin, *Americans and the California Dream, 1850–1915* (1973)

Starr, Kevin, *Inventing the Dream: California Through the Progressive Era* (1985)

Van Nostrand, Jeanne, *The First Hundred Years of Painting in California, 1775–1875* (1980)

Vincent, Stephen, Kevin Starr, and Paul Mills, *O California!: Nineteenth and Early Twentieth Century California Landscapes and Observations* (1990)

Walker, Franklin, *San Francisco's Literary Frontier* (1939)

Westphal, Ruth Lilly, *Plein Air Painters of California: The North* (1986)

Westphal, Ruth Lilly, *Plein Air Painters of California: The Southland* (1982)

Wheat, Carl I., editor, *The Shirley Letters from the California Mines, 1851–1852* (1949)

7. Great Expectations

Banham, Reyner, *Los Angeles: The Architecture of Four Ecologies* (1971)

Bottles, Scott Lee, *Los Angeles and the Automobile* (1987)

Brechin, Gray, *Imperial San Francisco: Urban Power, Earthly Ruin* (1999)

Davis, Clark, *Company Men: White-Collar Life and Corporate Cultures in Los Angeles, 1892–1941* (2000)

Davis, Margaret Leslie, *Dark Side of Fortune: Triumph and Scandal in the Life of Oil Tycoon Edward L. Doheny* (1998)

Fogelson, Robert M., *The Fragmented Metropolis: Los Angeles, 1850–1930* (1967)

Foster, Mark S., *Henry J. Kaiser* (1989)

Hise, Greg, *Magnetic Los Angeles: Planning the Twentieth-Century Metropolis* (1997)

Hoffman, Abraham, *Vision or Villainy* (1981)

Hundley, Norris, *The Great Thirst* (1992)

Kahrl, William L., *Water and Power: The Conflict over Los Angeles' Water Supply in the Owens Valley* (1982)

Kaplan, Sam Hall, *LA Lost & Found: An Architectural History of Los Angeles,* Julius Shulman, principal photographer (1987)

Kelley, Robert, *Battling the Inland Sea* (1990)

Reisner, Mark, *Cadillac Desert* (1986)

Sitton, Tom, and William Deverell, editors, *Metropolis in the Making: Los Angeles in the 1920s* (2001)

Starr, Kevin, *Material Dreams: Southern California Through the 1920s* (1990)

Tygiel, Jules, *The Great Los Angeles Swindle: Oil, Stocks, and Scandal During the Roaring Twenties* (1994)

Van Der Zee, John, *The Gate: The True Story of the Design and Construction of the Golden Gate Bridge* (1986)

Worster, Donald, *Rivers of Empire* (1985)

8. Making It Happen

Adamic, Louis, *Dynamite: The Story of Class Violence in America* (1929)

Arax, Mark, and Rick Wartzman, *The King of California: J. G. Boswell and the Making of a Secret American Empire* (2003)

Cronin, Bernard Cornelius, *Father Yorke and the Labor Movement in San Francisco, 1900–1910* (1943)

Cross, Ira, *A History of the Labor Movement in California* (1935)

Daniel, Cletus, *Bitter Harvest: A History of California Farmworkers, 1870–1941* (1981)

del Castillo, Richard Griswold, and Richard A. Garcia, *César Chávez* (1995)

Gregory, James N., *American Exodus, The Dust Bowl Migration and Okie Culture in California* (1989)

Halsam, Gerald W., photographs by Stephen Johnson and Robert Dawson, *The Great Central Valley: California's Heartland* (1993)

Kazin, Michael, *Barons of Labor: The San Francisco Building Trades and Union Power in the Progressive Era* (1987)

McWilliams, Carey, *Factories in the Field: The Story of Migratory Farm Labor in California* (1939)

Roney, Frank, *Irish Rebel and California Labor Leader: An Autobiography,* edited by Ira Cross (1931)

Schwartz, Stephen, *Brotherhood of the Sea: A History of the Sailors' Union of the Pacific, 1885–1985* (1985)

Selvin, David, *Sky Full of Storm: A History of Labor in California* (1966)

Starr, Kevin, *Endangered Dreams: The Great Depression in California* (1996)

Street, Richard Steven, *Beasts of the Field: A Narrative History of California Farmworkers, 1769–1913* (2004)

Whitten, Woodrow, *Criminal Syndicalism and the Law in California, 1919–1927* (1969)

9. War and Peace

Davis, Mike, Kelly Mayhew, and Jim Miller, *Under the Perfect Sun: The San Diego Tourists Never See* (2003)

Douglass, John Aubrey, *The California Idea and American Higher Education: 1850 to the 1960 Master Plan* (2000)

Johnson, Marilyn S., *The Second Gold Rush: Oakland and the East Bay in World War II* (1993)

Lotchin, Roger W., *Fortress California 1910–1961: From Warfare to Welfare* (1992)

Nash, Gerald D., *World War II and the West* (1990)

Rarick, Ethan, *California Rising: The Life and Times of Pat Brown* (2005)

Starr, Kevin, *Embattled Dreams: California in War and Peace, 1940–1950* (2002)

Verge, Arthur C., *Paradise Transformed: Los Angeles During the Second World War* (1993)

10. O Brave New World!

Berlin, Leslie, *The Man Behind the Microchip: Robert Noyce and the Invention of Silicon Valley* (2005)

Bronson, Po, *The Nudist on the Late Shift* (1999)

Gillmor, C. Stewart, *Fred Terman at Stanford* (2004)

Hanson, Dirk, *The New Alchemists: Silicon Valley and the Microelectronics Revolution* (1982)

Lowen, Rebecca S., *Creating the Cold War University: The Transformation of Stanford* (1997)

Reid, T. R., *The Chip* (1985)

11. AN IMAGINED PLACE

Albright, Thomas, *Art in the San Francisco Bay Area 1945–1980* (1985)

Boas, Nancy, *Society of Six: California Colorists* (1988)

Davis, Mike, *City of Quartz: Excavating the Future in Los Angeles* (1990)

Dijkstra, Bram, *American Expressionism: Art and Social Change 1920–1950* (2003)

Ferlinghetti, Lawrence, and Nancy J. Peters, *Literary San Francisco: A Pictorial History* (1980)

Fine, David, *Imagining Los Angeles: A City in Fiction* (2000)

Gebhard, David, *Schindler* (1980)

Gioia, Dana, Chryss Yost, and Jack Hicks, editors, *California Poetry from the Gold Rush to the Present* (2004)

Haslam, Gerald W., *Workin' Man Blues: Country Music in California* (1999)

Hicks, Jack, James D. Houston, Maxine Hong Kingston, and Al Young, editors, *The Literature of California* (2000)

Hines, Thomas S., *Irving Gill and the Architecture of Reform* (2000)

Hines, Thomas S., *Richard Neutra and the Search for Modern Architecture* (1982)

Karlstrom, Paul J., editor, *On the Edge of America: California Modernist Art, 1900–1950* (1996)

Landauer, Susan, *The San Francisco School of Abstract Expressionism* (1996)

Livingston, Jane, *The Art of Richard Diebenkorn* (1997)

Longstreth, Richard, *On the Edge of the World: Four Architects in San Francisco at the Turn of the Century* (1983)

McClung, William Alexander, *Landscapes of Desire: Anglo Mythologies of Los Angeles* (2000)

Nelson, Kevin, *The Golden Game: The Story of California Baseball* (2004)

Reid, David, editor, *Sex, Death, and God in LA* (1992)

Scott, Allen J., and Edward W. Soja, *The City: Los Angeles and Urban Theory at the End of the Twentieth Century* (1996)

Solnit, Rebecca, *River of Shadows: Eadweard Muybridge and the Technological Wild West* (2003)

Spaulding, Jonathan, *Ansel Adams and the American Landscape* (1995)

Starr, Kevin, *The Dream Endures: California Enters the 1940s* (1997)

Walker, Franklin, *A Literary History of Southern California* (1950)

Ward, Elizabeth, and Alain Silver, *Raymond Chandler's Los Angeles* (1987)

Wilson, Charis, and Wendy Madar, *Through Another Lens: My Years with Edward Weston* (1998)

12. ECUMENOPOLIS

Balderrama, Francisco E., and Raymond Rodriguez, *Decade of Betrayal: Mexican Repatriation in the 1930s* (1995)

Chan, Sucheng, *Asian Californians* (1991)

Daniels, Roger, and Spencer C. Olin, Jr., editors, *Racism in California* (1972)

Krouchett, Lorraine, *Filipinos in California* (1982)

Mazon, Maurice, *The Zoot Suit Riots* (1984)

McWilliams, Carey, *North from Mexico* (1949)

Wollenberg, Charles, *All Deliberate Speed* (1976)

13. ARNOLD!

Baldassare, Mark, *A California State of Mind: The Conflicted Voter in a Changing World* (2002)

Boyd, Nan Alamilla, *Wide Open Town: A History of Queer San Francisco to 1965* (2003)

Davis, Mike, *Ecology of Fear: Los Angeles and the Imagination of Disaster* (1998)

Didion, Joan, *Where I Was From* (2003)

Gerston, Larry N., and Terry Christensen, *Recall!: California's Political Earthquake* (2004)

Leamer, Laurence, *Fantastic! The Life of Arnold Schwarzenegger* (2005)

Mowry, George, *The California Progressives* (1951)

Putnam, Jackson, *Modern California Politics, 1917–1980* (1980)

Rorabaugh, W. J., *Berkeley at War: The 1960s* (1989)

Schrag, Peter, *Paradise Lost: California's Experience, America's Future* (1998)

Starr, Kevin, *Coast of Dreams: California on the Edge, 1990–2003* (2004)

Wyatt, David, *Five Fires: Race, Catastrophe, and the Shaping of California* (1997)

Index

Page numbers in *italics* refer to illustrations.

ABOUT THE AUTHOR

KEVIN STARR is University Professor and professor of history at the University of Southern California in Los Angeles. From 1994 to 2004 he served as the state librarian for California. He received his Ph.D. in American literature from Harvard in 1969 and the master of library science degree from UC Berkeley in 1974 and has taught primarily at Harvard, the University of San Francisco, and the University of Southern California. The author of ten books, he has won a Guggenheim Fellowship, gold and silver medals from the Commonwealth Club of California, and election as Fellow to the American Antiquarian Society and the Society of American Historians, the California Historical Society, and the Historical Society of Southern California. He divides his time between Los Angeles and San Francisco.